Governments and Marriage Education Policy

Also by Elizabeth van Acker

DIFFERENT VOICES: Gender and Politics in Australia
GOVERNING BUSINESS AND GLOBALIZATION (*co-editor*)
GLOBALIZING GOVERNMENT BUSINESS RELATIONS (*co-editor*)

Governments and Marriage Education Policy

Perspectives from the UK, Australia and the US

Elizabeth van Acker
Department of Politics and Public Policy,
Griffith University, Australia

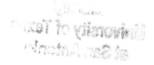

palgrave
macmillan

First published in 2008 by
PALGRAVE MACMILLAN
Houndmills, Basingstoke, Hampshire RG21 6XS and
175 Fifth Avenue, New York, N.Y. 10010
Companies and representatives throughout the world.

PALGRAVE MACMILLAN is the global academic imprint of the Palgrave Macmillan division of St. Martin's Press, LLC and of Palgrave Macmillan Ltd. Macmillan® is a registered trademark in the United States, United Kingdom and other countries. Palgrave is a registered trademark in the European Union and other countries.

ISBN-13: 978–0–230–00337–8 hardback
ISBN-10: 0–230–00337–0 hardback

This book is printed on paper suitable for recycling and made from fully managed and sustained forest sources. Logging, pulping and manufacturing processes are expected to conform to the environmental regulations of the country of origin.

A catalogue record for this book is available from the British Library.

Library of Congress Cataloging-in-Publication Data

Van Acker, Elizabeth.
     Governments and marriage education policy : perspectives from the UK, Australia and the US / Elizabeth van Acker.
         p. cm.
     Includes index.
     ISBN 0–230–00337–0 (alk. paper)
         1. Marriage – Government policy – English-speaking countries – Case studies. 2. Marriage – Government policy – United States. 3. Marriage – Government policy – Great Britain. 4. Marriage – Government policy – Australia. 5. Family life education – Government policy – English-speaking countries – Case studies. 6. Family life education – Government policy – United States. 7. Family life education – Government policy – Great Britain. 8. Family life education – Government policy – Australia. I. Title.

HQ515.V36 2008
306.872'0973—dc22   2008011267

10 9 8 7 6 5 4 3 2 1
17 16 15 14 13 12 11 10 09 08

Printed and bound in Great Britain by
CPI Antony Rowe, Chippenham and Eastbourne

For
Jessica, Declan, Jake and Kieran

Contents

Abbreviations

AAME	Australian Association for Marriage Education
ACF	Administration for Children and Families
AFA	Australian Family Association
AFDC	Aid to Families with Dependent Children
AGD	Attorney General's Department
AGMARS	Advisory Group on Marriage and Relationship Support
ALI	American Law Institute
BCFT	Bristol Community Family Trust
BSA	British Social Attitudes
CALD	Culturally and Linguistically Diverse
CLASP	Center for Law and Social Policy
CMPs	Community Marriage Policies
CSME	Catholic Society for Marriage Education
CWA	Catholic Welfare Australia
CYPF	Children, Young People and Families
DCA	Department for Constitutional Affairs
DFES	Department for Education and Skills
DHHS	Department of Health and Human Services
DOMA	*Defense of Marriage Act*
FaCS	Department of Family and Community Services
FaCSIA	Department of Families, Community Services and Indigenous Affairs
FFRF	Freedom from Religion Foundation
FOCCUS	Facilitating Open Couple Communication Understanding and Study
FLA	*Family Law Act*
FPI	Family and Parenting Institute
FRCs	Family Relationship Centres
FRSA	Family Relationships Services Australia
FRSP	Family Relationship Services Program
FSA	Family Services Australia
FTF	First Things First
HMGR	Healthy Marriages Grand Rapids
HMHR	Healthy Marriages Health Relationships
HMI	Healthy Marriage Initiative

HRSCFCA	House of Representative Standing Committee on Family and Community Affairs
HRSCLCA	House of Representatives Standing Committee on Legal and Constitutional Affairs
IPPR	Institute for Public Policy Research
IRBs	Industry Representative Bodies
LCD	Lord Chancellor's Department
MAREAA	Marriage and Relationship Education Association of Australia
MARENC	Marriage and Relationship Education National Conference
MARS	Marriage and Relationship Support
NOW	National Women's Organization
NFI	National Fatherhood Initiative
OMI	Oklahoma Marriage Initiative
PAIRS	Practical Application of Relationship Skills
PREP	Prevention and Relationship Enhancement Program
PREPARE	Premarital Personal and Relationship Evaluation
PRWORA	*Personal Responsibility and Work Opportunity Reconciliation Act*
RA	Relationships Australia
RECC	Relationship Enhancement and Couples Communication
SJPG	Social Justice Policy Group
TANF	Temporary Assistance for Needy Families

Preface

Why on earth is a political scientist studying marriage education? I asked myself this question many times over the past few years. I was initially interested in the role of romance which has such powerful meanings in our individualistic society and how government policies deal with it. This led me to examine marriage and relationship support in Australia and I soon discovered that policy developments were also occurring in the US and the UK. In 2003, I decided to conduct a comparative study of what was happening within this area in these three liberal democracies.

Marriage and families are the focal point of a number of important, contentious public debates. Should the institution of marriage be shored up as vital to the social health and well-being of citizens? Can governments do anything to stem the tide of cohabitation, divorce and out-of-wedlock child bearing? This book sheds light on some of the shadowy spots of the measures underway in the three countries to address the 'marriage problem'. By including the voices of a range of people who passionately champion – or oppose – marriage and relationship education, I hope to contribute to a clearer understanding about the issues and to illuminate some of the misapprehensions. The research for this book discovered that although there is much enthusiasm and active support for marriage education policies, there is also cautious resistance and in some situations downright opposition. Some view marriage programs as an important element in enriching people's intimate relationships, or as a useful measure in the fight against child poverty and family breakdown. Others oppose funding programs that have not been sufficiently evaluated because they may be wasting taxpayers' money. A further criticism suggests that more funding should be provided for basic economic support and services that are necessary for family welfare. Another response is that strengthening marriage is none of the government's business. My interviews revealed that the various players in this story have not only an intellectual but also a passionate engagement in the issue of marriage support. Any policies influencing citizens' intimate relationships go to the heart of people's lives and many of the participants have an emotional investment in improving relationships in society.

The book utilizes my interviews with staff and stakeholders from a range of organizations involved in different ways with marriage education.

This includes policy makers, researchers, civil servants, service providers, representatives from think tanks, community organizations and religious groups, as well as couples who have taken classes. Some of the people have a public profile and were pleased to be quoted, while others wished to remain anonymous. Therefore, in accordance with their wishes, some of the interviewees are named, while others are described by their work title. To all of those who took the time to talk to me, thank you so much for your willingness to cooperate and for your generosity. Apart from the interviews, I attended forums and conferences, participated in reference groups and presented seminars, conference papers and keynote addresses. Many participants allowed me access to data and information about marriage education programs. I conducted approximately 70 interviews from 2003 to 2007 across the three countries to obtain people's views on a range of issues such as marriage and relationship education programs, policy developments and the role of governments.

Naturally I have many people to thank. I would like to express gratitude to Bill Coffin from the Administration for Children and Families in Washington, DC who provided an enormous wealth of information. Thanks also to Belinda Hartsell for her friendship and to Nisa Muhammad for generously allowing us to sit in on her relationship classes. This of course leads to a big thank you to the friendly couples in those classes. Bob Lerman and the staff at the Urban Institute provided support during my visits in 2006 and 2007 when I was a visiting scholar. I also appreciate the kindness and help of Penny Mansfield, Fiona Glenn, Laura Dimmock and all the staff from One Plus One in London when I was based there. Their 'Cake Wednesdays' should be mandatory in all work places.

I would especially like to thank those who read and commented on some of the chapters: Bill Coffin, Giorel Curran, Robyn Hollander, Wade Horn, Kerri Kellett, Theodora Ooms, Robyn Parker, Penny Mansfield and Anne Tiernan. The book has benefited greatly from their feedback. For taking the time to discuss the book's ideas and progress, the following people were supportive along the way – Catherine Althaus, Janis Bailey, Kaye Broadbent, Sharon Broughton, Kim Halford, John Kane, Joanne Kelly, Brendon O'Connor, Haig Patapan, Mike van Acker and Pat Weller. For research assistance, I thank Colleen Knight and Cliff Smith. For production of the book I thank Daniela di Piramo. Thanks also to Julie Howe and to Jean Norman. The editorial assistance of Philippa Grand and Hazel Woodbridge from Palgrave Macmillan is much appreciated 'as is all the great work of the team at Newgen Imaging Systems'. Needless to say, any errors in this book are my own.

I am grateful to the Centre for Governance and Public Policy which supported this project and provided some travelling funds. I also acknowledge the funding provided by a Faculty of Commerce and Management Research Grant and a Griffith University Research Grant. Colleagues at the Department of Politics and Public Policy provided encouragement and cheered me on. Finally, thanks to the many engaged and newly married couples who graciously indulged my curiosity at weddings, parties, functions – any event really – where I asked all and sundry whether they had taken marriage and relationship education classes. This book is for my younger niece and nephews – Jessica, Declan, Jake and Kieran – in the hope that when they grow up, they will enjoy happy, healthy and loving relationships.

LIZ VAN ACKER
Griffith University

Introduction: Government and Marriage: Strange Bedfellows?

In previous times, when people considered marriage, a fitting phrase for many couples may have been 'what's love got to do with it'? Yet at present, when many people marry for love, this is not the case. Romance is alive and well – starry-eyed lovers enthusiastically consume all the trimmings associated with romantic love. If or when the romance dies, many people move on because for them, marriage and relationships are disposable. Today, marriage is typically understood as a very personal matter. One might therefore question any connections between government policies and marriage. Can governments influence the progress of blossoming love? Is it possible for them to encourage couples to work on their intimate relationships? Why is marriage the last area of family life to enter the realm of national family policy? Without a doubt, it is difficult for governments to regulate what goes on behind closed doors or get involved with how people relate to each other in the privacy of their own homes, especially when couples are not facing any particular difficulties in their relationships. Nonetheless, government interest in this most private domain has been expanding over the past few decades.

This book examines the role that governments play in managing policy challenges in response to social changes in marriage. It analyses some of the marriage education policies that attempt to foster lasting and satisfying marriages, especially a broad range of programs and marriage and relationship support services. The new governmental measures seem to stand against and resist the romantic tide, reminding those citizens who will listen that 'all you need is love' is just a love song; that a healthy and happy marriage needs much more. In attempting to address social changes such as increased cohabitation, divorce and out-of-wedlock births, the three governments under study have

1

adopted quite different approaches although they all wish to avoid being seen as 'interfering' in private matters. The US government is particularly anxious about the wider context of changing social relations, but wants to introduce support for one family form that has been absent from government policy: marriage. The intent is to add a new service – marriage education – to the myriad of social services already being offered. In contrast, the key objective for the UK government is to assist in developing positive outcomes for children and families. For Australia, the main goal is to strengthen families at different times in the relationship cycle, from pre-marriage to post-divorce.

Within these three nations, many relationships have become more equal and fluid, and based on individual needs. Given this context, it seems to make common sense that relationships should be robust, whether they are founded on marriage or not. With this in mind, it is worthwhile to note at the outset that some programs refer specifically to marriage education, though for other programs, the more appropriate term is 'marriage and relationship education'. Thus the book covers the various types of education, ranging from marriage preparation, support during marriage and helping people to stay married. Other programs may have less emphasis on marriage *per se* and more emphasis on developing the knowledge and skills needed for a successful relationship. In any case, marriage education is conducted in group settings making it distinct from face-to-face individualized counselling and therapy which focuses specifically on marriages in difficulty. This approach is based on a diagnosis and treatment by a therapist or counsellor, while marriage and relationship education is not.

The book considers whether governments in the UK, the US and Australia can or should intervene in the area of marriage and relationship support. To various degrees, these governments are facilitating and funding programs because they deem it necessary to protect and preserve the family. Politicians are not only attempting to restore and acknowledge the social and economic benefits of stable families for society, but are also attempting to instil the values of personal responsibility for individuals. This illustrates the close connections between the public and the private. Accordingly, the book examines the challenges that governments face in their attempts to deal with issues relating to marriage in both the public and the private spheres. The public sphere encompasses institutional features such as social norms, as well as legal and economic regulations, while the private domain refers to the area where individuals make intimate decisions and choices. Historically, the divide between overtly public institutions and the domestic sphere of the family meant that there have been many areas of civil society where governments could not intrude. The public nature of the wedding ceremony, the legal contract and social customs surrounding marriage, however, indicate that marriage is not a completely private arrangement between two individuals. Over the years, governments have developed many public policies that have favoured married couples, by providing a number of special entitlements, rights and duties in relation to matters such as tax, welfare, inheritance and caring for children. These measures interact with other policy areas such as immigration, citizenship and social security. What is different and interesting about the recent policy agenda is the growth of policies which specifically assist training for marriage.

Governments are concerned with four main indicators which influence the family: marriage; divorce; out-of-wedlock births and cohabitation. Many politicians and policy makers are anxious about the changing patterns of intimacy in relationships. Over the long term, first marriage rates are declining, while age at first marriage is higher for both men and women. Birth rates have plummeted, while cohabitation rates and out-of-wedlock births have risen. There is political uneasiness about the high divorce rates and the effects of single parenthood. Governments are therefore seeking appropriate policy responses to these trends. The perceived solution to the 'marriage crisis' is to protect the traditional family unit: married heterosexual parents with children. This idea is especially prevalent in the US, where the federal government has developed strategies specifically designed to create 'healthy' marriages by offering early intervention and prevention activities, with the intention of providing people with the tools to bolster and sustain their relationships and to prevent difficulties from expanding into unresolvable problems. There is milder support in Australia for these programs, while the focus in the UK appears centred more on the well-being of children, with no spotlight on strengthening marriage.

The book compares government policies, categorizing the range of available programs in the three case studies. By facilitating access to education and support services, governments are encouraging partners to safeguard their marriages and avoid relationship distress which has detrimental effects not only for the individual but also for families and communities. The political message is that couples have to rescue themselves from the potential of poor relationship behaviour and can do so by participating in government-funded programs. Although public efforts to strengthen marriage have the potential of considerably influencing the future development of family policy, the expansion of relationship education and support services has been quite contentious. Governments are experiencing pressure from conservatives who argue for the defence of heterosexual marriage. In addition, some progressives argue that marriage is a public health issue and that two-parent married families fare best, financially and emotionally, as do their children. Alternatively, libertarians see government attempts as intrusive meddling in people's most intimate relationships, while feminists argue that the policies will do little to improve the lot of women and children.

Aims of the book

Government intervention in family life is not new. Books on family policy and comparative family policies have been written before. But none of these has dealt with a critical, core component of family life – marriage and the relationship between couples. This is because couples and marriage education is a brand new field for public policy. This is the first book to identify and describe these developments from a political perspective. This book does not assume that conditions in any of the three case studies under investigation are necessarily applicable to any of the others. Despite the evidence of a divorce revolution worldwide among wealthier nations, it is unlikely that policy proposals of different countries can realistically be transferred to others. Nevertheless, it is timely to examine policy developments and it is possible to glean some nuanced understanding of the different policy approaches. In any case, the goal here is to compare and contrast government policies concerning marriage education and to provide answers to the following questions:

Should governments facilitate people's preparation for successful and stable marriage?

What difficulties and problems do governments face in attempting to support marriage programs?

Who advocates and who opposes government policies in marriage and relationship support?

How do governments manage this complex area, made more complicated by the disparate demands from various lobbyists and community groups?

How do factors such as class, race, religion and people's romantic expectations influence the goal of promoting marriage?

My argument is that governments in the UK, Australia and the US confront many challenges in seeking to implement policies that encourage couples to participate in relationship and marriage education services. This book considers the similarities and the differences in the development of marriage education policies across the three countries. Governments adopt practical strategies that are concerned not only with financial costs but they also draw on particular beliefs and values about the place of marriage in society.

It is important to do research that goes beyond national borders to compare trends and policies. Accordingly, the book uses a comparative approach with two dimensions. The first is a historical one, comparing policies over time. The research on each country begins with a chronological overview, commencing from the late 1940s, and then providing a more detailed analysis of the 2000s. The second dimension is cross-national. The three case studies demonstrate many contextual similarities; for example, they are liberal democracies with similar political systems and cultures, facilitating close comparisons. In the UK, the US and Australia, governments have by and large embraced neo-liberal principles, stressing the values of freedom, the market and small government. Protecting the rights of the individual is imperative as citizens are recognized as the source from which society derives its moral standing. Liberal democratic governments see their role as establishing a framework in which a free society can thrive, while simultaneously championing a decrease in the role of government. This reinforces the notion that the individual should be self-sufficient, taking personal responsibility for his or her actions. Although primacy is given to individual choice, these governments also promote ideals of social harmony within the family.

Notwithstanding neo-liberal commitments, personal matters such as relationships are not beyond the scope of government intervention. The US and Australia have a federal system and have conservative governments: President George W. Bush has led the US federal administration since 2000, while John Howard has been the Australian Prime Minister since 1996.[1] In a paradoxical division between the public and the private, encouraging independence and individual freedom makes it difficult for governments to be part of the solution to personal problems, even at a distance. Yet this is precisely what they are attempting to do, because marriage education policies focus on individual characteristics such as values, behaviour, relationship skills and preparation. Despite the many similarities, the main difference between the three countries when comparing marriage education policies concerns political partisanship. In Britain where Tony Blair's – and Gordon Brown's – Labour government has governed since 1997, public funding of marriage education is now virtually non-existent and strengthening marriage is no longer viewed as an important policy objective.

Governments are developing policy measures for three main reasons to do with economics, health and morality. First, they intervene for economic reasons. Governments understand and articulate the problem of marital instability in terms of the high financial, legal and social costs of divorce, not only for the public purse but also for society as a whole. Closer facilitation of strengthening heterosexual relations is designed to reduce the high rates of divorce. For example, in Australia, the approximate expense of marriage and family separation is more than $3 billion per annum (House of Representatives Standing Committee, 1998, p. 51). The amount doubles with indirect costs, in addition to the personal and emotional suffering for parents and children. In America, more recent calculations estimate that the direct and indirect costs of divorce are $33.3 billion annually (Schramm, 2006, p. 133). The cost of separation and divorce for the public purse and society is much higher than the cost of early intervention and prevention programs.

Second, the social health argument provides governments with what they consider a legitimate rationale for privileging marriage in their policies. Research shows that good marriage contributes to good health not only for the adult couple but also for children. As a social good, therefore, it is in the public interest to keep couples together (Wood et al., 2007). By encouraging those getting married to undertake prevention focused programs, designed to assist in learning the skills needed for lifelong and successful marriages, governments intend to serve the health interests of the community.

Third, governments are intervening for moral reasons – to uphold traditional family values – particularly in the US and Australia. Encouraging and supporting marriage is an important variant of government intervention, because it is a mechanism for regulating morality. In response to panic about the 'marriage crisis', governments are promoting marriage in an attempt to assert universal moral standards and improve family life. They perceive marriage as a rock of stability while also endeavouring to define marital obligations and boundaries. The US government in particular seeks to enhance self-reliance and personal responsibility via marriage, while in the UK and Australia, there is more recognition of different forms of parenting and partnering that exist outside marriage as modern lifestyle choices. Furthermore, in the UK, gays and lesbians have similar rights and obligations to those of married couples after the passing of the Civil Partnership Act in 2004. Nevertheless, civil partnerships and marriage are not recognized as the same thing: marriage remains exclusively the preserve of heterosexual couples. At the federal level in the US and Australia, however, same-sex marriages are strongly opposed – marriage is defined as a union 'between a man and a woman'.

Marriage education policy has been available for decades, but it has waxed and waned as a policy issue receiving different degrees of attention at different times. While every policy development is distinctive with its own sets of characteristics, supporting healthy marriages is now on the policy agenda, particularly in the US. In 2002, President George W. Bush announced a $US1.5 billion plan to promote marriage and the federal government now provides more than $100 million per annum – over five years – for marriage support and related programs. The Blair government spent £5 million on marriage support in 2002–2003, but direct funding no longer exists. In contrast, the Howard government spent approximately $AUS 4 million annually in the early 2000s on similar programs, although this has recently increased quite substantially as part of a broader package. These figures suggest that governments are becoming involved in marriage services, albeit to varying degrees. In spite of the diversity of responses the policies represent certain powerful themes recur and dominate.

Book overview

The central purpose of this book is to investigate the role of governments in attempting to strengthen marriage and relationships and the challenges they face. Accordingly, marriage is discussed in the first two chapters. Chapter 1 examines the problem of marriage and the changing trends in marriage and divorce. The chapter establishes the wider framework for the book's discussion by setting out the debates concerning the changes to marriage. Some of the literature argues that marriage is in decline, while other literature argues that marriage is resilient. It is important to explain the different perspectives because governments need to manage these divergences. The chapter also describes the various marriage and relationship education programs which are – broadly speaking – available in the three countries.

Chapter 2 traces the tensions between the roles of marriage in the public and the personal spheres in a context of social change. The chapter highlights challenging matters for governments and society about how marriage is changing. Marriage remains a key social institution, but in the modern world, individualism and choice have become paramount. The second chapter examines many factors that create tensions – marriage entails not only certain obligations and duties but is also about meeting individual needs and making people happy. It traces some of the major transformations such as the shifting relevance of religion and the increasing importance of love and romance. It also investigates feminist critiques which suggest that the institution of marriage oppresses women. Some feminists argue that it should be abolished, while others argue that this is unnecessary because although marriage has problems, it can be reformed. The chapter also discusses debates about same-sex marriage. Supporters of same-sex marriage claim that marriage is a fundamental human right that should not discriminate on the basis of gender. Exploring these different viewpoints and understandings of marriage provides a clear map of the complexities of modern relationships and issues which governments are expected to address, whether directly or indirectly.

Chapter 3 begins the empirical study of the three countries by examining the UK where the government has pursued a low profile effort to strengthen marriage. The chapter's historical overview traces the development of marriage and relationship support in its discussion of various government reports and policy recommendations. The chapter argues that since 1997, the Labour government has not implemented consistent marriage education policies, although there was a push for increasing programs in the early 2000s. An Advisory Group on Marriage and Relationship Support (AGMARS) delivered a report in 2002 recommending that the government should play an active role in leading policies to deliver services. Consequently, marriage and relationship support organizations received increased core funding, but this did not prevail for long. Since 2003, there has been a clear policy shift focusing on the well being of children rather than married couples. Other strategies have included attempts to reform divorce laws, increase support for lone parents and examine legal protection for cohabiting couples. A particular focal point, however, is improving the lot of children.

Chapter 3 also considers various criticisms of government strategies, illustrating that marriage education, while currently off the political agenda, is a contested terrain. Some groups are criticizing the government for not supporting marriage much more explicitly. The Tory Party has published a report and recommendations arguing that the government is neglecting marriage support at the expense of robust families and that its primary focus on children and young people is misplaced (see Social Justice Policy Group, 2006, 2007).

Chapter 4 provides details of the Australian example. It argues that in Australia, marriage education does not receive a great deal of public attention and is not a particularly controversial policy. This may be due to the long term evolution of marriage support that has been embedded in legislation such as the 1960 *Marriage Act* and the 1975 *Family Law Act*. The federal government has gradually increased its spending on marriage education policies and support since the 1960s, broadening the definition to 'marriage and relationship' education programs by the 1990s and providing millions of dollars annually to approved community-based organizations. The federal government has recently been more concerned with what happens when marriages break down than with preparing people for marriage. In response to tackling issues such as shared parenting, child support and the role of the Family Court, the government has established Family Relationship Centres (FRCs) with the objective of smoothing the process of mediation when couples are separating and going through divorce. The FRCs also offer marriage and relationship education and support.

Chapter 5 examines the US government and its marriage education policies. While historically, both the UK and Australia have considered marriage education policies – albeit to varying degrees – for decades, the US has only recently become involved in this area. The chapter argues that it is here that marriage programs are now the most advanced in terms of political support. Before the 1990s, US government policy makers did little to push policies strengthening marriage; indeed, for many years the US federal government considered marriage as private and 'off limits' to government policy. They became concerned with strengthening marriage and reducing illegitimate births, viewing this as a main cause of welfare dependency as well as other economic and social problems. In 1996, Congress passed the *Personal Responsibility and Work Opportunity Reconciliation Act* (PRWORA). The accompanying welfare reform package provided Temporary Assistance For Needy Families (TANF) programs, including support for marriage. Low-income, unmarried families have been increasingly noticed by policy makers and are being targeted by the government. The clear message of the government's Healthy Marriage Initiative is that healthy marriage benefits women, men and children as well as the community at large.

Much lobbying from various community groups and think tanks, service providers and scholars has assisted in the push for marriage. Chapter 5 discusses the marriage movement – which is much more vibrant in the US than in the UK or Australia – playing quite a critical role in placing marriage on the policy agenda. The chapter offers examples of available programs. It also canvasses the critiques offered by feminist organizations and social justice advocates who argue there is too much focus on pro-marriage policies at the expense of other public services that would assist in alleviating poverty, and provide better access to services such as child care and health care. In their study of the transformation of marriage in the US, Amato et al. (2007) argue that strengthening healthy marriages has become a central focus of social policy which remains highly controversial (2007, p. 35). Nevertheless, from the government's perspective, it is hoped that opposition will weaken as more people become comfortable with and understand what marriage education involves.

Chapter 6 begins analysing the challenges for governments in supporting marriage education programs by considering the traction that various factors have had on marriage. It examines variables that primarily affect the private sphere such as religion, romance, class and race which inspire people's decision to marry or not to marry, to cohabite or not to cohabite (and perhaps to divorce or not to divorce). These issues lead to different outcomes – for example, the US population is overall much more religious and therefore respectful of marriage than the citizenry of the other two countries. The problem for governments is that matters such as religious values or romantic love lie beyond the scope of political influence, not simply because they fall on the private side of the public-private divide, but because governments can do little to regulate personal aspirations or expectations, except try to prepare couples for marriage and offer them the skills and information to sustain their relationships and avoid relationship breakdown.

Chapter 7 examines additional challenges for governments which are linked to the policy process. It endeavours to understand how effectively governments can facilitate success in personal relationships and with what results. Policy makers have not sufficiently linked marriage education policies to other initiatives as part of a 'whole-of-government' approach. This includes dealing with structural issues that underlie social problems such as poverty, poor health and child care services and unemployment. These public measures have not been included as part of a wider package of marriage policies. Another contentious issue is balancing work and family which could not only improve people's economic security, but their well being. These are pressing concerns which must be confronted effectively before marriage education policies can have significant impact in many sections of society. The chapter also develops more nuanced insights about policy capacity concerning marriage education. Finally, the chapter examines evaluation which is a critical part of the policy cycle and is crucial in uncovering whether the programs do contribute to preventing relationship difficulties and creating healthy stable relationships. One of the main differences between the three case studies is evident here: the US government is funding the facilitation and ongoing conduct of research and evaluation, but there is a lack of evaluation in the UK and Australia.

The conclusion provides some final comments about the question of whether governments should become involved in marriage education and how they should do so. It briefly revisits love, marriage and the role of government policies. Ultimately, there is only so much that governments can do. Marriage education can teach skills and provide information about how to develop rational steps to strengthen relationships. However, people develop complex relationships based on a range of rational and irrational factors. If commitment is missing or sexual attraction fades, couples may not remain together. This fundamental point about couple dynamics along with the myriad challenges that this book discusses may help to explain and provide some understanding about why governments have been slow to enter the realm of marriage education.

Part I

Changing Perceptions of Marriage

1
The Problem of Marriage

This chapter sets out some recent changes in relationship trends in the United Kingdom, Australia, and the United States which explain the intense debates concerning the marriage problem. It explains why the marriage debate is so contentious and sets out a constructive framework for considering the challenges that governments face in developing marriage education policies. On the one hand, from the 'marital decline' perspective, marriage is perceived as disintegrating and in need of rescuing, while on the other hand, from the 'marital resilience' perspective, marriage is perceived as just one relationship option among many that people can choose. This frame sets out the clear distinctions in the debate, but it is necessary to keep in mind that marriage itself is constantly changing. Therefore, as the remaining chapters will illustrate, the key issue is how or whether it can be revitalized or recreated as an important social institution in the three countries. The chapter also offers a brief overview of marriage and relationship education which has been receiving public support for strengthening marriage.

Recent relationship trends in the UK, Australia and the US

Marriage education policy has developed as a political response to the perceived social problem of a crisis in marriage, where many couples have moved away from the altar or exchanging marriage vows as the ultimate goal. Trends in family arrangements are not dissimilar in the UK, Australia and the US, where there has been a general decline in marriage rates and age at first marriage, while rates of divorce, cohabitation, and out-of-wedlock births have increased. As more people retreat from marriage, the political and policy debates about the purported marriage crisis are particularly lively in the US, where the policy focus is on whether marriage offers unique benefits for couples and their children. In the UK, marriage tends to be a rather taboo subject in public debate and dialogue concentrates more on how to support all children and families, regardless of the marital status or sexual orientation of the parents. In Australia, recently there has been little public discussion about marriage *per se*, but there has been an increasing interest in protecting the family unit, especially at the point of divorce.

Tables 1.1–1.3 illustrate the changes in relationship trends. Couples living together as 'husband and wife' in informal marriages have been difficult to identify and quantify in the past. However as cohabitation – or *de facto* relationships – became more socially acceptable, more data has become available, although it is presented in different measures. In the UK, the percentage of non-married men and women under the age of 60 cohabiting increased between 1986 and 2005 from 11 per cent to 24 per cent for men and 13 per cent to 24 per cent for women (National Statistics, 2007). The Australian 2006 census showed that just over 85 per cent of couples were in registered marriages, while 15 per cent of couples were in *de facto* relationships. Couples with children are slightly more likely to be married (89 per cent) than couples without children (81 per cent).[1] The US Census figures in 2000 showed that 5.5 million couples were living together but not married. This was up from 3.2 million in

Table 1.1   Marriage rates: Australia, UK, and US (marriages per 1000 people)

	Australia	UK	US
1993	6.4	–	–
1994	6.2	11.00	–
1995	6.1	11.32	–
1996	5.8	11.18	8.8
1997	5.8	10.99	8.9
1998	5.9	10.93	8.4
1999	6.0	10.98	8.6
2000	5.9	10.53	8.5
2001	5.3	10.32	8.2
2002	5.4	10.29	7.8
2003	5.4	10.33	7.7
2004	5.5	09.80	7.8
2005	5.4	09.74	7.5

Sources – Australia: ABS (2006a), UK: Eurostat, US: National Center for Health Statistics, *National Vital Statistics Reports* (2005, 2006).

Table 1.2   Divorce rates: Australia, UK, and US (divorces per 1000 people)

	Australia	UK	US
1993	2.7	–	–
1994	2.7	–	–
1995	2.8	2.8	–
1996	2.9	3.0	4.3
1997	2.8	3.0	4.3
1998	2.7	2.8	4.2
1999	2.8	2.8	4.1
2000	2.6	2.7	4.0
2001	2.9	2.7	4.0
2002	2.7	2.7	3.8
2003	2.7	2.8	3.7
2004	2.6	2.8	3.6
2005	2.6	2.6	–

Sources – Australia: ABS (2006a), UK: Eurostat, US: National Center for Health Statistics, *National Vital Statistics Reports* (2005, 2006).

Table 1.3   Births out-of-wedlock (as a percentage of total live births)

	Australia	UK	US
1993	–	32.2	31.0
1994	25.6	32.4	32.6
1995	26.6	33.9	32.2
1996	27.4	35.8	32.4
1997	28.1	37.0	32.4
1998	28.7	37.8	32.8
1999	29.2	38.9	33.0
2000	29.2	39.5	33.2
2001	30.7	40.0	33.5
2002	31.3	40.6	34.0
2003	31.6	41.4	34.6
2004	32.2	42.2	35.8
2005	32.2	42.8	–

Sources – Australia: ABS (2005a), UK: National Statistics (2006), US: Centers for Disease Control and Prevention (2006).

1990 (Census, 2003). Put in percentage figures, nearly 60 per cent of US adults are married, 10.4 per cent are separated or divorced, 6.6 per cent are widowed, 19 per cent are never married, and 5.7 per cent are living with a partner (Centers for Disease Control and Prevention, 2006).

The marriage debate: disintegration or progress?

The challenge for government is to manage marriage at a time when there are differing views about its function and role in the twenty-first century. If we ask the question 'what is marriage for'? the perceptions that marriage is a productive public institution or a fulfilling private one can both provide convincing, if distinct, explanations. There is an enormous literature on the value of modern marriage, especially from the US.[2] This literature on the marriage debate is divided into two main camps. Marriage is perceived as a form of public commitment and the most appropriate institution for raising children, or as a private emotional relationship which does not concern governments. Therefore, as the institution of marriage undergoes rapid changes, some social scientists and legal scholars argue for restoring it, while others disagree. This debate forms the framework of the book's analysis. While it should be acknowledged that much of the discussion draws on American research, due to similar trends in the UK and Australia, it is possible to draw out some relevant insights.

Amato (2004) and Amato et al. (2007) offer a very useful framework which contributes to a better understanding of the conflicting views in the marriage debate. Contemporary marriage possesses multiple meanings and wide-ranging objectives. Both the 'marital decline' perspective (situated in an institutional framework) and the 'marital resilience' perspective (situated in an individual framework) are valuable for charting and appreciating the difficulties in developing public policies. These perspectives assess the changes in marriage in different ways and many of the factors that we will be examining can be regarded as markers of institutional or individualistic marriage. For example, in keeping with the argument that marriage is an important institution, it represents the favoured entity for raising children, a lawful contract, a religious directive, an economic bond, a measure to avoid poverty and welfare dependency. It may embody a calculated agreement on the basis of negotiating a mutually beneficial arrangement. From the standpoint that marriage is more about fulfilling individual needs, it signifies commitment, an exclusive sexual attachment, self-gratification, proof of one's sexual appeal, the fulfilment of romantic hopes and dreams or relations of power. Not surprisingly, marriage for many couples probably features various parts of these elements.

The 'marital decline' perspective

Those who are concerned about the retreat from marriage adopt the 'marital decline' perspective which emphasizes an institutional world view; that is, marriage is more than the individuals within it and therefore should be protected by institutions such as the law and the churches. This perspective considers how marriage has played a role in meeting the needs of society and sustaining the family structure over time. Due to the shift towards individualism and the pursuit of personal happiness, people no longer remain married 'for better or for worse' and this leads to the major question: 'how can we save marriage'? The answer, from this perspective, is to develop a marriage culture and government policies that strengthen the institution of marriage through measures such as premarital and relationship education programs. Divorce should be made more difficult so that people take marriage vows more seriously and make a commitment to stay together even when their relationships are under duress. The solution is to dismantle and repeal the culture of divorce and to encourage unwed parents to marry.

As the forms, values and arrangements of marriage are changing around the world, some social scientists and legal scholars – along with politicians and policy makers – are concerned that marriage is a fragile institution which should be restored. For example, *Rebuilding the Nest* edited by Blankenhorn et al. (1990) argued for recreating the privileged status of lasting heterosexual marriage. Voices from various political persuasions celebrated the term 'family values' and helped launch a conservative ascendancy about the importance of marriage. In 1992, US Vice-President Dan Quayle attacked the television character of Murphy Brown for becoming a single mother. The following year, Barbara Dafoe Whitehead wrote an op-ed piece on Murphy Brown declaring that 'Dan Quayle Was Right'. Her volume on *The Divorce Culture* (1997) discusses the dangers of single parenthood and divorce. Works such as Maggie Gallagher's *The Abolition of Marriage* and David Popenoe's *Life Without Father* both published in 1996 added to the growing debates about marriage. These authors place the well-being of children at the centre of the marriage debate. 'Marriage is an institution in crisis. Close to half of new marriages end in divorce. A third of our children are born out-of-wedlock. The majority of children, at current estimates, will experience a fatherless or motherless household' (Gallagher, 2003, p. 21). Popenoe (1996, p. 24) bemoans the fact that

> Marriage has been losing its social purpose. In place of commitment and obligation to others, especially children, marriage has become mainly a vehicle for the emotional fulfilment of the adult partners. 'Till death do us part' has been replaced by 'so long as I am happy'. Marriage is now less an institution that one belongs to and more a vehicle to be used to one's own advantage.

These authors extol the virtues of marriage and two-parent families – a husband and wife. They oppose same-sex marriage, arguing that only heterosexuals should be permitted to marry (George and Elshtain, 2006).

The work of scholars such as Waite and Gallagher (2000), Whitehead and Popenoe (2003, 2004, 2005, 2006), and Wilson (2002) is used to support policy developments to strengthen marriage. Waite and Gallagher's book *The Case for Marriage: Why Married People are Happier, Healthier, and Better Off Financially*, attempts to counter what they regard as a 'sustained and surprisingly successful attack' (2000, p. 1) on the institution of marriage. They argue that married people tend to lead longer, healthier, happier lives than divorced or single people. In addition, they suggest that children in intact, two-parent families tend to earn more and learn more. Because of this, these children generally require fewer government-paid social services, such as remedial learning, criminal justice, drug and alcohol rehabilitation, depression counselling, and medical, income and housing-aid programs. There are also economic benefits for married couples, according to Waite and Gallagher, who draw on data which indicates that married men earn at least 10 per cent more than single men, and that married families have the highest amount of assets. They argue that 'married men and women report less depression, less anxiety, and lower levels of other types of psychological distress than do those who are single, divorced, or widowed' (2000, p. 67). Therefore, they conclude, 'when it comes to building wealth or avoiding poverty, a stable marriage may be your most important asset' (2000, p. 123). Marriage provides many benefits, and protects the interests of children and families by upholding the foundational institution of social order.

The 'marital resilience' perspective

Others disagree: for them, marriage is changing, but it is a robust institution which is not necessarily in decline. Those who adopt the 'marital resilience' perspective do not mourn the shift to individualism and the focus on self-interest (Amato, 2004, p. 960) intimating that marital instability is not necessarily a problem. Personal development and self-fulfilment are important factors in shaping people's decisions about marriage, cohabitation, divorce and having children out-of-wedlock. At present, love is the central reason for marriage. This has created a paradox according to Coontz (2005), because 'no sooner did the ideal of marrying for love triumph than its most enthusiastic supporters started demanding the right to divorce if love died' (2005, p. 307). Before divorce became easy to obtain, troubled couples would have had 'stable' marriages at least to the outside world, even though they may have been sleeping in separate bedrooms or have been dissatisfied with their relationship. The advent of no-fault divorce, from the marital resilient perspective, is a positive development as it has offered unhappy couples more options about how to live their lives. People do not divorce because they are more 'promiscuous or irresponsible than their forebears were; they divorce because the social role of marriage has changed' (Shumway, 2003, p. 226). While in the past, many individuals remained in unhappy marriages because divorce was difficult, expensive and stigmatized, this is no longer the case. In fact, divorce offers people another chance for happiness and an escape from dysfunctional homes for children.

The argument that marriage is in decline has also sparked a range of rejoinders that underscore and sometimes cheer the changing nature of marriage for endorsing flexibility and championing individual rights and needs. At the time when the works mentioned above denounced the decline in marriage, Judith Stacey (1996) a US family studies academic, responded that these authors were part of a strong network of 'scholarly and policy institutes, think tanks and commissions' which effectively mobilized 'to forge a national consensus on family values that rapidly shaped the family ideology and politics of the Clinton administration' (1996, p. 54). She continues:

> through the sheer force of categorical assertion, repetition, and cross-citation of each other's publications, these social scientists seem to have convinced most of the media, the literate public, and Clinton himself that a fault-free bedrock of social science research validates the particular family values that they and most Americans claim to favour, but fail to practice. (1996, p. 58)

Deliberations about the resilience of marriage developed in reaction to these developments. The central question is 'how can we make relationships personally and socially fulfilling'? This recognizes the pressures and anxieties experienced by families in all living arrangements and across class, racial and ethnic lines. An important point for those who adopt this perspective is that relationship decisions are private choices and governments have no business in endorsing or privileging the nuclear family at the expense of other types of family. Promoting marriage, therefore, offers few solutions. Governments should address problems such as poverty and poor access to education, health and child care, which threaten the well-being of children, more than the growth of individualism and the corresponding decline in the two-parent family. Problems in social relationships indicate that wider measures such as family-friendly work policies, parental leave, flexible work arrangements, and access to good quality child care should be available not just for married couples but also for all families. Improved public policies providing effective support systems would make life easier and put less of a burden on all relationships, not just married ones. Developing policies to restrict no-fault divorce are unhelpful and harmful for those trapped in abusive relationships. Divorce should not be made more difficult, as this may discourage many people from entering marriage in the first place. The high rates of divorce heighten the impression that marriage is a risky investment (Kiernan, 2004).

Those coming from a 'marital resilience' standpoint criticize some of the authors who view marriage as the avenue to better life chances. Coltrane cites one reviewer who claims that Gallagher and Waite's *The Case for Marriage* 'reads like and infomercial for marriage. ... Marriage, in their treatise, becomes a kind of universal wonder product, Prozac without the side effects' (cited in Coltrane, 2001, p. 395). Coltrane suggests that the simple comparisons offered in Gallagher and Waite's work 'overstate the potential benefits of marriage and lapse into treating correlation as causation' (2001, p. 395). Making a similar point to Stacey above, Coltrane argues that the pro-marriage movement is

> guilty of oversimplifying and often misrepresenting research on marriage, divorce, and parenting. Through sheer frequency of repetition, their public proclamations and media rhetoric about the dangers of fatherlessness and the evils of divorce come to be seen as 'facts'. In truth, the social science evidence on these topics is much more mixed. (2001, p. 405)

Marriage's perceived benefits need to be evaluated carefully. Huston and Melz (2004) call for caution when interpreting findings that support marriage, claiming that it is necessary to pay greater attention to details. Making generalizations, as Waite and Gallagher (2000) do, tell us very little about the benefits of marriage. Using broad-scale statistics that treat all groups the same, Huston and Melz (2004) claim 'obscures substantive differences in family-building behaviour for different racial and income groups' (2004, p. 946). To prove convincingly that marriage provides health, economic and other benefits it is necessary, they say, to compare married, single and divorced people on a range of indicators.

Marriage's advantages, Huston and Melz assert, cannot be limited to those who establish good marriages – those in conflict-ridden marriages should also experience benefits. Good marriage should be better for people than good forms of other lifestyles such as *de facto* or gay relationships. The benefits of marriage should exist for all couples, and demographic differences such as being rich or poor, gay or straight should not matter.

Several scholars have challenged the 'marital decline' argument that because married people, are, on average, better off than divorced or single people, lifelong marriage should be promoted for all and sundry, while divorce and cohabitation should be opposed. Coontz (2005, p. 310) disagrees with using averages to bestow personal advice to individuals or to develop social policy for everyone. Typically, she argues, marriage has substantial benefits for both husbands and wives. That is because, she acknowledges, most marriages are reasonably content. But, she insists, 'individuals in unhappy marriages are more psychologically distressed than people who remain single, and many of marriage's health benefits fade if the marriage is troubled' (2005, p. 310). In any case, according to Judith Stacey (1996), changes in family life are here to stay. It is more important to provide good public services and support all types of families, not just those which consist of heterosexual, married parents with children. She argues that there are two choices:

> Either we can come to grips with the postmodern family condition by accepting the end of a singular ideal family and begin to promote better living and spiritual conditions for the diverse array of real families we actually inhabit and desire. Or we can continue to engage in denial, resistance, displacement, and bad faith, by cleaving to a moralistic ideology of *the family* at the same time that we fail to provide social and economic conditions that make life for the modern family or any other kind of family viable, let alone dignified and secure. (1996, p. 11)

From this point of view, the objective of reviving marriage in its traditional form of the nuclear family is misguided. Any movement that sets a goal of re-establishing heterosexual marriage as the main site of child raising, dependent care or interpersonal commitments misunderstands how irrevocably marriage and family life have changed (Coontz, 2005). The claim for equality in marriage has centred on the reliance of love as the crucial element for legitimacy. This has implications for gays and lesbians. If love is the true foundation of marriage, and queer love is no different in passion or sincerity from straight love, then the institution of marriage cannot exclude gays and lesbians, except on the improper grounds of discrimination based on sexual orientation (Graff, 1999). Moreover, if gays and lesbians raise children, then their children should not be prevented from enjoying the rights and protection provided by marriage for heterosexual families.

Research indicates that successful marriage can be partially explained by self-selection, that is, people who choose to marry in the first place are more likely than unmarried couples to have steady employment, higher education and higher wages. From this perspective, governments can do little, because they cannot be involved in this selection process. Clearly though, marriage does not actually cause these differences, but people with good prospects are more likely to marry (Smock and Manning, 2004). Studies have shown that economically disadvantaged groups are just as likely to marry as non-disadvantaged groups. However, being economically disadvantaged does not result in successful marriage: couples with low income or income instability are more likely to divorce (Raley and Bumpass, 2003).

As Amato (2004) argues, the conflicting perspectives on marriage depend on whether marriage is perceived from an institutional point of view or from an individual point of view (2004, p. 962). Indeed, he reveals that the clash between these two perspectives 'reflects a fundamental contradiction within marriage itself'. On the one hand, marriage is designed to promote social stability and tradition, but on the other hand, it should nurture personal freedom and happiness (2004, p. 962). Ultimately, Amato supports marriage policies, citing studies that demonstrate that children have the best life chances if they are raised by two happily married parents. In a later study, Amato et al. (2007) investigate major changes in marriage in the US by comparing data from 1980 and 2000. They examine different dimensions including couples' social connections with friends, family and community organizations, and their expectations and attitudes about marriage and divorce. They document complex patterns of marriage, which 'have become stronger and more satisfying in some respects and weaker and less satisfying in other respects' (2007, p. 238). They noticed no consistent support for either the 'marital decline' or the 'marital resilience' perspective. For example, their findings indicate that attitudes towards life-long marriage have become more traditional and strongly value marital commitment, while the majority of people believe that personal happiness is more important than remaining in a bad marriage (2007, p. 201). Thus it is possible to support different perspectives on the state of marriage, depending on the selected evidence.

As a consequence of changing expectations which structure marriage, all the previous precedents have been challenged. As Coontz expresses it, society is now entering 'uncharted territory', and there is no clear guide to the new marital landscape. Most of what was taken for granted about who marries and why, or how to make a marriage work, is 'in flux' (2005, pp. 11–12). A return to traditional values of commitment, responsibility and sacrifice in marriage require what Cherlin calls a 'reinstitutionalization of marriage' and a 'reversal of the individualistic orientation toward family and personal life' (2004, p. 857). This would be difficult because today, as never before, decisions about marriage and family life rest with the individuals involved, not with society as a whole.[3]

Certainly there have been claims that Western society is accepting a wide variety of relationships. Giddens (1992) and Beck and Beck-Gernsheim (1995) have identified a loosening shift in family meanings and structures, suggesting that emotional and egalitarian attachments are replacing traditional bonds. They theorize about the greater acceptance that relationships are an essentially private subjective agreement. Giddens (1992) provides an interesting argument about the transformation of intimacy from a sociological perspective. He describes the shift in the late eighteenth century as 'the intrinsically subversive character of the romantic love complex' (1992, p. 46). Intimate relations are more fluid and no longer fixed by laws and customs or morals. People have the autonomy to deliberate, judge, choose and act on different possible courses of action (1992, p. 185). 'Love used to be tied to sexuality, for most of the sexually "normal" population, through marriage; but now the two are connected more and more via the pure relationship' (1992, p. 8). This relationship, Giddens argues, is entered into for its own sake, based on sexual and emotional equality, offering participants the likelihood of mutual respect and personally satisfying love. Accordingly, marriage is 'just one life-style among others' (1992, p. 154). Giddens reasons that this approach to relationships is reconfiguring popular as well as academic culture.

What is significant about Giddens' approach is that he sees the development of new types of intimacy holding the prospect of radically democratizing the personal sphere. However, he seems to be exaggerating his case. He does not consider sufficiently the inequality of gender, class and race. And as Cherlin (2004, p. 858) points out, Giddens does not take into account the effect of children on the pure relationship. It may be the case that couples who are well educated, earn good wages and have no children have a casual view about responsibility and can enjoy fluid relationships. However, people who are, or who intend to have children, or are not well-off, also want steadfastness and financial support from their partners. Ultimately, Cherlin (2004) concludes, it is marriage which can offer commitment and stability. This final comment points to the continued value of marriage for children and of relevance to governments who share public responsibility for their welfare. Those who argue for bringing back traditional marriage as well as those who defend diverse range of relationships would agree that children need a stable and happy environment if they are to flourish.

Marriage education programs and relationship support

Couples may no longer be content with having a 'stable' marriage if they are unhappy. Although governments may be limited in what they can do to address this discontentment, they can support a range of marital and relationship education programs as a way of strengthening relationships. As I will discuss in the empirical chapters, marriage and relationship education programs are similar in the UK, the US and Australia, ranging from early intervention and preventative strategies to strengthening approaches for those already married to rejuvenate their relationships, or assist those considering separation. In all three countries, a distinction is made between marriage and relationship education and marriage counselling. Marriage education programs suggest that people need to nurture their relationships and can benefit from accessing information, learning new skills or changing their behaviour (Gottman, 1994). This is different from counselling which is offered to already distressed couples experiencing specific problems.

Marriage education embraces pre-marital preparation when couples are happy with each other and willing to invest effort into their relationship. Entry to marriage is a good time for educational measures to prepare couples for the challenges they may encounter in the future. While newly weds report high levels of relationship satisfaction initially, after the first year or two couples find the attraction moderates and are confronted with the need to develop new roles and routines in their relationship and also with the need to find ways to negotiate conflict (Halford, 2004, p. 561). Other forms of marriage education include mentoring programs, relationships skills training, campaigns and information about the value of marriage. The aim of the marriage and relationship education, more broadly, is to assist committed couples (whether cohabiting, engaged or already married) to move through the various phases of their relationship.

There are numerous approaches to marriage education, some focus on role playing, or showing empathy, some are content driven, others focus on updating and revising skills. While marriage education programs provide a variety of learning options, the common objective is to teach people the behaviours that predict marital success and those that predict failure, to teach them about the advantages of marriage for families and what to expect along the path of matrimony. The assumption is that the earlier couples learn relationship skills, the fewer problems they will experience once married. Various studies have shown that these programs produce large improvements in relationship skills immediately after completion and that these improvements persist over time (Halford and Simons, 2005; Stanley et al., 2001). Benefits of pre-marriage education include slowing couples down to allow time to deliberate over their relationship and reduce impulsive decision making; sending a message about the importance of marriage and the commitment it entails; raising awareness of support and resources if couples require it and reducing the risk of subsequent distress (Stanley, 2001).

Marriage education provides information designed to help people achieve 'long-lasting, happy, and successful marriages. It aims to impart knowledge and attitudes and teach the skills and behaviours needed to have successful intimate relationships' (Ooms, 2005, p. 1). Ooms refers broadly to the field of marriage and relationships education which includes information for people in different life-cycles from single to divorced. Marriage and relationships education is available through classes and also via media campaigns, fact sheets and brochures, self-help books, DVDs and self-guided web courses and other informations available via the Internet. Most commonly, however, this form of learning refers to 'structured programs, classes, and work-shops for couples and individuals offered on a voluntary basis in the community, churches, campuses and schools' (Ooms, 2005, pp. 1–2). It uses an educational approach, providing information and understanding about relationship choices, behaviours and challenges. The idea is to equip individuals and couples with the skills and knowledge they need to deal with any relationship issues. The programs employ various teaching methods, lecture material and experiential exercises. They are often supplemented with videos and movie clips, role-playing, workbook exercises and practice assignments between sessions. Most courses run from eight to twenty hours and are delivered over a weekend or one night per week for six to ten week periods.

While differences exist between the three countries, there are two main approaches: skills training and inventories. One of the main approaches to marriage education programs (particularly in the US), uses skills-based programs focusing on active training of skills, although these approaches usually include other components such as building awareness and cognitive change (Halford and Simons, 2005, p. 150). Examples include Practical Application of Relationship Skills (PAIRS), Prevention and Relationship Enhancement Program (PREP), Relationship Enhancement and Couples Communication (RECC). The programs offer married or unmarried couples skills for maintaining a lasting relationship. They are designed in different formats and can be delivered in a range of settings by clergy, trained para-professionals, religious and lay leaders and teachers. Courses and activities cover issues such as positive communication, managing conflict, balancing work, home and relationships, sharing responsibility, intimacy and sexuality. The goal of providing information and self-awareness is important. Many programs involve sharing information, for example, about issues such as financial budgets and awareness raising, particularly about expectations and attitudes, communication and conflict. There is evidence on the short-term effectiveness of skills training, in particular, immediately after programs (Hahlweg and Markman, 1988) and that improvements continue over time (Halford et al., 2003) Studies have illustrated that even short programs of a few hours duration can strengthen relationships over a period of one to five years (Carroll and Doherty, 2003). A study of 3,000 families in the US discovered that divorce rates were 30 per cent lower over the first five years of marriage for those who had completed a marriage preparation course (Stanley et al., 2006a).

A widely used approach is based on pre-marital assessment by utilizing couple inventories. Examples of inventories include Premarital Personal and Relationship Evaluation (PREPARE) and Facilitating Open Couple Communication Understanding and Study (FOCCUS). These programs involve completing a self-diagnostic inventory assessing a range of relationship issues or completing a questionnaire which seeks to help couples identify their strengths and areas for growth. Used as an introduction to the marriage preparation process, the programs open up issues for discussion and couples consider the results of their surveys with a trained facilitator, educator or clergy person. According to Halford and Simons (2005, pp. 149–150), the benefit of these programs is the focus on adult learning processes which allows self-directed learning and negotiating curricula between participants and educators. For example, FOCCUS surveys a respondent's perceptions of his or her partner as couples complete a premarital inventory that assesses relationship issues. A facilitator considers the results of these questionnaires with the couple, addressing their strengths and weaknesses. Couples can then reflect on issues where they disagree and consider ways of improving their relationship. A positive aspect of the inventory-based approach is that programs such as PREPARE and FOCCUS can predict the trajectory of relationship satisfaction in the initial years of marriage (Larson and Olsen, 1989; Williams and Jurich, 1995). They provide the opportunity for couples to evaluate their personal risk and resilience. In some instances, couples realize they have problems that they need to resolve and may delay or even cancel their wedding. And the structured approach to using the inventories and the available training might help to explain their widespread application (Halford and Simons, 2005, p. 150). However, outcomes studies on the use and effects of assessment instruments such as PREPARE have not been carried out (Stanley, 2001, p. 276).

Some settings offer couples skills programs after they have completed the inventories. It has been argued that inventories are a supplemental tool and should not be called marriage education because they do not teach skills (Sollee, email 2007). At any rate, inventories continue to be widely used, particularly by religious organizations; many of these receive public funding in the UK and Australia.

While the divorce rate is high in the three countries under study, it is important to acknowledge that over 50 per cent of marrying couples remain married for the rest of their lives. This suggests that many couples sustain marriages without participating in relationship education (although this tells us little about the quality of their relationship and it does not necessarily follow that these couples are happy). However, of more concern is the need to target 'high risk' couples. Predictors of high risk for future relationship problems include 'negative family-of-origin experiences, certain personality characteristics, patterns of couple communication, and low religiosity' (Halford and Simons, 2005, p. 153). Particular groups have been identified as being 'at risk' or 'high risk' and susceptible to developing unsuccessful marriages. Halford (2004) argues that relationship education is of particular benefit to these high-risk couples. Assessing risk indicators such as parental divorce, previous marriage, amount of time that the partners have known each other, whether they have cohabitated or will be forming stepfamilies are relatively easy to measure. While some of the programs such as PREP focus on negative behaviour which is particularly relevant for high-risk couples such as withdrawal, escalation, negativity and invalidation, the problem is that high-risk partners are less likely to go to education classes than are low-risk partners (Halford, 2004, pp. 562–563). A recent study by Fincham et al. (2007) argues that forgiveness, sacrifice, commitment and sanctification in maintaining and regulating marital quality are important. This finding is connected to the transformation of marriage itself – these factors may not be present in relationships given the current trend towards individual fulfilment. However, the analysis concludes that those who do place the stability of the marriage above their own personal needs are more likely to enjoy happy and successful marriages.

Various studies indicate that not all couples require the same intervention, so a 'one size fits all' approach may not be particularly useful. While some couples may need communication skills training, others may benefit from learning stress-management techniques or how to deal with conflicts with in-laws. Others may be experiencing emotional problems or physical illness (Larson, 2004; Halford et al., 2004). Ooms (2005) argues that in the US, some attention has been paid to 'best practice' curricula thereby avoiding a model based on traditional family roles and tasks within marriage. She claims that 'the processes and skills taught in these programs are clearly egalitarian and carefully structured to create and model a level playing field' (2005, p. 5). She goes on to acknowledge, however, that marriage education does not 'explicitly discuss the dark side of couple relationships and marriage, nor what constitutes violent and abusive intimate behaviour' (2005, p. 5).

Government subsidies for many of these programs allow the service providers to charge inexpensive fees. Moreover, governments are gradually funding programs that have been designed for the specific needs of diverse populations in different situations. For example, programs that were initially designed for fairly small numbers of white, middle class, committed couples are being adapted for stepfamilies, military families, prisoners and their partners and couples dealing with substance abuse or chronic illness. Particular racial and ethnic groups, refugees and migrants are also being targeted. In the US, marriage educators are now working with domestic violence groups. Self-directed learning kits are available for people living in regional and remote areas in Australia. Evidently, marriage and relationship education takes place in assorted arrangements and settings. Service providers often develop their programs in response to local needs or to address the requirements of particular cohorts.

Recent studies show the different participation levels in marriage and relationship education. In the US, 44 per cent of couples who married in the 1990s attended some form of program (Stanley et al., 2006a). In Australia approximately one third of marrying couples attend some form of premarriage education (House of Representatives Standing Committee on Legal and Constitutional Affairs, 1998), while in the Britain, it has been estimated that less than one in 100 couples per year seek relationship support of any kind (Social Justice Policy Group, 2007). These low figures suggest that governments and service providers face many challenges if they wish to increase this amount.

Conclusion

This book considers how differing perceptions about marriage play out in interactions between the various actors in the public realm. Those who view marriage as a traditional institution wish to see it revived through government support and individual effort, arguing that a strong *marriage* is far superior to a strong *relationship*. In contrast, those who perceive marriage as a private institution are not automatically opposed to governments enhancing marriage education, but are concerned about the implicit message that single-parent families are inferior. They recommend that the focus of the debate should be on developing policies that support *all* family relationships, regardless of their form. They are also concerned about an approach that is directed toward changing couples' behaviour, rather than tackling wider societal or environmental problems. While there is therefore some overlap between the two perspectives, there are nonetheless fundamental disagreements. The following chapters will demonstrate the ways in which the issues surrounding the marriage debate remain contested.

Marriage educators agree that the attitudes, skills, and behaviours needed for a successful marriage can be learned; that marriage education is more easily accepted, reaches more people and is more cost-effective than individual couples therapy. Moreover, happy couples can profit from education – it is not necessarily for those whose relationships are already under stress. In short, marriages naturally decay unless energy is put into them (Ooms, 2005, p. 4). These programs focus on practical, technique-based measures to sustain successful relationships. Their underlying theme is for couples to reduce any unrealistic expectations that they will 'live happily ever after' and to adopt responsible attitudes by working on their relationships. This may occur via feedback through completing an inventory; accessing resources materials;

or learning skills which provide people with the ability to strengthen their relationship through programs such as PREP.

The next chapter examines the changes and different understandings about marriage because they impact on the role of governments. As the above account illustrates, there have been many explanations and discussions about shifts in people's relationships and changes in marriage's functions. Governments not only have to deal with these numerous, wide reaching developments but also with a range of particular variables which in turn influence marriage education and public policy.

2

Tensions within Marriage: Public Institution or Private Choice?

The status of marriage in the twenty-first century is a contested issue and there is much disagreement about marriage's nature and purpose in Western societies. The march of history has seen shifts in emphasis from the communal to the personal as the bonds of marriage weaken. Indeed, the many justifications for marriage can be organized along a continuum between its collective components and its current focus on the individual. Marriage has been historically organized as a public institution which works for the common and social good for the benefit not only of individuals but also of society as a whole. The move to personal satisfaction and individual fulfilment as a priority has altered the meaning and the confidence in marriage. The changing circumstances surrounding relationships are important in explaining why government attempts to strengthen marriage are so challenging. The chapter highlights the tensions between marriage as a fundamental social institution with a formal, legal and religious status regulated by public opinion and norms and marriage as a form of emotional bonding chosen by two autonomous individuals. Even though marriage and relationships are now in many ways a 'private' concern, marriage continues to function as a public institution in so far as it is governed by political and legal acts. Governments contribute to our understanding of marriage, its financial benefits and cultural meaning because it regulates marriage in different ways, for example, via tax and other policies. Public policies provide a range of benefits and rights for married people. Laws govern the entry into and exit from marriage.

The chapter examines broad historical shifts in marriage as its primary purpose has moved to encompass the increasing importance of love and individual choice. It then analyses a range of factors which have not only contributed to the long-term structural transformation of marriage as framed by the 'marital decline' and 'marital resilience' arguments but also have changed marriage and influenced the role of government. These dimensions incorporate religion and the sacred aspects of marriage; feminism and the gendered nature of marriage; romantic love in marriage; and same-sex unions and their legal status. These interconnected trends contribute to the complexity of modern relationships and are influential in developing marriage education policy.

The factors triggering the flight from unhappy marriages are intertwining and multifaceted. It is difficult to pinpoint whether any particular factor is a cause of the flight or a consequence of it, because most factors can be understood as both cause and consequence (Smock, 2004). For many different reasons, people postpone or dissolve their marriage, while some do not marry at all. While marriage can be very fulfilling, providing people with a sense of belonging, predictability and security, it is also disposable when their needs are not being met. Marriage has also changed within the social context of greater sexual freedom and improved birth control. Thanks to feminism, there is more equality between women and men and attitudes about women's roles are changing as their participation in the paid workforce increases. There is growing tolerance for diverse lifestyles, illustrated by greater acceptance of homosexuality and of couples living together. The stigma surrounding divorce has declined and there are fewer reasons for remaining in miserable marriages. Social policies and legislation have changed as attitudes and behaviour in relationships have shifted towards 'greater individuality, autonomy, equality, and privacy as driving factors in refashioning existing social norms related to marriage and family life' (Brotherson and Duncan, 2004, p. 460). Within this changing context, the political promotion and policy development of marriage education is occurring. As we shall see, these changes have important implications for the role of governments.

Historical changes in the meanings of marriage

The meaning of marriage and its purpose in people's lives have altered dramatically. Governments have engaged with marriage in different ways and there have been different expectations placed upon the state. Many historical and sociological records document the functions of marriage and how the institution has changed in Western societies (Stone, 1977). Historically, the purpose of marriage was not primarily to meet the needs and desires of a man and a woman. In previous centuries, marriage had as much to do with economic decisions, family connections and political advantage as it did with an emotional connection. Until the late eighteenth century, the accepted wisdom was that matrimony operated as an institution with financial objectives rather than an alliance founded on love and mutual support of the partners. Luhmann (1986) suggests that in pre-modern societies love was restricted to certain groups and was highly delimited in terms of who could love whom, when and where (as, for example, in the case of court society). According to Stone (1977, p. 5), 'marriage was not an intimate association based on personal choice'. Rather, it was a rational affair, based on a private contract between two families exchanging property. Stone argues that the subordination of freedom of choice was for the benefit of ancestry, parents, neighbours, kin, Church or state. Parents, relations and community often chose suitable mates who would wed. Among the upper classes, marriage was a way of binding kinship groups, gaining collective economic benefits and securing advantageous political alliances. For peasants, artisans and labourers, marriage partners contributed to the economic unit. Matrimony was also a way of controlling sexual desire, because of a presumption that any acceptable person of the opposite sex could satisfy this urge. Meeting someone special and falling in love was not important. Romantic love was perceived by 'moralists and theologians as a kind of mental illness, fortunately of short duration' (1977, p. 5). Thus 'romantic love'– a strong emotional connection involving sexual desire, a yearning to be with one's lover and a readiness to excuse his or her faults and to see only their good features – was not considered a sensible reason for marriage. Indeed, the common belief was that short-lived factors such as sexual attraction or romantic love were less likely to produce lasting happiness than a prudent and mature arrangement. Marriage based on personal selection or passion was therefore not encouraged (1977, p. 181). Marriage was considered a success if it survived economically. Consequently, if marriages took place without providing mutual emotional support or feelings of love that we expect today, so be it.

With the rise of industrial society, passionate love began to spread throughout the population. Historians generally agree that novels communicated the idea that love and marriage were connected. The literature on love in the eighteenth and nineteenth centuries incorporated confessions, novels and pornography and developed socially important 'codes' between men and women, especially in the increasingly urbanized world of strangers. Luhmann (1986) suggests that as this discourse of steady information flowed, romantic love became prominent as an important measure of symbolic exchange. In effect, the growing predominance of passionate love had the function of encouraging strangers to meet and converse (Luhmann, 1986). A parallel market to the economic market, the market of free emotions started to develop. Thus, falling in love was a product of learned cultural expectations, which became fashionable through practices such as the spread of novel reading (Stone, 1977, p. 286). Stone suggests that

> romantic love and the romantic novel grew together after 1780, and the problem of cause and effect is one that is impossible to resolve. All that can be said is that for the first time in history, romantic love become a respectable motive for marriage among the propertied classes, and that at the same time there was a rising flood of novels filling the shelves of the circulating libraries, devoted to the same theme. (1977, p. 284)

Fiction contributed to the development of new practices involving courtship and marriage. Marriage became more than a rite of passage to adulthood and parenthood, more than an economic necessity for women or a means of assuring inheritance rights for men.

By the mid-twentieth century, the social functions and internal dynamics of traditional marriage had been transformed. Cherlin (2004) argues that marriage has experienced a process of deinstitutionalization – 'a weakening of the social norms that define partners' behaviour' (2004, p. 848) offering examples such as the increasing number of cohabiting couples and the emergence of same-sex marriage to support his case. He contends that these developments are 'the result of long-term cultural and material trends that altered the meaning of marriage during the 20th century' (2004, p. 851). He discusses two major changes. First, in the middle of the twentieth century, there was a move from institutional to companionate marriage, reaching its zenith in the 1950s with the stable breadwinner–homemaker model. In these marriages, emotional satisfaction and friendship were highly valued as well as fulfilling the traditional gender roles of breadwinner and homemaker. Then a second transition occurred from companionate to 'expressive individualism' in marriage from the 1960s.

> When people evaluated how satisfied they were with their marriages, they began to think more in terms of the development of their own

sense of self and the expression of their feelings, as opposed to the satisfaction they gained through building a family and playing the roles of spouse and parent. (Cherlin, 2004, p. 852)[1]

Consistent with the idea of individualization, Cherlin (2004) argues that marriage has experienced a process of 'a weakening of the social norms that define partners' behaviour' (2004, p. 848). If people's individual needs were not being met, spouses move on, seeking new partners.

Contraception – becoming more readily available in the 1960s – and legal abortion – becoming more readily available in the 1970s – disconnected sex from reproduction. This had momentous significance for the dominance of marriage. Wilcox (2006, p. 243) argues that 'marriage promotes social order by regulating sexual and romantic relations, providing a long-term vehicle for the accumulation of property, and – most importantly – fostering a strong, life-long bond between men and women that confers considerable social, economic, and spiritual benefits on any children'. From this perspective, Wilcox identifies legal abortion and the availability of the contraceptive pill as contributing to the separation of sex and procreation from marriage. This had dramatic consequences for the institution of marriage and society as a whole. Wilcox draws on research which demonstrates that contraception allowed married women to focus on careers rather than childbearing, decreasing their economic dependence on husbands and therefore their investment in marriage. Contraception 'changed men and women's basic assumptions about the nature and character of marriage by allowing men and women to focus more on their relationship, leisure, consumerism, and careers, and less on children' (2006, p. 246). Women wanting to marry could no longer hold the threat of pregnancy over their male partners, either to withhold sex or to elicit a promise of marriage if a pregnancy did occur. Wilcox thus contends that the sexual revolution left traditional women unable to compete with women who did not object to premarital sex. Contraception and abortion also allowed young men to postpone marriage and hence they 'missed out' on the benefits of 'the civilizing influence of wives and children' (2006, p. 248). This was especially the case for poor and working class men who were unable to access educational and economic opportunities. These various historical developments led to increasing attention from governments on the place of marriage, which still resonates today.

Marriage and religion

Religion is a very powerful factor. It has played a complex and important role in influencing what constitutes marriage, connecting it with religious values such as commitment, acceptance and sacrifice. Indeed, according to Browning, marriage has 'been seen as a profoundly religious reality'. He elaborates:

> the first two chapters of Genesis and their theologies of creation have been foundational for views of marriage in Judaism, Islam and Christianity, as well as for the culture and law in the societies they have influenced. These texts establish marriage as an 'order of creation' that expresses the will of God for all humankind. This order is preserved and enhanced through covenant promises between god and humans and between God and husband, wife, their families and the wider community. (2001, p. 5)

By the twelfth century, a wedding ceremony was attached to the church. Around the late twelfth and early thirteenth century, marriage came to be viewed as one of the church's official sacraments. As a sacramental reality, the marriage bond could not be dissolved and consequently, the Catholic prohibition against divorce arose. Many Judaeo-Christian religious doctrines accept that marriage embodies the Christian way of life. The most well known wedding ceremony comes from the *Book of Common Prayer* (1662), spelling out the obligations of marriage beyond procreation, fidelity and sacrament. Husband and wife promise to love, to comfort, to honour and to keep each other, for richer or poorer, in sickness as in health. The Book states that the procreation of children is the first reason for marriage. For this reason, most contemporary churches oppose legalizing same-sex unions because they do not contribute to reproducing the human race (Cretney, 2006, p. 14).

The importance of religion for marriage has been argued by scholars such as Kohm (2003) who argues that religion should be used in public decision making relating to marriage. Matrimony must be protected to defend religious liberty and moral freedom (2003, p. 88). Marriage, Kohm says, was 'not invented, codified or planned' by governments, rather, 'governments gave the stamp of approval to a design already evident, honoured, maintained and flourishing'. Any government that 'ratified marriage as an institution did so only after organized religion had established a methodology for upholding the marriage concept as a good to be promoted in human civilization' (2003, p. 82).

Religious observance and religious convictions carry great importance for marriage which 'symbolized the eternal union between Christ and his church, bringing sanctifying grace to the couple, the church, and the community at large' (Kohm, 2003, p. 82). Scruton (2006, p. 6) agrees that marriage is an institution designed by the church to symbolize the eternal union between Christ and his church. He proposes that religion is important in contributing to the 'long-term interests' of society by stimulating the 'short-term decisions' of its members. Therefore, it is natural, he contends, that marriage should be regarded as something 'divinely ordained, with a sacred aura that reinforces' the duties associated with raising children. Scruton goes on to argue that civil unions cannot have the function of marriage as traditionally conceived, because they cannot guarantee security for children and they show no evidence of sacrifice by the parents for their children's future. 'When the Church first declared marriage to be a sacrament, to be administered before the altar in the presence of God, it was attempting to give institutional form to a vow' (2006, p. 13). This is because marriage was perceived as 'a form of adhesion contract, to be accepted or rejected in toto, but not individually renegotiated' (Witte, 2003, p. 45). Marriage was viewed as the appropriate place for enjoying sexual activities. Indeed, Witte argues, those 'who practiced sex elsewhere, with self or others, were subject to various moral and criminal sanctions' (2003, p. 45).

Eventually marriage came to be viewed as the consent that heterosexual spouses gave to each other at the beginning of their married life. 'The bond of marriage could be understood as a metaphysical reality that existed in the souls of the spouses from the moment that they spoke the words of the sacramental sign' (Martos, 2001, pp. 41–42). Cooke (2001) argues that in a Christian marriage, the communication between the two people intends to 'embrace the sharing of faith and hope in that salvation that comes through Jesus. The Christian family is meant to be the most basic instance of Christian community, people bonded together by their shared relationship to the risen Jesus' (2001, p. 57). Religious faith can be challenged in times of a relationship crisis, but strengthens the bonds between husband and wife.

Marriage has been recognized as both an important public contract and private promise. Browning describes this very well:

A public philosophy of marriage cannot be ruled directly by religious ideals of creation, covenant, and sacrament. But it must understand our society's indebtedness to what these concepts did to form western marriage. A public philosophy of marriage must take a generous and supportive attitude toward how these great ideas worked in communities of faith and shaped both secular law and wider cultural sensibilities. Furthermore, it should allow these ideas to sensitize public debate on how the deep experiences of marriage tend to call forth the kind of transcendent aspirations generally associated with religion. Whether it is the deep metaphors of covenant as in Judaism, Islam, and Reformed Protestantism; sacrament as in Roman Catholicism or Eastern Orthodoxy; the yin and yang of Confucianism; the quasi-sacramentalism of Hinduism, or the mysticism often associated with allegedly modern romantic love, humans tend to find values in marriage that call them beyond the mundane and everyday. (Browning, 2001, p. 6)

With the widespread secularization of Western culture, the meaning of marriage began to move away from its religiously grounded definitions. As Mack and Blankenhorn (2001) suggest, until recently, religion was the preeminent influence on the ideals governing marriage and the marital relationship. It was regarded as 'a sacred covenant, a union of higher spiritual and moral purpose which could not be dissolved without serious justification' (2001, p. xv). Now, however, it is 'less a spiritual covenant than a simple legal and economic agreement – entered on for the good of society, perhaps, but less for spiritual purposes than for material and natural purposes' (2001, p. xv). Nonetheless, as Amato et al. (2007) contend, religion continues to play an important role in marriage for those with religious beliefs. Most religions promote marital quality and stability, emphasizing the importance of family life and strong marital bonds. In addition, church involvement draws families together into communities of people with similar beliefs. This network provides social support for married couples and can be helpful for those experiencing relationship problems (2007, p. 29). Moreover, the symbolism of religion remains, for example, brides wear the white dress, many couples still wish to marry in a Church and to celebrate the spiritual rituals of the occasion.

The progressively more *laissez-faire* attitude towards marriage's religious aspects has implications for governments. Scruton (2006) argues that

when the state usurped the rite of matrimony, and reshaped what had once been holy law, it was inevitable that it should loosen the marital tie. For the state does not represent the Eternal, nor does it have so much regard for future generations that it can disregard the whims of the merely living. (2006, p. 19)

In response to public demands, it has been politically convenient for governments to authorize a simple divorce process and to relegate marriage from a vow to a contract. Browning (2001) draws the public and private aspects of religion together. He argues that marriage 'as a public institution, sanctioned by law, in service to the common good, and blessed by religion, must protect its private, personal, and intersubjective dimensions' (2001, p. 8). Most importantly, the procreation and education of children should remain marriage's most crucial function. But the option of divorce if happiness is not forthcoming and the possibility of improved marital happiness with a new partner have resulted in less support for the belief that marriage entails a life-long commitment. One of the key explanations in this shift is the seduction of romance as the primary reason for marriage.

Romantic love and wedded bliss

One important variable that governments need to take seriously when considering marriage education policies is the role of romance. In Western popular culture today, romantic love provides an important explanation for why people get married in the first place. If liberal democracy makes possible marriages founded upon romance, what are the political consequences of such an understanding of marriage? Of course this is a large and complicated question, linked to a range of political concerns including those of privacy, reproduction rights and the separation of church and state. Here we want to focus on one aspect – the question of marriage and the stability of marriage as a matter of public concern. People grow up dreaming of falling in love, getting married and growing old together.[2] Many believe that 'love conquers all'. Contemporary expectations of relationships are very high and include romance as an important aspect of love. In popular culture, movies, television and women's magazines depict the perfect form of matrimony via images and stereotypes reinforcing the perception that love is effortless if you meet 'the one'. Marriage and relationship education does not fit in this ideal, although many of the classes actually consider the role of romance. The problem is that romantic ideologies are reproduced again and again, colouring many people's idealistic expectations and leaving little room for exploring the normality of relationships.

Romance has been assumed as natural, but Shumway (2003, pp. 2–3) argues that fictional narratives in novels, movies and other forms of entertainment 'teach readers and viewers even if they are often unaware of the lesson'. Therefore, many people do not think about the fact that 'love stories permeate our lives', but 'probably assume that all these representations of love are themselves a response to people's natural concerns and therefore a reflection of reality' (2003, p. 2). The fictional narratives, he suggests, lead to 'the expectation that marriage will be a continuation of the romantic state' (2003, p. 3).

The notion of the inevitability and enchantment of 'true love' is now a crucial ingredient for marriage and an important vehicle in close gender relations, as women and men exercise far greater choice over marriage partners than in previous times. From the perspective of romance, matrimony becomes the accepted goal for personal fulfilment. In this context, the stricture of romantic love defines the grounds and boundaries of a 'true' marriage. Couples should not marry unless they are 'in' love – mere affection is rather inadequate. Honesty and sincerity demand that such a love be 'pure'; base considerations, such as wealth, may taint the entire marriage. In this light, children become an 'expression' of love, rather than a continuation of the family line, or a provision for old age as they may have been in times gone by. Finally, a 'loveless' marriage, understood in the elevated terms of romantic love, is a sham that should not be tolerated. All those who marry for other than love are thus fraud, made to feel guilty for their illegitimate unions. This, at any rate, is the world that is depicted in modern literature, plays and poetry and especially by Hollywood.

Romance has become easy to acquire, because we are able either to buy it or to use its manufactured form. Illouz (1997) charts the development of romantic proclivities and the expansion of economic activities in purchasing the trappings of romance as consumer capitalism expanded. Men and women adopted new rituals and dating appeared alongside the rise in income and acquisition of material goods. In this 'romantic utopia', love and marriage incorporated romance with courtship. Advertising, movies and media images advanced a vision of love as a utopia to courting couples (1997, p. 43). People have been overexposed to the ideal of romance in the mass media and consumer culture. Consequently, Illouz maintains that romantic love penetrates everyday life via images, technologies of leisure and commodities (1997, p. 15). This is not to suggest that people consume romance in its many forms as unthinking dupes, but that they do yearn for – and expect – romance in their lives and relationships.

Interestingly, it has been primarily feminist scholars who have been critical of romance as a foundation for marriage. Feminists in the 1970s condemned the way romance reinforces patriarchal power structures, distorting women's self-understanding. Thus following de Beauvoir (1987),

Greer (1971, p. 188) argues that 'romance sanctions drudgery, physical incompetence and prostitution'. Firestone (1970, 139) sees romance as a 'cultural tool of male power to keep women from knowing their ('real') conditions'. More ambiguous, yet still critical, is Grymes (1996) who claims that women's unconscious contradictions and illusions affect lives in dangerous ways, and Evans (1998, 273) who argues that 'romance distorts and limits the possibilities of human relationships'. Though recent scholarship has been more sympathetic (see, for example, Radway 1991; Jackson 1995; Stacey and Pearce 1995), the general tenor of this research has emphasised the power of romance and its destructive potential, especially for woman.

As Jackson (1993, p. 42) argues, the 'ideology of heterosexual romance tells us that falling in love is the prelude to a lasting, secure and stable conjugal union'. Contemporary cultural representations evident in the genre of romantic discourses continue using clichés, focusing on the central couple who, after some obstacles, realize they have found 'the one', leading to the cue of 'living happily ever after'. In cinematic magic, romance's narrative drive is the traditional one, often depicting the man's pursuit of the woman. In this way, conventional forms of masculinity and femininity remain intact. Understanding the texts from a gendered perspective highlights the fact that regardless of changing gender relations, motion pictures reinforce long-established expectations about love. For spectators, heterosexual relationships are constructed in particular ways: shaping love, sexuality, marriage and the family. Yet audiences negotiate meanings, conforming to and resisting gender codes and relations in their own lives. Indeed, we may view the predictable outcomes in conventional romances with pleasure, enjoying the escapism. As Pearce and Wisker (1998, p. 17) argue, the majority of romantic texts will continue to be as 'interesting, pleasurable and valuable' in their failure to achieve any 'sort of ultimate transgression as the few that do'. The point to underline, however, is that as audiences negotiate various cultural meanings and messages, the ideal of romance perseveres, operating as a discourse that marks all of us, whether we resist it or not. It is difficult to link this discourse to the possibility that even couples in love could benefit from marriage education.

The extravagant wedding is another indication of the changing meaning of marriage. Feminist critiques of marriage have expanded to emphasize what are perceived as troubling connections between marriage and romance. One area that has received attention is the wedding industry, resplendent with rich choices of diamonds and dresses, flowers, cakes, receptions and honeymoons, encouraging brides to throw themselves into planning the perfect wedding day (Paul, 2000). This stressful attention to every minute detail deflects from reflecting about the seriousness of the couple's legal obligations and social commitments once the marriage begins. Couples are therefore ill-prepared for the adjustment to daily married life. Research on contemporary weddings shows how people indulge in them as a celebration and consumption of romance. Boden (2003) argues that the wedding has become 'a fantasy-laden cultural event that is dependent upon consumption' (2003, p. 74). She argues that the 'superbride' focuses so much on planning her wedding that she does not consider the marriage she is entering.

Ingraham (1999) explores white weddings and their various practices, arrangements and rituals, investigating television sitcoms, advertisements, films and magazines. Arguing that weddings in popular culture 'contribute to the creation of many taken-for-granted beliefs, values, and assumptions' concerning heterosexuality, Ingraham says this works to organize gender while preserving racial, class and sexual structures (1999, p. 128). The ensuing belief system creates and maintains the illusion of well-being, setting up expectations of couples easily pairing together forever. One of the central ways that this belief system survives is by convincing couples that romance is not only essential but also revered, far outweighing the realities of the marketplace and its consequences for consumers and communities. Ingraham's work on weddings demonstrates how ideology has been used to represent and highlight gender. Weddings 'work as a form of ideological control...to signify that the couple is normal, moral, productive, family-centred, upstanding, and most importantly, appropriately gendered' (1999, p. 18). The happy ending is usually fulfilled with the promise or the visualization of a wedding. Indeed, the wedding has become a 'personal achievement' and a 'status symbol'; an event focused on and 'controlled by the couple' (Cherlin, 2004, p. 856).

The problem with depictions of romance and weddings is that the various discourses of popular culture rarely raise issues about how the pair will adapt and negotiate domestic duties, paid work or children 'till death do us part'. Different feelings from romantic longing tend to ensue as domesticity takes over, but these are not the romantic film or novel's concern. As Wilson states, romance is performed around motifs of 'compulsion and denial' so the story ends at the point of final consummation. This is because 'sexual gratification destroys the compulsion little by little' (1983, p. 43). But in reality, new and often confronting responsibilities overtake romance. Love has disruptive social consequences as people move to a new area, find different jobs and lifestyles or change partners. Evans (2003, p. 5) argues that the promises of 'romance and sexual pleasure within intimacy which are the subject matter of the various dream factories of the West endlessly threaten the fragile possibilities of human happiness'. The 'industries and institutions of romance' may become more problematic as our expectations (and sense of entitlement) about the rewards of personal relations increase (2003, p. 142). She advises that we abandon love in its romanticized and commercialised form. It should be retrieved from 'those careless and irrational spheres to which it has been assigned. ... Rather than regarding the rational as the cold and uncaring enemy of love, we might well regard it as its only defender in a social world awash with deadly cocktails of romance, hedonism and personal entitlement' (2003, p. 143). One suspects that Evans would approve of marriage education where people can learns skills about how to strengthen relationships.

Of course people who get swept away by romance may be unprepared for the realities of marriage. This is part of the problem that governments have to deal with – the aftermath when romance 'goes wrong'. Whitehead and Whitehead (2001, p. 107) argue that the expectations of marriage are now very high and romance is an important aspect of married love. Celebrity weddings of Hollywood movie stars contribute to many taken-for-granted beliefs, values and assumptions about finding 'soul mates' and 'living happily ever after' which do not eventuate. Alternatively, people may avoid marriage to protect themselves and prevent disappointment. A variety of research shows that people getting married want mutuality, intimacy, happiness and self-fulfilment. As Gillis (2004) notes, it is 'precisely this purity that makes marriage so vulnerable to disappointment and renunciation. Promoted to a level once reserved for sacred callings, marriage raises expectations it cannot fulfil' (2004, p. 990). Linked to these high expectations of relationships is the destabilization of traditional forms of male control over women, which provides another important explanation for changes in marriage.

Feminist views of marriage

Woven throughout investigations of marriage are key questions about the role of gender. While there are many differences in methods, emphasis and objectives, feminism offers some compelling political arguments about marriage and how it shapes and defines women and men. Feminists have raised a number of issues about the role of marriage, arguing that gender inequality is one of the main barriers to successful heterosexual relationships. A major feminist critique is that marriage is a site of gendered power relationships that entails rigid gender roles buttressed by legal rules and sanctions. The supposedly private domain of the family is not immune from operations of power. From a public policy viewpoint, marriage caters for individuals to bear and nurture children and care for other dependants such as aged parents or sick friends and neighbours. Therefore, 'the state has an interest in guaranteeing that people marry, procreate, and take care of one another' (Tronto, 2004, p. 38). Thus, marriage is premised on the normative gender stereotype of men as husbands, fathers and the main breadwinners and women as wives, mothers and domestic carers.

The claim that women benefit from marriage as much as men is an argument disputed by many feminists. According to Shanley (2004), while marriage laws themselves are gender-neutral, 'cultural norms and employment practices perpetuate a division of labor at work and at home' that results in gender hierarchy (2004, p. 20). This can have implications for women who are financially dependent on their husbands. Different wage-earning capacities between men and women give men more material resources and this in turn affects dynamics within the family. Moreover, wives who are out of the paid workforce for a number of years lose earning power. This diminishes their authority within marriage and their ability to leave unsatisfactory ones. 'The division between workers and caregivers not only harms women in the workplace but makes it less likely that men will develop interpersonal and caregiving skills' (2004, p. 22). According to Folbre (2001), within a marriage the person who works in the home (usually the woman), 'has no legal right to any more than the partner earning a wage or salary chooses to give them' (2001, p. 92). Tronto (2004) points out that for the state, marriage is not about individuals expressing themselves, but it is a way to guarantee the care of those who are vulnerable, for example, young children and the elderly (2004, p. 38). An understanding of marriage requires more, therefore, than considering a neutral role of the individuals within it.[3]

Changing economic structures have also influenced family and gender roles, with diverse effects on the poor and children. Folbre (2004, p. 235) argues that economic and legal systems have not kept pace with changes in the types of caring relationships that individuals form. It is difficult, she states, 'to disentangle the causes of changes in family structure' and economic development, but proposes that 'the destabilization of traditional forms of patriarchal control over women' plays a part. Women's increased participation in the paid workforce has undoubtedly led to 'increased freedom of choice' and 'additional bargaining power within the family' (2004, p. 235). Nevertheless, women in both dual-earner and single parent families need better access to child care, health care, housing subsidies and improved working conditions. Thus, there is a need to recognize the needs of human interdependence within the family with the needs of those in the workplace. Public policy seeks to promote healthy relationships, but should not 'stigmatize or punish families that do not conform' to the ideal of marriage (2004, p. 236).

Brook (2002) sets out a framework of feminist analysis that highlights the tensions between the public and the private aspects of marriage. She argues that feminists treat marriage as either a sexist institution which should be reformed because there is nothing inherently oppressive in marriage, or as a patriarchal institution which should be abolished because men will always be husbands with power over their wives. Those arguing that marriage is sexist, criticize the openly different treatment of men and women in identical or similar circumstances. For example, usually wives rather than husbands are expected to change their surname and title when they marry; women's 'marital status is a marker of discrimination in employment, banking and housing'; and women perform domestic work that is 'undervalued and often unrecognized' (2002, pp. 47–48). From a sexist perspective, the problem is that marriage tends to disadvantage women rather than men. The source of the problem is not intrinsic to marriage itself, but is due to women's 'limited opportunities and choices both within and outside of marriage' (2002, p. 48). Those who perceive 'sexist' marriage as an essentially benign institution argue that equality should provide the same treatment for women and men. Thus, gender neutrality is an effective foundation for reform.

Numerous studies have shown that women still do the 'double shift', performing housework and looking after the children, even if she works in the paid workforce. To quote from just one study by Blaisure and Allen (1995), marital life is problematic for women, because

> Women are the marital partners responsible for a family's emotional intimacy, for adapting their sexual desires to their husbands', for monitoring the relationship and resolving conflict from a subordinate position, and for being as independent as possible without threatening their husbands' status. (1995, p. 6)

Gender inequality is thus perpetuated by subtle, often hidden practices. Marriage would be enriched, feminists suggest, if more men contributed to childrearing, household chores and caring roles for which women have traditionally taken responsibility.

In contrast, feminists who view marriage as a patriarchal institution censure the calls for reforms as treating the symptoms rather than the root of the problem. They argue that there are limits to how much marriage can be improved. It is impossible, for example, to employ measures of law reform to change how people experience sexual and emotional relationships (Brook, 2002, p. 49). From a patriarchal perspective, feminists perceive marriage as fundamentally and structurally oppressive for women. Brook draws on the work of Delphy and Leonard (1992) who argue that marriage is a coercive relation of sexed and sexual labour in which women's work, both paid and unpaid is undervalued *because* it is work performed by women. They argue that wives support their 'husbands' occupations', their 'leisure activities' and attend to their 'emotional and sexual well-being'. These tasks, however, become completely lost because they are 'so varied, so personalized and so intimate' (1992, p. 226). Delphy and Leonard (1992, p. 265) suggest that 'women enter marriage "freely" in the West, persuaded (or pressured) largely by love for their partner – though behind that lie the social and economic advantages of conforming to the norm and of allying oneself with a member of the dominant group: sharing his income and getting his protection'. But marriage (or cohabitation) is not a personal relationship that is independently decided upon by each particular couple. Delphy and Leonard (1992) concede that individuals can make choices about which partner to marry, and how couples choose to organize their lives within marriage (to an extent); for example, how often to see their extended families and whether or not to have children. They do not, however, choose the nature of marriage, kinship or heterosexual relations. Delphy and Leonard specify that they do not wish to portray women as 'victims', or all men as 'exploitative or physically abusive'. They nonetheless insist that men have advantages within heterosexual couples and that they benefit because of the social structure within which their interpersonal relations operate (1992, p. 261).

These contested debates about gender and marriage demonstrate that it is as unreasonable to condemn matrimony as it is to inflict it on all couples as a panacea for the social ills in contemporary policy discussions. The institution of marriage cannot be offered as *the* distinctively appropriate form for social policies targeting personal relationships. Feminism's lasting critique of marriage is articulated in the well-known phrase that 'the personal is political'. Liberal democratic governments in theory view the sphere of personal life as exempt from government intervention, but marriage is not removed from politics in practice. The division between the public and private realms is an artificial construct, because the world we live in cannot be divided so neatly. This not only acknowledges that marriage is a location of gendered power relations but also raises thorny issues for feminism because many women marry for emotional reasons, based on personal choice. While feminist debates are useful in setting out women's role in marriage, the majority of women will continue to marry or aspire to marry. Women may wish for better gender relations, but do not want to renounce marriage, particularly when their domestic situation offers them a range of benefits and personal satisfaction.

Changing gender relations

Marriage is not a historically fixed institution. Coontz (2005) provides a quite positive analysis of relations between married women and men, tracing the replacement of the old system of arranged, patriarchal marriage with the love-based male breadwinner/female homemaker marriage, with its ideal of lifelong monogamy and intimacy. This model of marriage with a traditional gender division of labour began to shift in the late 1960s, gathering force during the 1970s as women gained more independence, participating in the paid workforce and negotiating roles of income earner and caring for their children. Birth rates lowered and education rose. She describes 'the perfect storm' that swept over marriage and family life since the 1970s and how it changed the role of marriage. Coming from a 'marital resilience' perspective, Coontz is optimistic because men and women now 'can customize their life course. They can pick and choose whether they want to marry at all, when they want to marry, whether they want children, how many children they want, and when they want them' (2005, p. 301). She does however, acknowledge that while people have more choices, they also have the opportunity to make poor decisions: 'the bad news is that the institution of marriage will never again be a universal or stable as it was when marriage was the only viable option. But that is also the good news' (2005, p. 301). Coontz (2005) argues that a positive change in marriage is that husbands have to respond well to their wives' requests for change. This is challenging, because 'for thousands of years marriage was organized in ways that reinforced female subservience'. Although a husband has little authority over his wife, people have 'inherited unconscious habits and emotional expectations that perpetuate female disadvantage in marriage. For example, it is still true that when women marry, they typically do more housework than they did before marriage. When men marry, they do less' (2005, pp. 311–312).

Numerous studies have shown that gender equality is imperative for sustaining strong and satisfying relationships (McLanahan and Sandefur (1994); Amato and Booth, 1997; Pocock 2003).[4] Despite the ambivalence towards marriage, many feminists have reconciled their politics and their personal relationships with men. This can perhaps be partially explained because, as Coontz (2005) argues, marriage

> remains the highest expression of commitment in our culture and comes packaged with exacting expectations about responsibility, infidelity, and intimacy. Married couples may no longer have a clear set of rules about which partner should do what in their marriage. But they do have a clear set of rules about what each partner should *not* do. (2005, p. 309)

Coontz contends that marriage has steadily become fairer, 'more fulfilling and more effective in fostering the well-being of both adults and children than ever before'. It has 'also become more optional and more fragile' (2005, p. 301). The roles of wives have changed as more women work outside the home. Women have gained economic independence and domestic roles are more flexible and open to negotiation, breaking down the male provider/female caregiver model. At the same time, the norm of lifelong marriage continues to enjoy support. These changes are entangled and hence contradictory developments concerning marriage and gender persist.

Less confidence in marriage

The contradiction between the weakening of its meaning and the continued high esteem in which it is held has resulted in a loss of confidence in marriage. Scholars have found that many people do not see themselves as 'the marrying kind' because they are not confident that marriages last forever. They fear what will happen if they marry and then divorce. Gillis argues that when people's expectations of 'big marriages' are unattainable, they choose 'little marriages' instead. These *de facto* unions offer a 'downsized version of the conjugal, a less demanding version that will suffice until something bigger is possible' (2004, p. 989). What marriage supporters see as the limitations of living together are in fact what make it attractive to more people. People resist marriage as an option because 'they set the bar too high' (2004, p. 989). Couples are aware that they do not have what it takes to make a perfect couple, so they opt for something with a lower standard. In contrast to marriage, cohabitation requires only a private commitment which is not so difficult to break. Gillis argues, therefore, that 'clearly the barriers to marriage are not only material but also mental' (2004, p. 989).

The reasons why people marry are as unique and different as the couples themselves. But there seems to be increasing difficulties in finding the 'perfect partner'. For governments that are encouraging stronger relationships amongst its citizens, it can do little to provide suitable 'marriageable' men or women. One of the inroads (or problems, depending on your point of view) that feminism has made on gender relations is that many women have become choosier in finding a partner. Studies such as the aptly titled *Mismatch: The Growing Gulf between Women and Mmen* argue that as women have become more assertive, independent and critical of men, it is difficult for them to find good men to date, let alone marry. Indeed, both sexes have very high standards and are more demanding than in the past. 'Earlier, the decision was easier, since it involved less choice. Upon arriving a certain age, it was something one did' (Hacker, 2003, p. 15). Marriage was socially expected and most people conformed. Yet today, young people do not feel ready for marriage. Hacker suggests that because men and women have more freedom about how they live their lives, terms such as 'husband' and 'wife' do not have the authority and constraints they previously had. Therefore, couples 'show less willingness to make the concessions and incur the obligations that a workable marriage requires' (2003, p. 20).

Another problem which is difficult for governments to spearhead is that there are fewer opportunities for individuals to meet new people or potential partners. (No, I am not suggesting that governments should establish publicly sponsored dating agencies.) Many people are extremely busy with work commitments, they are less involved in their community or churches, they move to new cities, states or countries. More people are using avenues such as dating services, personal advertisements and the Internet which is changing initial practices of romance and the way people interact and relate to each other. There are many opportunities to meet faceless lovers and become involved in anything from a short dialogue to virtual sex. However, some people meet in 'real time', fall in love and marry, while others experience conflicts, difficulties and disenchantment. Websites offer contradictory possibilities for romantic rituals and intimacies. While cyberspace celebrates the fantasies of romance and encourages individuals to search for their 'soul mate' or their 'one and only', it also offers gendered advice on 'how to be romantic', etiquette on the net, and dealing with online harassment. Therefore, the Internet reinforces traditional myths and codes about romance and marriage while simultaneously introducing practical ways of managing relationships (van Acker, 2001). People communicating on the Internet are developing different types of relationships, but many hope that they will find a suitable partner. If a relationship does not work, it is easily disposed of, and a new search can commence. People can keep trying as there are many others searching for their own 'flawless' significant other.

Because people have higher expectations about marriage and how it should satisfy their personal needs, they take a long time to search for suitable mates which has led to an increase in the age at first marriage (Amato et al., 2007, p. 31). Marrying late then can create concerns, especially for women who desire children as they may face fertility problems. Couples wish to have achieved certain life goals firsts, such as putting their career on track, having money in the bank and travelling. It is to be expected, moreover, that women choose to marry those men who are likely to be good breadwinners (Penman, 2005). Indeed, many studies show that low-income couples (just like middle-income couples) want secure employment, good housing and future prospects before considering marriage (Edin and Kefalas, 2005).

Women and divorce

Governments are concerned about divorce. In the 1970s, feminists such as Jessie Bernard (1972) argued that the new culture of divorce offered women a future of creativity, experimentation and freedom. A well-known feminist who strongly disagrees with this argument and supports the 'marital decline' perspective is Jean Bethke Elshtain (2006). She acknowledges that in the early 1970s, there was a great deal of discussion about the rights of women who were trapped in unhappy marriages. Elshtain argues, however, that because the debate about divorce was directed towards individual rights, any opposition was interpreted as 'anti-feminist, despite the fact that many of the concerns expressed were precisely about the well-being of women who faced divorce' (2006, p. xi). She denounces the insufficient discussions about

> what effects no-fault divorce would have on the institution of marriage; how social perception of marriage as a normative institution

would subsequently change; how its purpose in society might be altered; what historical and philosophical roots anchored the movement; what effect widespread no-fault divorce might have on how we raise children and prepare them to become responsible citizens. Certainly people did not consider the negative impact no-fault divorce would have on women themselves! (2006, p. xi)

Approximately two-third of divorces are initiated by women.[5] Therefore, if governments and society wish to lower the divorce rate, it is necessary to address public policies which may actually steer women towards divorce (Morse, 2006, p. 95). Moreover, Morse argues, it is necessary 'to address the dreams and aspirations of women that also encourage them to believe that divorce is a solution to their problems, or a step toward larger goals' (2006, pp. 94–95). Numerous studies show that when women divorce, one of the major repercussions is that they experience declining living standards and poverty.

Feminist scholars such as Judith Stacey (1996) raise different issues, contending that as marriage has become 'increasingly fragile', it exposes the 'inequity and coercion' of companionate marriage for women. Stacey argues that despite the harsh consequences of divorce, many women find it a better option than remaining in unjust and difficult marriages:

Even in a period when women retain primary responsibility for maintaining children and other kin, when most women continue to earn significantly less than men with equivalent cultural capital, and when women and their children suffer substantial economic decline after divorce, that in spite of all this, so many regard divorces as the lesser of evils. (1996, p. 69)

Furthermore, Folbre (2004) argues that any government-sanctioned economic incentives and benefits to marriage such as tax policies, 'almost by definition, impose economic penalties on those who are not married', have never married or are divorced. 'These penalties have a double edge that can lower the welfare of many children living in non-traditional households' (2004, p. 236).

Many feminist issues are still relevant to matrimony and divorce. This includes domestic violence, the sexual division of labour in the paid workforce and in the home, women's welfare rights or dependency and child support. Marriage and divorce are regulated and governed through acts, statues and policies; they are contemplated, safeguarded and modified in political and legal discourses of government. A pessimistic view is that

> Whatever we may have accomplished in legislation, the gap between women's and men's understanding of relationships, marriage and home life has remained wide. For many women, relationships are the centre of our universe, often to a fault. We tend to subordinate ourselves and our work to our relationships. We depend on them, and they on us, so much that we may expect the relationships in our lives to define life itself. (Grymes, 1996, p. 23)

Relationships remain important for women; therefore, it is imperative that feminist investigations into contemporary marriage inquire into the nature of governmental investments in marriage. The allure of marriage remains, not only because it 'continues to be identified with the emotional security of regular companionship' but also because marriage offers 'promises of romance and intimacy' (Shumway, 2003, p. 229). The emotional life of marriage is thus linked to romantic love which is a significant factor in modern relationships, not only for heterosexuals but also for homosexual couples.

Same-sex marriage

The role of governments is very important when considering same-sex unions and whether to allow gays and lesbians the right to marry. The issue of same-sex marriage draws the distinction between the 'marital decline' perspective and the 'marital resilience' perspective into sharp relief. A vocal promarriage movement has developed within the gay and lesbian community since the 1990s and early 2000s. Reformists make the case that allowing same-sex couples to marry legally would significantly undermine the historically heterosexist and patriarchal constraint of marriage. If couples could marry without considering their sexual orientation, marriage would cater for all individuals and their relationship choices. In response, collections such as the edited volume by George and Elshtain (2006) find the arguments advocating same-sex marriage unconvincing. Those opposing same-sex marriage base their arguments on traditional moral and religious values. Gallagher (2003, 2006) perceives marriage as a collective public institution which can never accommodate same-sex unions. Marriage describes

> a public sexual union between a man and a woman that creates rights and obligations between the couple and any children the

union may produce. Marriage as a public tie obligates not only fathers, but fathers' kin to recognize the children of this union.... Above all, normal marriage is normative. The society defines for its young what the relationship is and what purposes it serves. Successful societies do this not only because children need fathers, but also because societies need babies. (2003, p. 18)

Wolfson (2003) strongly advocates same-sex marriage. In response to Gallagher (2003), he retorts that much of what preoccupies her – deficiencies in parenting, divorce and failures of existing marriages, absent fathers – 'does not have any logical connection to depriving gay people of the commitment, responsibilities and support that come with marriage'. Excluding gay people out of marriage, he argues, does nothing to help heterosexuals 'treat their spouses better, or behave more responsibly' or spend more time with their children. He continues:

isn't it a lie to say that committed gay couples taking on the responsibilities of civil marriage threaten this most resilient of social institutions – when nongay convicted murderers, deadbeat dads, and for that matter, even games-show contestants on Who Wants to Marry a Millionaire? who never met before are all free to marry at will? (2003, p. 26)

Another proponent of the 'marriage for all' argument is offered by Jonathan Rauch whose book *Gay Marriage* has the message that marriage is 'good for gays, good for straights, and good for society' in its subtitle. He argues that discrimination against same-sex marriage in the US is evident because domestic partnerships and civil unions receive legal privileges and protections that same-sex unions do not (2004, p. 42). For Rauch, marriage is about sexual love, commitment and mutual dependency. Moreover, having children is not the defining element of marriage, calling attention to the fact that infertile couples, the elderly and couples who do not intend to have children are not prevented from marrying. Therefore, Rauch (2004) argues, gays and lesbians should not be prohibited from marrying either. Gay advocates value marriage and wish to create a new marriage culture. Eskridge (2003, p. 183) supports marriage for everybody because of its 'civilizing, domesticating features' and notes that both sides of the debate fear that 'sexuality is becoming a consumer good' which gives pleasure without 'deepening any interpersonal features'. Despite this strong approval of marriage by gays and lesbians, they have been unable to convince supporters of heterosexual marriage that they too should enjoy the right to marry.

Those arguing for same-sex marriage insist that marriage is a basic human right that should not discriminate on the basis of gender. Activists such as Graff see marriage as intrinsically benign, suggesting that marriage laws will have to become gender blind. If marriage is about letting equal partners willingly share responsibility for each other's lives and fortunes, then same-sex couples belong (1999, p. 52). Consequently, the legalization of same-sex marriage would signal a triumph not only for homosexuals and lesbians but also by and large for all women. Nonetheless, other activists have become opponents of same-sex marriage because they perceive marriage as not only oppressive and misogynistic but also as naïve and imprudent. From this standpoint, same-sex marriage would merely buttress and reproduce heterosexual beliefs, standards and roles. For instance, Nancy Polikoff (2003) opposes campaigns advocating marriage for gays and lesbians because this detracts from attempts to unlock economic and health benefits from marriage. Moreover, this would require a rhetorical strategy that emphasizes similarities between gay relationships and heterosexual marriages, valuing long-term monogamous relationships and denying the potential to transform the gendered nature of marriage (2003, pp. 223–224). Therefore assimilating into the questionable form of marriage is counterproductive.

To demonstrate the influence of the concept of romantic love on contemporary governments, it is sufficient if we note the arguments employed by gays and lesbians to justify same-sex marriage. From this standpoint, marriage is an intimate and emotional relationship formed by two people on the basis of their personal decisions and choices. The goal is to enhance their well-being. It is discriminatory, not to mention unconstructive, therefore, for governments to favour particular types of private relations over others. It stands to reason, from this standpoint, that everybody should be free to enjoy his or her own vision of marriage, family and sexuality on an equal basis. Their claim for sexual equality has focused precisely on the centrality of love for a legitimate marriage (Eskridge, 2003; Wolfson, 2003; Rauch, 2004). Procreation is not a proper basis because many heterosexuals do not (or cannot) have children. In any case, adoption and modern reproductive technologies allow queer couples to bring up children.

Graff (1999, p. 229) argues that changes to marriage result in romantic love becoming marriage's new 'public philosophy', displacing everything from finances to babies. Gays and lesbians want to have their bond treated with full respect and public benefits just as heterosexual couples do (1999, p. 209). They argue that love in the private sphere is not something that governments should regulate. Given the widespread changes in sexual and family relations and the diversity of households that had occurred during the past century, supporters of same-sex marriage do not perceive any threat to other families in permitting two adults of the same-sex to make a legal commitment to each other. They have yet, however, to convince the US and Australia federal governments – two of the countries under study in this book – of their arguments.

The complexity of modern relationships

For policy makers (and social scientists, legal scholars and family advocates), the complex changes surrounding marriage and relationships make it difficult to manage the diverse and contested variables, whether political, social, economical or cultural. The complexities of these issues, the different expectations and understandings of marriage have implications for public policies. Governments are engaged in different ways with trends that reflect changes concerning religion, love, feminism and same-sex unions. As we have seen, love and relationships are influenced by diverse social and cultural forces, both in the public and the private spheres. Marriage is no longer the primary source of commitment and care giving and we live in a society where individuals have many choices about marriage, cohabitation, divorce, re-partnering and remarrying. Marriage provides important contributions to larger public and social systems while simultaneously providing personal enrichment for couples. As much as it conflicts with religious or romantic sensibilities, we cannot understand how love and marriage are socially organized or politically recognized without thinking about some idea of bargaining and negotiating. Gender is particularly important to our understanding of these issues, because men and women are not only exposed to different messages about love and marriage but they are also encouraged to play different roles in scripted courtship rituals. The legitimacy of same-sex unions raises further complexities.

Giving couples' relationships the best possible chance of success depends on a range of public and private factors which impact on particular couples in diverse ways. The fundamental message of marriage education policies is that being in love is not enough for a successful relationship; the romance will inevitably subside or disappear, and accordingly couples need to be taught how to deal with the daily reality of living together. Policymakers and marriage educators are aware that people may have unrealistic expectations and desires, so they are trying to counteract this by educating people about how to have a good marriage. Caught in the paradoxes between romance and reality, everyone involved must negotiate a delicate path, trying to implant the message of moderating dreamy hopes, while shoring up the solid foundations of marriage. Governments are attempting to implement early intervention and prevention strategies, rather than merely taking on a corrective role when marriages dissolve. Public policies adopt measures that can be interpreted and understood as attempts to secure successful intimate relationships. In this light, government promotion of marriage education is an attempt to enhance relationships by turning to self-reliance and personal responsibility as a much stronger basis for marriage.

Conclusion

Whether government policy choices endeavour to strengthen marriage rather than accept change and try to understand the complexities and expectations of modern relationships, the public–private divide provides significant obstacles for governments attempting to promote and encourage marriage and relationship education. An important principle flowing from these historical changes is that people who perceive marriage as a free and individual choice will not get married because of political compulsion, however slight. While useful in learning positive skills for dealing with relationships, marriage and relationship education are located in a context of wider social forces. It remains uncertain whether governments can implement a pragmatic or technique-based strategy to improve marriage when structural supports such as religion are weak. Moreover, focusing on more practical measures to sustain successful relationships may be difficult because romantic love is based on people's emotions and cultural expectations, making it unpredictable and mystifying. It is difficult for public policies to deal with these complexities. Variables such as higher expectations about what marriage should offer, the need for economic viability, the acceptance of cohabitation, the difficulty in meeting suitable marriageable partners and the fear of failure provide some explanations for why people are not marrying. These factors highlight some of the challenges that governments and society face in trying to sustain robust relationships.

Marriage education implies that marital problems cannot only be managed and solved but also be prevented in the first place. Therefore, how governments have addressed marriage in public policy initiatives merits consideration and forms the basis of the following empirical chapters, beginning with the UK.

Part II

Marriage Education in Three Liberal Democracies

3
The UK – Governments Supporting Children

Like the US and Australia, the UK government views stable families as pivotal for a well-functioning society. Yet unlike these countries, particularly the US, the UK government is less concerned about strengthening marriage as the best way to enhance the well-being of families and children. Stable unions, whether married or not, heterosexual or gay, rather than robust marriages are the key drivers of policy objectives. The government's emphasis on children is clearly pivotal in protecting and supporting all forms of families. Its choice of such a wide definition has perhaps unintentionally yet significantly broadened the range and scope of personal dealings that may be subject to governmental attention. In the last decade the policy focus has oscillated from supporting the adult relationship to improving children's welfare. Policy measures have often been framed by sharply diverging understandings and ideologies, raising complex dilemmas about how far the government can and should assist the personal lives of its citizens. Some participants – believing in a 'marital decline' perspective in the policy debate – may wish to return to a 'golden age' of marriage, but the government's policies indicate that support for the couple relationship is currently weaker than support for children.

Policies have developed and arisen from how particular problems have been perceived at a particular historical moment. This chapter illustrates that the UK government is adopting a 'marital resilience' perspective. It has not attempted to push back the individualistic tide in respect of marriage – instead it has attempted to implement stricter policies regarding childhood. The government supports non-abusive relationships and would consider any form of domestic abuse intolerable and a good reason for the relationship to end.[1] Although it is reviewing the legal rights for cohabitants, it is not advocating marriage to this particular cohort. In these policy developments, the couple dimension of family life has been consumed by the concentration on children and parenting.

This chapter begins to discuss the empirically based research, drawing on my interviews with a range of players. It maps the various conflicting political positions and demonstrates the ways that marriage education has received attention from policy makers since the 1940s. An ongoing political challenge for policymakers in the UK concerns how social policies can promote stability in families, particularly when marriage is not a priority and individual choice is highly valued by citizens. This has been debated in various documents at different times. The present Labour government increased funding for a short period in the early 2000s, but no longer prioritizes or funds marriage education as such – relationship support is funded under the children, young people and families fund and is for parental relationships. By contrast, the Conservative Party has recently shown interest and renewed the debate about the importance of marriage for developing stability in society. For all political parties, the danger is being regarded as moralistic, on the one hand, and attempting to operate a 'nanny state' on the other. These politically conflicting views have important policy implications because promoting marriage above and beyond other relationships does not match the circumstances of many parents and partners. Thus political responses have shifted and are often confused, sometimes developing policies which suit a variety of family categories and activities, while at other times, the impetus has been on marriage as an ideal family type, understood as somehow socially superior. While the Conservative Party supports the US government's policies which offer skills training as a way of alleviating the decline in marriage, the view of the Labour government is different. Broadly speaking, the prevailing governmental consensus is that families are changing their forms but are resilient: marriage is one option and whether people marry or cohabit does not matter.

After providing a brief historical and political overview of the development of marriage policies, the chapter draws on evidence from various players. This includes policy makers, participants from community and faith-based organizations, research centres and think tanks as well as the Conservative Party. The chapter offers an account of the fiercely contested terrain concerning governments and families and how marriage education has moved on – and off – on the policy agenda. The government plays a complex role as it attempts to strike a balance between intervening in the private sphere of the family while not interfering unnecessarily. Here we see the divide between the 'marital decline' and the 'marital resilience' perspectives in their starkest forms. Although there is political concern about the breakdown of families and divorce, the government does not regard marriage as the solution to cohabitation and bearing children out-of-wedlock. Therefore, unlike the US, there is no prioritizing or considering the place of marriage and relationships skills training.

Political context and historical roots

The provision of marriage support and services has been a public policy issue for over 50 years. The new approach to families emerging in the 1990s can be traced back to the 1940s when marriage preparation was first recommended and political support began for what was then termed marriage guidance. Due to concerns about the increasing number of marriage breakdowns and divorces, an enquiry was established. In 1947, consequently, Lord Denning chaired the Report of a Committee of Inquiry on Procedure in Matrimonial Causes. His report recommended that public funds should be provided for marriage education and training programs for marriage counsellors. In 1949 the Home Office provided some funding to the National Marriage Guidance Council, the Catholic Marriage Advisory Council and the Family Welfare Association (Marshall, 1996, p. 11). Many marriage guidance counsellors were women who had given up their jobs as social workers and doctors, working part-time as non-paid volunteers. The stereotype of a marriage counsellor was a 'twin set and pearls lady' doing 'good works' (Blaisure, 2003, p. 16). Because of these stereotypes and a lack of thorough training programs, marriage guidance was not taken seriously in social service provision for many years. Nevertheless, David Mace, one of the founders of marriage guidance, argued that marriage preparation was critical for improving the quality of married life in works such as *Does Sex Morality Matter?* (Mace, 1943) and *Marriage Crisis* (Mace, 1948). Mace's work also became very influential in Australia and the US.

Since the late 1940s, marriage guidance has gradually evolved with an increasing emphasis on education for personal relationships and preparing for marriage (Mansfield, 2000, p. 31). At the same time, the belief that love is the basis for marriage prevailed. Accordingly, the perception that morality could be imposed, that marriage was a discipline and an order with wider purposes could not be sustained (Kiernan et al., 2004, p. 83).[2] Nevertheless, the New Right's focus on 'family values' throughout the 1980s targeted single mothers as 'political scapegoats by blaming them as the cause of a collapse of the moral infrastructure of society' (Chambers, 2001, p. 146). The conservative government viewed non-traditional families as the major problem; it did not focus on marriage and relationship support services as an important plank in its policy platform. For example, John Major government's 1993 'Back to Basics' campaign had a high moral tone, aiming to 'recover the golden era of economic self-reliance, prescriptive morality and traditional family values' (2001, p. 146). Although the campaign focused on issues like the economy, education and policing it became undone when various politicians were humiliated and disgraced with the sensational media publicity of their rather lurid affairs and financial wrongdoings (2001, p. 146). Politicians found it difficult to moralize about the virtues of marriage and family when the messiness of their own relationships was revealed. Moreover, the failed campaign left a legacy of cautious politicians who wished to avoid being perceived as 'preaching' to the public about issues such as moral virtues and marriage. In fact, many of the people I interviewed mentioned this legacy as a primary reason for the present lack of enthusiasm for publicly supporting marriage education policies.

In 1995, with the introduction of the *Family Law Bill*, the Lord Chancellor's Department (LCD) took over responsibility for policy development and funding for supporting adult couples from the Home Office. At this time, the state bore the rising costs of broken relationships by providing financial support to one-parent families, most of whom were created by relationship breakdowns. Consequently, marriage support was placed on the public agenda as a policy issue public with the development of the *Family Law Act 1996* (FLA). This Act attempted to influence relationships by promoting strategies to strengthen marriages and making people more responsible for their actions. Part I of the Act emphasized the importance of saving marriage, promoting a conciliatory approach to divorce and supporting continuity in parenting. There was also much debate about the failure of the divorce system because the existing arrangements did not help to 'save saveable marriages', a phrase which became the widely publicized objective of Part II of the FLA. Part II included the most controversial elements: removing fault-based facts as evidence for divorce, including a period of reflection and consideration before dissolution and compulsory information meetings.

There was disagreement, however, about how best to implement measures to meet the desired objectives. While marriage counsellors and mediators welcomed pre-divorce information meetings and the new-style mediated settlements of dispute, lawyers displayed a lack of enthusiasm (Walker, 2000, pp. 4–6). As Kiernan et al. (2004, p. 284) point out

> marriage and divorce law cannot stop married people separating and living with other people, or from cohabiting rather than marrying. If divorce is perceived to have been made more difficult, then the legislation may have the unintended outcome of discouraging people from marrying in the first place.

The goal of this Act and of child-support legislation has been to provide a framework so that couples recognize their obligations to each other and to their children (2004, p. 284). The traditional emphasis on the duties of marriage shifted to the quality of the relationship as a way of achieving individual satisfaction. Due to this change in the perception of marriage, both divorce and cohabitation dramatically increased and became ever more socially acceptable (2004, p. 96). In line with the 'marital resilience' perspective, we see the significance of marriage subsequently diminish as a public institution. Kiernan et al. argue that 'the quality of a relationship based on romantic love rather than duty can only be decided by the individuals involved. In this context, a high divorce rate, while by no means welcomed by policy-makers, becomes difficult to stop' (2004, p. 63).

The new Labour government in 1997 piloted Part II of the FLA. As a result of these pilots much of Part II of the Act was never brought into force. This decision follows what the Lord Chancellor described as 'disappointing' results from pilot testing in respect of information meetings, which showed the difficulty in attempting to juxtapose social work and family law. However, s22, which gives the power to provide grants to marriage support organizations was introduced. It also bestowed funding for mediation on relationship breakdown. At the time, Roberts (1997) argued that the new Labour administration made no clear policy statements about marriage, although its leadership and its manifesto were less ambiguous about the importance of the family. She maintained that there were indications of potential policy tensions, for example, from welfare to work for lone parents – but little understanding of the financial or economic basis of committed or married relationships. Little would happen, Roberts predicted, to bolster marriage through government action in the short term. While the churches, especially the Catholics and evangelical Christians are pro-marriage, a weak political constituency was not wide enough to move the issue of marriage support to centre stage (1997, p. 105). The government advanced a policy that 'attempted to demonstrate its commitment to marriage while also acknowledging the reality that many in the UK are in nonmarital relationships' (Blaisure, 2003, p. 20).

The thorny issue of government responsibility and funding for programs to encourage not just lasting relationships but also marriage is evident in several policy documents. First, in 1998, the new government's consultation document *Supporting Families* proposed practical measures to support families and to strengthen marriage, arguing that marriage provided the best choice and the foundation for stable relationships. Here the government acknowledges the problem of marriage breakdown, though this is not perceived as damaging the essential advantages of marriage: 'Divorce statistics take the headlines, but marriage still works for the majority' (Home Office, 1998, p. 30). Marriage preparation, as well as programs for parenthood and post-divorce parenting, was strongly recommended in this document. The tension between the different government roles becomes apparent. On the one hand, the consultation paper proclaims that the goal of intervention is to help the parenting relationship – whether married or not – to succeed. Therefore, the government must be cautious about interfering in areas of private life, and is limited in what it can do because 'families do not want to be lectured about their behaviour or what kind of relationship they are in.... But they do want support: advice on relationships; help with overcoming difficulties; support with parenting' (1998, p. 30). Furthermore, the Home Office report adds that 'family matters are essentially private matters, and individuals must live their own lives (1998, p. 31). Yet on the other hand, the Home Office asserts that the ideal parenting arrangement is marriage, stating that: 'marriage does provide a strong foundation for stability for the care of children' and therefore 'it makes sense for the government to do what it can' (1998, p. 31). The articulation of the government's family policy seemed at this time to privilege two-parent married families.

The aim of New Labour was to remould family structures and practices in a way that would better promote social cohesion. Yet chapter 4 in *Supporting Families* reveals the limitations of Labour's vision in this field. Like the Conservative government before it, Labour was anxious about the move away from marriage into other family forms and argued for strengthening the institution of marriage. According to Barlow and Duncan (2000, p. 141), this was at the expense of supporting other types of families. Despite the heavy focus on how marriage can be supported and encouraged, other options of partnership and parenting are scarcely mentioned and there is silence on the issue of same-sex parenting. The legal position of cohabitants remained complicated and confusing. When it comes to cohabiting families, only two proposals are suggested. First, the introduction of a non-religious and public child-naming ceremony and second, producing a guide setting out legal rights of cohabitants in relation to income, property, tax, welfare benefits and responsibility towards their children (Home Office, 1998, p. 32). These proposals do not, however, address reforming the complex and inadequate laws that regulate cohabitation relationships. Barlow and Duncan (2000, p. 131) criticize the report for not considering counselling to save cohabitation relationships which is at the expense of the proposed efforts and investments in saving marriages. They argue that from the perspective of a child, the improvement of the parents' relationship – irrespective of their marital status – is of critical importance (2000, p. 140). Barlow and Duncan maintain that New Labour should be trying 'to develop supportive and flexible legislative frameworks' that recognize the different ways that people make moral and economic decisions. This was the real challenge for the 'joined-up thinking' that the government extols (2000, p. 142).

The Lord Chancellor commissioned an independent review of funding for marriage support which Sir Graham Hart completed in 1999. The Review recommended that the LCD should establish strategies for developing marriage support services in partnership with the voluntary sector, professional bodies, statutory services and other government departments. The Hart *Review* argued that it is necessary to help couples reduce conflict and avoid divorce and that marriage support can be effective in saving marriages and assisting couples to improve their relationships. This could not only assist individual couples but also save the government large amounts of money (1999, p. 12). The cost of family breakdown and divorce was estimated to be approximately 5 billion pounds in 1999. The Hart *Review* advocated a strategic approach, emphasizing research and development and increased funding. The government accepted the recommendations and funding for marriage support programs increased from 3.2 million pounds in 1999–2000 to 4 million pounds in 2001–2002 to 5 million pounds in 2002–2003. Finances provided core funding for national organizations and grants for research and development projects. It was anticipated that consultation would occur between government, service providers and researchers in developing future strategic and funding decisions within a coherent policy framework.

One of the outcomes of the Hart *Review* was the recognition that the LCD should play a more active role in policy: consequently, an Advisory

Group on Marriage and Relationship Support (AGMARS) was established. The AGMARS first met in 2000 to develop guidelines and assess funding for marriage and relationship support. The Lord Chancellor's AGMARS published *Moving Forward Together: A Proposed Strategy for Marriage and Relationship Support for 2002 and Beyond* in 2002. Including 'and Relationship' is a significant shift in the terminology, illustrating an unambiguous change of direction away from marriage as the pivotal point which was the explicit focus of both the *1996 Family Law Act* and the Hart *Review*. The 2002 report recommends an inclusive approach to adult–couple relationships, maintaining that it is 'vital that Government funding can be directed to offer support for all adult relationships, whether or not these are marital, or familial' (2002, p. 12). It states that 'the Government has no desire to tell people how to live their lives. But if couples' lives can be improved – and those of their children – then that is something worth doing' (2002, p. 3). The role of the government was to provide 'a lead in developing policy and strategy to deliver the agreed outcomes' while the statutory sector should provide education and training, services to clientele with health problems and referrals to specialist services and couples support services. The voluntary sector, the report states, is 'best placed' to develop and provide services, good practice, innovative ideas, training, education and information (2002, p. 29). Accordingly, relationship funding was spread across more organizations, but most of the funding ultimately was devoted to crisis intervention rather than early intervention (Mansfield, 2000, p. 31).

There were strong criticisms that some of the recipients of funding did not meet the core objectives of the original AGMARS strategy. Civitas published a report by Nadia Martin (2003) who contended the government 'finds itself supporting and promoting marriage on the one hand and chipping away at the institution of marriage on the other' (2003, p. 3). She emphasized that too many groups with alternative agendas to marriage were receiving marriage and relationship support (MARS) funding, while more appropriately pro-marriage organizations and initiatives were being disadvantaged. She argued that the LCD must re-evaluate its funding process because groups that have agendas outside the objectives of MARS received grants. This included organizations such as Aquila Care Trust which helps people to deal with the problems of separation, divorce and broken relationships. In addition, the Lesbian and Gay Foundation offers a variety of services for homosexuals such as self-help groups for transsexuals, and support for those coming out. The Project for Advocacy, Counselling and Education provides services for lesbians and gay men, including counselling and therapy, mental health advocacy, HIV prevention, employment and training. Martin also criticized the LCD for not supporting initiatives such as Futureway Trust which organizes National Marriage Week. It had received government funding in the past, but their last successful application was for the year 2000–2001. She contends that it is not clear why its application failed.

The government's initiative of establishing the National Family and Parenting Institute (now known as the Family and Parenting Institute (FPI)) in 1999 eventually contributed to what was to become an entrenched focus on children. The aim was to influence policy and transform the environment for raising the next generation (Family and Parenting Institute, 2006). This goal focused on providing support for children and for parents through a range of services, rather than developing programs that supported the relationship of parents between each other. Indeed, the FPI's manifesto – making families matter – does not mention the 'M' word – marriage – at all. It advocates an overarching family policy which addresses concerns such as housing, education, health, work, childcare, taxation, the law and community safety. Honor Rhodes, the former Director of Services, for the Family Welfare Association, acknowledges that

> While couple work features in its (the FPI's) remit, it is not seen as the bread and butter, the very stuff, of family life. This is what needs changing. We have to persuade our family and parenting colleagues, and government, that we have answers to many of the questions they are asking themselves: what promotes children's resilience? What supports educational attainment? We must persuade them that we have answers to questions they haven't yet thought of: what is the main building block of strong, healthy happy communities? (2005, p. 291)

It becomes evident, however, that Rhodes's hopes for concentration on the couple have not been realized as we trace the developments and recommendations of policy documents.

The shift in focus to children and their parents is clearly elucidated with the creation of the portfolio covering Children, Young People and Families (CYPF) in 2003. The government published a green paper entitled *Every Child Matters* (2003) which aimed to improve preventive measures to protect all children, whatever their background or circumstances. This landmark paper led to the passing of the *Children Act 2004* which legislated for more effective and accessible services to support the needs of children and young people. At the same time, the Department for Constitutional Affairs (DCA) took over many of the LCD's responsibilities. According to a government official, the DCA was created as 'a department responsible for upholding justice, rights and democracy. Justice – responsibilities include running the courts and improving the justice system. Rights – responsibilities include human rights and information rights law. Democracy – responsibilities in the family arena for law' (interview, 2007). Responsibility for children and marriage support and for the children and family court advisory and support services moved to the Department for Education and Skills (DfES). With these changes, the department 'is sometimes involved in social policy' (interview, 2007). It continues to invest in research into family justice matters.

The machinery of government changes in 2003 saw the DfES take over the development of children's services from the Department of Health. At the same time, it took on responsibilities for family policy areas from Health, the Home Office and the DCA. In 2004, the Children's Minister announced the provision of new support services with £22.6 million funding for local and national projects. The primary goal is that 'children grow up in a safe, stable, and loving family environment' (DfES, 2004). The focal point of government policies is children's well-being, overriding concerns about adults' relationships and marriage. MARS funding moved – in combination with funding from the Family Support Grant – into the Strengthening Families Grant under the auspices of the Sure Start program (which delivers services for children). The goal of the amalgamation was to provide information materials, advice, training and mentoring to adults. Within this program, funding for marriage and relationship support continued with 4.9 million pounds in 2004–2005. The funding was validated because it would assist in ensuring that more children grow up in a safe, stable and loving family environment. The government has sought to reduce its spending on the adult relationship in favour of promoting the responsibility of women and men as mothers and fathers. There is a policy shift towards placing the welfare of children at the heart of programs and services, but there is little vision or sense that this is connected to ensuring the interests of the parents. As one researcher explained it: 'parent to parent relations are too uncomfortable because of the view that adult relationships are private. Anything to do with "traditional family values" – the department won't go there' (interview, 2007).

The implication of the political focus shifting away from the couple to protecting and supporting children has resulted in an absence of government policy that provides skills training for couple relationships.

While service providers continue to receive core grants, Rhodes (2005) censured these shifts because

> research and development funding is now directed to telephone help lines, to identified excluded groups and (to my particular chagrin) to 'fundamentalist' Christian organisations that have a very particular ideological approach and what seems like a hotline to government. It is also being offered to other religious groups supporting couples, and I have much less anxiety about them, but I am aware of the desperate fragmentation (perhaps better termed 'divorce' or 'separation') that is going on in our field of work. (Rhodes, 2005, p. 291)

Rhodes also offers a rather dire warning, claiming that if policies do not discover a path 'through the prevailing fog of mistrust about couple and relationship work then it really feels as if we are doomed. The couple dimension of family work stands poised to be swallowed up by the focus on parents and parenting issues' (2005, p. 291).

In 2006, MARS funding was reduced to less than four million pounds per annum. According to a government official, the political rationale for this shift is as follows: 'adults are old enough to make their own mistakes; government should look after the children...The priority must be children'. Furthermore, the civil servant noted that 'there's very little money and what there is, is used to resolve problems rather than prevent them in the first place' (interview, 2007). Clearly, marriage and relationship education is no longer priority areas on the policy agenda. Given the various scandals in politicians' personal lives, the campaign to support children and parents was 'a relatively safer political step than potentially being perceived as interfering in adult relationships' (Blaisure, 2003, p. 28). Moreover, as the Social Justice Policy Group (SJPG) points out, many politicians, policymakers and academics 'are aware of their own frailty' and because they have experienced difficulties in their own families 'they are understandably determined not to moralise. They are also reluctant to support an institution which may not have served them well, either because their own parents parted or because their own marriages and partnerships have faltered' (2006, p. 9). A researcher's comment is appropriate here: 'public policy is very confused about how much government should be involved and how much responsibility comes back to the family' (interview, 2007).

Policies were directed to a greater extent towards children as a 'social investment' (Lister, 2003; Featherstone, 2006) as well as reconciling work and family life (Kilkey, 2006) as a way of sustaining the family unit. Jane Lewis, from the National Centre for Social Research, argues that not only the policy agenda but also the language and discourse has changed over the past ten years. There is less stigmatizing of lone-parents, less talk about 'absent fathers' or 'feckless teenagers on benefits' (interview, 2007). Correspondingly, the changing role of fathers has become more important, but Lewis stipulates that 'whether parents are together is only a small part' of the wider focus which is 'all about children and healthy lives in the broadest possible sense' (interview, 2007).

Drawing on the right for individuals to choose, a policy maker states, 'in the 1950s people felt a sense of duty, but now couples want to be together, they're very clear about their choices'. He elaborated:

> From the government's point of view, it doesn't see its role as influencing lifestyle choices people make....It quite clearly recognizes that stable, adult relations are the best foundation for children, whether it should be marriage or otherwise, is not for the government to say. It won't dictate for people choices they make. (Interview, 2003)

Moreover, another government official pointed out that 'Treasury looks for a bankable result. If we put up a nebulous idea about marriage education programs that might work, but said we're not sure they're any good, they wouldn't even look at it. We would be unlikely to receive funding' (interview, 2007).

Studies such as those by Barlow et al. (2001) and Duncan et al. (2005) examine the British Social Attitudes (BSA) survey and come to the conclusion that there is no straightforward 'decline' in marriage, but a more complicated sequence of cohabitations, separations, marriages and divorces. Their findings indicate that while marriage is still widely valued as an ideal, it is regarded with ambivalence when it comes to partnering and parenting. At the same time, cohabitation is widely accepted as a prelude to marriage or as an alternative (Barlow et al., 2001, p. 41). The government has removed the term 'marital status' from official documents, replacing the words 'husband' and 'wife' with 'partner'. This political move to recognize different forms of relationships and households also helps to explain why the term 'marital status' was abolished in most government-supported family research in 2003, so that statistics about the labour force, social trends and the Families Resources Survey refer to 'couple parent families' (SJPG, 2006, p. 31).

Beverley Hughes, the Minister for Children, has written a chapter on children, parenting and families with Graeme Cooke, a researcher (2007). They point out that while the best marriages may be beneficial for children, hostile and conflictual relationships are not. Moreover, children growing up with cohabiting or lone parents can do well. They argue that

> What children need is not marriage itself but the love, stability, financial well-being and positive parenting that ideal marriages often provide – and it is fostering these attributes that public policy should focus on. (2007, p. 238)

Thus the policy agenda should focus on promoting active fatherhood, healthy relationships among married, cohabiting and separated parents and supporting families when they are separating (Hughes and Cooke, 2007, pp. 239–240). These objectives ultimately focus on parental responsibilities rather than the quality of the adult relationship.

In 2007, marriage was undoubtedly off the policy agenda in departments such as the Treasury, the DCA and DfES. As a matter of fact, the DfES was replaced by the Department for Children, Families and Schools in mid-2007. An academic explained it in the following way: 'The hot issue was mediation, but now it is fathers' rights and the Child Support Agency. What drives government policy is the headlines in the Daily Mail – votes are what matter, therefore the fathers' organizations did well' (interview, 2007). A government official affirmed that

> no one is working on marriage law reform. We are undertaking programs to help when marriages break down. We are trying to ensure that when relationships end the parties reach the solution which is least acrimonious and which provides the best outcome for any children involved. (Interview, 2007)

This suggests that marriage education is not on the political radar and that there is little political will to consider early prevention programs.

Service providers and marriage support programs

Local charities and service providers have been important in delivering marriage and relationship education programs. There is no reliable data on the number of couples taking marriage education, as the programs are so varied and not co-ordinated by any central agency. There are however, records of the main organizations which receive strategic funding for developing infrastructure such as salaries, utilities and rent. These include Relate, the Tavistock Marital Studies Institute, Marriage Care, One Plus One and 2 as 1.[3] As Blaisure notes, service providers 'are perplexed that the government seems unaware of the connection between the quality of adult relationships and the well-being of children, at least when allocating funds and the lack of "joined up thinking" among government departments' (2003, p. 28). I interviewed many people working in the field who support this view. They argue that while funding goes to parenting and children's services, they are unsure why there is minimal financial support for services to couples.

A civil servant claimed 'the government realizes that it can't deliver things itself'. While he was not sure of the content of various programs, he added that 'we trust the providers to deliver them'. He also believed that 'no male breadwinner/women at home type organizations exist' (interview, 2003). Nevertheless, various agencies received funding in the early 2000s, including National Marriage Week and 2 as 1, both of which support this model of traditional marriage.

In the early 2000s, there did not appear to be much collaboration among MARS organizations or between MARS representatives and the administering government office. Blaisure (2003, p. 70) therefore recommended that the government, MARS organizations and researchers should increase collaboration. She suggests that MARS organizations could benefit from a closer working relationship. 'Organizations were not as cohesive as they once were and thus were not as effective as they could be in their collective interactions with Government' (2003, p. 31). However, some of the interviews suggested that various agency representatives did network quite closely and regularly. A number of government officials have maintained that they have 'a good close working relationship' with the directors of the agencies. One noted that 'there may be a bit of jealousy between different organizations about funding, but that's just human nature' (interview, 2003). As funding has decreased, the service providers are competing for the same public funding which may affect networking, particularly between agencies which disagree on issues such as the place and importance of marriage in society.

Relate, formerly the Marriage Guidance Council, has been operating since 1943 and was renamed in 1988 to reflect support and services for a wider clientele than married couples. Relate is the UK's largest provider of relationship counselling and support. The agency's aim is 'to enhance the quality of couple and thereby marriage, parental and family relationships and thus help avoid marriage and relationship breakdown' (Relate, 2006). Most of its funding is provided through counselling fees, but it has consistently been the major recipient of MARS funding, for instance receiving 45 per cent of grants for the year 2002–2003. Thereafter, however, as one of the core funded agencies, Relate suffered quite substantial decreases in funding which reduced their capacity to introduce programs focusing on preventive work (SJPG, 2006, p. 95). Counselling received over 50 per cent of the funds and no funding has been allocated for new development projects in MARS work.

According to Jenny North, the Head of Public Policy at Relate, there is little political consensus about the place of marriage.

> This is a result of shrinking back funding and discomfort about talking about relationships. There is a battle on the left about whether to intervene and about autonomy. ... the conservatives are framing a new way to talk about couples, but it comes from a deeply conservative and moral framework. The danger in all this is that the debate is about cohabitation or marriage rather than whether people are good or bad at relationships. (Interview, 2007)

Relate, North explains, supports a more nuanced approach than either side of the political divide. She is cautious about the US government's approach: 'we are interested in what works rather than marriage *per se*. We want healthy relationships rather than healthy marriage initiatives' (interview, 2007). Relate (2006) comes from a 'marital resilience' perspective and has clarified the description of being 'pro-marriage' which was quoted in the SJPG's report *Breakdown Britain*. In the clarification, Relate (2006) explained that it was 'pro-marriage' because many of its clients are married and seek help in saving or strengthening their marriage. However, Relate pointed out that it also supports dating and cohabiting couples, same-sex couples, those ending a relationship and families and individuals seeking support in their relationships. It went on: 'we are not a marriage promotion agency' and urges the Social Policy Justice Group to focus its support on healthy and enduring relationships and not marital status (2006).

Marriage Care, formerly the Catholic Marriage Advisory Service, commenced operation in 1946 to relieve the pressure on family relationships which emerged in the aftermath of World War II. Marriage Care provides support in three main areas related to matrimony – preparation, enrichment and counselling. The marriage preparation component caters for adolescents, engaged couples and Catholic or Christian couples. A number of centres offer FOCCUS inventories, face-to-face classes, resource materials and lesson plans which are available via the web. Many service providers were dissatisfied when marriage education was taken off the government's policy agenda. For instance, in 2003 a spokesperson from Marriage Care said that the *Moving Forward Together* report was 'a bag of air'. He went on: 'the government is pouring money into children's services, but there's no strategy or long-term political view. I ask (X) [an LCD contact] "what are you doing?"' (interview, 2003). He acknowledged that politicians 'won't talk publicly about the importance of marriage' because this topic 'is a political football'. Indeed, he contends, 'politics directs policy' so that civil servants know that they should not mention marriage (interview, 2003). Marriage Care, he claims, actually has a watered down view about marriage as a traditional institution and is not concerned about how people live their lives or whether couples live together. He added that 'when the right wing part of the church claims that Marriage Care is supporting trial marriages, I say, no, we are helping people make choices' (interview, 2003).

Marriage Care has moved to a single, registered charity so that the various Centres are part of the collective owners (Catholic Marriage Care Limited, 2006, p. 3). While the organization relies on its volunteers, they have been trained to professional standards. Many of them work in the field and therefore bring their experience to bear. The cost of their services, currently provided for free, has been calculated at approximately 650,000 pounds (2006, p. 19), therefore saving a substantial amount for the public purse. Indeed, when I briefly met one of the spokespersons again in 2007, he lamented that 'nothing has changed. We still carry out the programs, but now get less funding' (2007).

One Plus One, formerly the Marriage Research Centre, identifies and examines the causes, effects and prevention of marital breakdown. In 2002, Penny Mansfield, the Director of One Plus One, praised the LCD's initiatives as 'highly constructive and based on recognition that much of the help currently available is too little, too late'. But she added that the LCD's commitment had so far not provided 'appropriate investment.... Innovative preventive projects will not get off the ground if funding is not increased. The LCD's vision is enlightened but will be constrained if the voluntary sector cannot afford to invest in development work' (cited in One Plus One, 2002). By 2007, however, Mansfield observed that 'marriage and relationships support has become a bit of a cul de sac – it's a left over from the Hart *Review* and the other government reports (interview, 2007).

One Plus One strongly supports an early intervention model which offers relationship support at vulnerable periods such as becoming parents for the first time and in times of change or crisis. Mansfield recommends that 'skills and information are necessary for general practitioners, health visitors, midwives – people brought up relationship difficulties in these visits' (interview, 2003). One Plus One has developed Brief Encounters, a brief intervention model used by frontline practitioners such as health visitors to identify relationship difficulties in routine visits with mothers in the post-natal period. Mothers and fathers have the opportunity to discuss their relationships, receive support and obtain referrals for other support services and receive assistance if necessary. One Plus One also offers training and resources for volunteers who work in home visiting and parenting programs. These services provide opportunities for assisting vulnerable families at a time of a major life transition. It is at these times that relationships may be at risk. Mansfield explains that

> this is a health issue – the evidence shows that relationship distress and breakdown is highly associated with poorer physical and mental health in adults and children. Parents of children under five are in routine contact with health practitioners. If those offering support to families can pick up a relationship issue, listening and normalizing may be all that's necessary for some couples. (Interview, 2003)

She maintains that many people

> resist counselling – they think there's no point. That if their relationship is so bad that counselling is needed, it is a sign that the relationship is over. But if they think they are going through a bad time, say their partner is difficult to live with, maybe s/he is depressed or going through a mid life crisis or unemployment, then they perceive it as a bad time for their relationships and being able to talk it through with someone can help them get through it. There's a difference between a bad time in a marriage and a bad marriage. (Interview, 2003)

The Head of Practice Development and Training, Clare Negreira, said that the aim is to build 'satellites' of various service providers such as housing support, the churches, clinics, drop in centres and post-natal organizations. The lack of attention on marriage was highlighted by Mansfield who pointed to evidence that the quality of relationships is what matters most (interview, 2007).

The Bristol Community Family Trust (BCFT) is a charity, offering short relationship and parenting courses and with over 100 volunteers is independently funded. The BCFT also runs ante-natal and post-natal relationship sessions. Harry Benson, its leader, adopts a 'marital decline' approach and is a member of the Family Breakdown Working Group which wrote the *Fractured Families* for the Conservative Party in 2006. He is a vocal critic of the Labour government's policies because there has been no implementation of key measures contained in the AGMARS (2002) proposals mentioned above. Benson argues that the government has not sufficiently encouraged the provision of pre-marriage education through civil registrars and has not shifted the focus of government support for relationship intervention towards a more preventive approach: 'the clear message from government is that marriage doesn't matter' (BCFT e-newsletter, October, 2006). More than 650 people have completed the BCFT's pre-marriage course since it began in 2002. Accordingly this represents 5–6 per cent of marrying couples in Bristol: 13 per cent of church weddings and 2 per cent of civil weddings. The BCFT aims to increase these low percentages and one of the ways of doing this is to support the mentoring component of the course. Like some of the mentoring programs provided by faith-based organizations in the US, no prior experience or expertise is necessary. The indispensable criteria encompass qualities such as caring about young couples and surviving the ups and downs of marriage. 'Mentoring is simply the transfer of experience. What you have to offer is the very fact that you're married' (BCFT, June 2006). The organization offers potential mentors the opportunity to learn 'a few tricks over just one weekday morning. The rest you learn through having a go' (BCFT e-newsletter, June 2006).

The following comments elicit the disconnection between offering a remedial approach and preventive programs. Jenny North from Relate criticized the brevity of the training which BCFT provides:

Volunteers receive no training on issues such as domestic violence, which, inevitably, they come into contact with. They're not able to recognize signs of violence and abuse, and this can be dangerous. Enthusiasm isn't always enough when working with couples. (Interview, 2007)

But Harry Benson argues that the mentors 'are taught to follow a clear format. The short training makes them well aware of their own limits and whom to refer more serious problems that may arise – if ever' (email, 2007). The role of volunteers is to facilitate the couple's discussion and share their own experience, but they do not provide advice or counselling. Moreover, he maintains that mentor couples do not 'inevitably' come into contact with domestic violence. He stresses that the focus of the BCFT is not on remedial work.

While there may be some disagreements among some of the organizations, they are fostering a spirit of partnership and cooperation between service providers as suggested in the recommendations of the government documents mentioned earlier. Most organizations preserve a continuing relationship with government departments. They do network and cooperate – the difficulty lies in how the service providers perceive the adult relationship and how to devise the best solutions to diverse problems.

Diversity and families

The UK government is willing to recognize diversity in people's relationships, whether they are married or cohabitating and includes gays and lesbians. Indeed, the Civil Partnerships Act 2004 permits same-sex couples to make a formal, legal commitment to each other. Gays and lesbians can now receive legal status similar to married couples. Homosexual couples are able to register their partnership in a civil ceremony; although the Act does not use the term 'marriage', it has been designed to resemble a marriage contract.[4] However, the government argued that cohabitating heterosexual couples did not require a civil partnership registration scheme because they had access to a religious or civil marriage. If these couples chose not to marry, that was their decision. More than four million people live together in England and Wales,[5] but they have few rights in comparison with married couples and civil partners. In fact, 'common law marriage' was abolished in the Clandestine Marriages Act of 1753. Thus, although the government does not publicly favour marriage, cohabitation in the UK lacks the formal and informal supports comprised in marriage (Seltzer, 2004, p. 927). Many British cohabiting couples, however, are unaware of the extent to which they lack the legal rights of married couples (Barlow et al., 2001; Seltzer, 2004).

The government has requested the Law Commission to examine ways of reforming legal rights that apply to cohabiting couples upon separation or death. This is because the government does little to support cohabiting couples in legal terms. For example, if the couple separates, a partner does not have to pay maintenance (although they do have to pay child support for their children). If there is no agreement in place, there is no entitlement to the other's savings and possessions. Moreover, fathers do not have parental responsibility if they have not jointly registered themselves with the mother as the child's parent. If one of the partners dies without leaving a will, however, the cohabitant may have the right to a share of their estate under the *Inheritance (Provision for Families and Dependants) Act*.[6] The main findings by Tennant et al. (2006) are that cohabiting couples do not resolve financial issues by reference to the law; they do not enforce their full legal rights, and the legal framework disadvantages main carers who are not property owners and their children. Public money, according to a government official, is being spent on advising individuals who cohabit of their rights, or lack of them, and how to safeguard their position as a cohabitant. It is taking account of the growing numbers of cohabitants in this country (interview, 2007). But the government is not encouraging these couples to get married.

Cohabitation is a pertinent issue, connected to the government's concern for protecting children's well-being. The Millennium Cohort Study surveyed more than 18,000 new parents and their children who were born in 2001–2002. This study, conducted by the Centre for Longitudinal Studies, estimates that 60 per cent of children born in the UK in 2001–2002 were born to married parents, 25 per cent were born to cohabiting parents and 15 per cent to parents who were not living together. The largest majority of non-partnered mothers – 86 per cent – were white. A service provider acknowledged their lack of well-defined legal obligations and privileges. As he explained it, 'people cohabiting do not lobby or ask for things. So no one asks cohabiting people what would their needs be? They are not a group or well organized lobby, this doesn't exist' (interview, 2003). So while there are many matters concerning cohabiting couples there is no lobby group to voice their problems. Moreover, they are not targeted in terms of opportunities to strengthen their relationships via education programs.

Patricia Morgan (2007) adopts a different angle. Marriage, she contends, 'can hardly exist unless it confers privileges and imposes obligations different from those on people who elect to cohabit or associate in some other way'. People who do not wish to undertake the responsibilities of marriage, Morgan asserts, should not receive its rights and they should not 'expect taxpayers to meet the financial costs of their decisions related to children, residence and so forth' (2007, p. 144).

Conflicting views about the marriage problem

Although the Labour government is not facilitating the development of marriage education policies to any great extent, the issue of whether to strengthen marriage has been receiving attention from different quarters. The debate often appears to come down to a conflict about differing views on marriage and a flood of intricate responses to specific problems. Players in this debate include not only politicians and service agencies, but also the media and various think tanks. In relation to families, a stark differentiation exists between right-wing moral panic about marriage and left-wing celebration and tolerance of diversity. The Conservative Party commissioned the SJPG to investigate family problems and poverty in Britain. Its *Breakdown Britain* report included its first *State of the Nation Report – Fractured Families* (2006) which argues that marriage lies at the heart of stable families and communities. Chaired by former Tory leader, Iain Duncan Smith, the group has identified five 'paths to poverty': family breakdown, educational failure, economic dependence and addictions and indebtedness. It argues that the cost of family breakdown is approximately 20–24 billion pounds per year including the direct costs of income support for lone parents, tax credits and inflation plus the indirect costs on employment, education, health, crime, police and prisons (2006, pp. 67–68). This is in sharp contrast to the four million pounds spent annually on supporting families via government funding.

Samantha Callan, one of the authors of the report, recommended that the government

> should normalize relationship support. I'm not saying that every couple should be morally induced by government rhetoric to stick with a dysfunctional, violent or profoundly unsatisfying relationship. But the idea that committed relationships necessitate hard work to maintain needs to be part of the rhetoric. So we should say that it's okay to have problems, but also be willing and able to say to people 'if you've made a commitment, it's good if you can stick with it'. (Interview, 2007)

Coming from a 'marital decline' viewpoint, she maintains that 'the current government policies are doing virtually nothing to address these problems – in this area the government appears to be impotent'. Callan argues that public and private commitment has been likened to two-part glue, where there is an adhesive and a hardener – it is necessary to have both in a good marriage. She explains:

> We all seem to know middle class cohabitees who have good relationships, which look a lot like marriages and the Millennium Cohort Study showed that the richest 20 per cent of cohabiting couples are as stable as the poorest marrieds, so there will be some similarities. But what about the people who are poor and cohabiting? There is no support for them. The idea of relationship support is not resonant in the policy community, or in the progressive media. Language about healthy marriage sometimes appears in the *Mail* and the *Mirror*. (Interview, 2007)

Moreover, illustrating the lack of policy focus on marriage, she commented that after *Fractured Families* was released,

> people came up to me to say they were pleased to see the move away from being politically correct, but Labour politicians avoid the issue. The 'M' word is unspoken – in this area the government won't come close to sending any kind of signal which might seem like telling people what to do. (Interview, 2007)

Callan and the SJPG made their final policy recommendations on ending the costs of family breakdown in 2007. Their report to the Conservative Party proposes a raft of policy reforms such as creating 'a positive policy bias in support of marriage' through tax incentives and reforms to the welfare system, childcare and housing. It also advocates an expansion of preventive relationship and parenting education by the voluntary sector through government-supported schemes. Another recommendation is implementing a competitive process so that service providers have to compete for funds, rather than receive block grants. Establishing a new Marriage and Relationships Institute to administer preventive initiatives and provide quality control is also proposed (2007, pp. 44–50).

The Family and Parenting Institute reacted to the *Fractured Families* report by agreeing that marriage is linked with longer lasting bonds than cohabitation. However, it cautioned that, 'it is over simplistic to assume that encouraging people to marry will automatically deliver more stable families and benefit children. Some families may benefit but marriage alone is not a magic bullet' (Family and Parenting Institute 2006, p. 1). Margo and Dixon (2006) argue that the Conservative Party's approach assumes, rather unconvincingly, that people make relationship decisions according to financial, rather than emotional factors. Furthermore, using the tax and benefits system to shape family formations would also divert resources away from those most in need.

The current leader of the Conservative Party, David Cameron, favours marriage above other family forms and recommends supporting marriage through the tax system, and endorses measures such as transferable tax allowances between a husband and wife. Cameron criticized the Prime Minster for failing to include measures to promote marriage in his draft Queen's Speech. In response, Gordon Brown argued that only one million families would benefit from the Tory plans. He added that politicians should not be trying to moralize or make judgements about other people's personal circumstances (cited in Russell, 2007). Here again, we see the clear distinctions between the different political views about marriage.

Contested responses to family values

Media responses about family values illustrate the conflicting views about marriage and relationships. For example, David Cameron's tax proposals signalling rewards for married people and providing incentives to stay married were ridiculed in some sections of the media. Aaronovitch (2006) responded:

> Middle-class people – Conservative MPS even – are prepared to take huge cuts in their standards of living so that they can divorce their spouses. They maintain second homes, move into poky flats, pay absurd lawyer's fees, endure social embarrassment and huge upset, and all so that they don't have to live with their once-chosen mates. Judged on an actuarial basis such behaviour is mad. So do they imagine that these others – the underclass single mums and their baby-fathers – are either so brute that they would ignore their own feelings of love, as we never would, or else so noble that, promoted by an extra couple of quid they'd stay put for the sake of the children? (2006, p. 15)

Richards (2006) provided another cynical response: 'People do not want to hang around together in a form of matrimonial hell for the sake of a few extra pounds. Even if a few pounds here and there compelled a reluctant couple to marry it would not necessarily result in magically stable families' (2006, p. 29).

Within the Labour Party, there has been disagreement over family values and the latest policy recommendations from the Conservatives. The Labour Party's Alan Johnson, the Education and Skills Secretary, repeated the political message that family policy should not focus on whether couples are married or not. Marriage is not for everyone and it is more important to focus on the needs of children. In his inaugural lecture at the Relate Institute, Johnson told the audience that

> Strong relationships represent the key to successful parenting. And marriage represents the pinnacle of a strong relationship: requiring a public commitment between two people. But not all children from married couples fare well, and other family structures are not irretrievably doomed to fail. (Cited in Relate Institute, 2007)

Johnson attacked David Cameron for 'moralising' on marriage instead of providing parents with practical support (cited in Mulholland, 2007). Labour had discarded the married couple allowance which provided tax relief for married couples because it unjustly penalized single mothers. It represented 'the state at its most pernicious and judgmental', unfairly discriminating against vulnerable children (2007).

Some other members of Cabinet disagreed with Johnson's stance. For example, the Work and Pensions Secretary, John Hutton, argued that two parents may be better than one for children and Gordon Brown criticized Downing Street for not responding quickly or coherently to David Cameron's recommendations and arguments (cited in Hinsliff and Temko, 2007). Another response to the *Fractured Families* report came from Natascha Engel, a Labour politician. In Parliament, she declared that she wished to 'vent my spleen' about the report, saying that 'to suggest that the breakdown of marriages is the reason why we have social exclusion in our society is not only wrong but deeply offensive' (cited in Hansard, 2007). This was in reaction to a comment made by her colleague, Graham Allen, who argued that the high percentage of out-of-wedlock births was 'a structural phenomenon that needs to be addressed.... The key thing is that we start to tackle causes rather than merely chase the consequences' (2007). These various tensions demonstrate that the government is uncertain about whether to champion the institution of marriage or not.

Another voice in the debate is the Institute for Public Policy Research (IPPR), a charity which describes itself as the UK's leading progressive think tank. It has strong relationships with the Labour government (Patricia Hewitt and David Miliband both worked at IPPR in the 1980s) and it recognizes the importance of family policy. It argues that stable and consistent parenting is more important than whether parents are married when predicting whether children will succeed in life. In an IPPR report that examines the role of fatherhood, Stanley and Williams (2005) make the case that providing relationships programs like the US's healthy-marriage programs would be 'an all too easy answer, for there are both limitations to the evidence and complexities around this issue' (2005, p. 36). For example, few studies have examined children's well-being and they have not been longitudinal. Class should also be considered because most studies have examined white middle class couples (2005, p. 36).[7] The IPPR argues for greater paternity leave and pay, flexible work practices and more support for fathers as measures to support families. From the IPPR's perspective, what occurs within a family is just as important as its structure and whether the parents are married.

In response to Conservative Party's 2006 report and 2007 policy recommendations, Kate Stanley, an IPPR spokesperson remarked that *Breakdown Britain* continued to represent the traditional conservative view rather than offer prescriptions for change (interview, 2007). The IPPR is more concerned with child outcomes as 'this is the centre of policy thinking' (Stanley, interview, 2007). Its *Freedom's Orphans: Raising Youth in a Changing World* by Margo and Dixon (2006) examines the 'problems of modern youth'. In this context, the study shows that having a warm and loving relationship with a parent can override the impact of living in a lone-parent family. This depends on whether the single parent is able to spend 'quality time' with the child. The study reveals that children who spend less quality time with their parents are more likely to commit antisocial behaviour than others (2006, p. x). Consequently, it is important to promote stronger bonds between children and adults, and more stable, consistent parenting. Adult role models are vital for children to learn social norms of behaviour and values. The report stipulates that it is unrealistic for governments to attempt to significantly lower the rates of divorce, cohabitation or single parenthood because these rates are socially and culturally driven trends. Margo and Dixon dismiss public policies that put emphasis 'on traditional family types', as this diverts resources away from those most in need such as sole parent families. Moreover, this approach 'is unnecessarily morally prescriptive' (2006, p. x). Instead, the report advocates supporting parents through measures such as improved childcare, more flexible working arrangements and increased funding for parenting education.

Freedom's Orphans also recommends investing in relationship education and support services for parents and couples, particularly lone parents. This should include providing skills training for professionals as part of workforce development in the National Health System and social services so that they are equipped to recognize and respond to couples' relationship difficulties. To engage fathers, information and support services should be available at key transition points, such as the birth of a baby or if they separate from their partners. The report also recommended establishing a UK cohort study to explore how relationships within families can best be supported by policy (2006, p. 188). Stanley was aware of the Fragile Families study in America which investigated low-income unmarried parents, adding 'we should leave out the marriage obsession and explore the nature of family relationships'. She continued that in relation to marriage education 'nobody quite knows what to do – if it's not counselling, what is it? … there is no credible alternative to Bush style programs' (interview, 2007).

Supporting the 'marital decline' viewpoint, Patricia Morgan (2000) in *Marriage-Lite*, a document published by the Institute for the Study of Civil Society, argues that cohabitation should be contained in ways that minimize its damage to marriage. In 2007, the Institute of Economic Affairs, a free-market think tank, published another document by Morgan which praises marriage because it 'may be the most important influence on poverty status in the long run; something which may be impeded to the degree that disadvantages or handicaps are imposed at the starting line' (2007, p. 36). She condemns the Labour government for providing large welfare payments and services such as childcare and long-term care for the elderly that families once provided for themselves. Morgan recommends policy solutions such as reforming divorce laws to ensure that parents are financially responsible for their children. Child support obligations should be strictly enforced. This is necessary because government policies 'are altering our demographics: policies that have progressively eradicated the links that bound families and communities together' (2007, p. 15).

Morgan denounces the lack of focus on family stability, arguing that 'we are meant to welcome and support "alternative" or "diverse" and "vibrant" new family forms – with disintegrative trends presented as self-affirming or self-justifying developments that must be embraced and "celebrated"' (2007, p. 49). The tacit consensus of government, the main political parties, academia, children's charities and public bodies is that the changing family structures can only be cheered on (2007, p. 49). Morgan adds that this typically means tiptoeing around the need to nurture marriage – despite its benefits for society. She argues that while it is not appropriate to 'denigrate other "lifestyles"', the tax and benefits system should 'stop discouraging family commitment and treating it as superfluous'. Further, she contends that compatible married couples are living separately, or pretending to do so, to avoid losing government benefits (Morgan, 2007, p. 142). The government, Morgan further asserts, does not have 'an obligation to support lone parents and spend vast sums mitigating the damage that results from the erosion of marriage', without supporting marriage itself (2007, p. 145).

Lone motherhood has been the focus of moral panic in the public domain for many years. Morgan (2007) condemns the government for not developing any proposals to support two-parent families since 1986. This was 'seen as retrograde by policy-makers. This has been felt to distract from and deprive the truly poor – exemplified by the campaign against the married couples' tax allowance' (2007, p. 57). While the US is attempting to encourage unwed women to marry, UK studies have shown that the restoration of the traditional two-parent family is unlikely. Kiernan et al. (2004) argue that the government has, however, attempted to reduce the amount of public expenditure available to support single mothers and to reduce the number of single mothers. As in the US, the hope is that the first goal will serve to promote the second (2004, p. 279).

The anxiety surrounding lone motherhood continued with the release of findings in Social Trends 37 (2007) calculating that 24 per cent of children in Britain were living in lone-parent families in 2006. This was more than three times the proportion in 1972 (National Statistics, 2007, p. 13). The statistic raised some media attention concerning single mothers, the stigma of being a single parent and the role of fathers.[8] For example on Radio 4 (11 April 2007), David Green from Civitas suggested in response to a single mother's comment that the quality of love that a child received was very important, that it was better to have two parents. In an on-air interview, he advocated trying to persuade couples 'to do the right thing' and get married, adding that governments could implement public campaigns to promote marriage. This was critical in changing the culture and people's attitudes towards marriage. Polly Toynbee, a journalist, responded that while governments cannot change climates about love relationships and marriage, they can implement practical measures and 'should make fathers pay' for their children's upbringing. This would assist in alleviating poverty and would improve public housing as well as relationship and parenting support.

Despite the conflicting views on marriage, people in the UK still value it, particularly younger people. A youth worker on inner-city estates suggests that young people support marriage and very few say they would not get married, especially women (cited in Dench et al., 2006). An academic explained the current situation succinctly:

> Marriage has become a status symbol. A child-centred policy has been adopted for political reasons – because it is less divisive. The government's not going to bang on about marriage. The DCA's approach is to avoid relationship breakdown rather than support marriage. Marriage education programs never found a comfortable home in government. (Interview, 2007)

The key point is that while some of the players lament this erosion of marriage, others celebrate autonomy and argue that couples should have freedom to choose their family forms or to move on if their relationship is unsatisfactory. For political reasons, therefore, the Labour government will remain cautious in its approach to marriage education and relationship support services.

Conclusion

In the UK marriage is a contested terrain – clearly illustrating that marriage is viewed as either in decline or resilient by different strands of the debate. As a vital policy issue it slips on and off the political agenda at various times. The problem is that policies are often perceived as being either 'for' or 'against' marriage. As Clulow (2005) argues,

> At the level of public policy it sometimes seems as if the choice is between a vociferous conservative moral argument for sustaining marriage at all costs and a liberal, family-friendly policy agenda in which children are placed centre stage and the couple features, if at all, in a shadowy background role. At all levels there is the potential for the link between partnering and parenting to be made or ignored. (2005, p. 266)

Like the Conservative government before it, the Labour government has fallen prey to the political anxiety associated with the drift away from marriage, but offers a different approach to implementing policy solutions. The Conservative Party adopts a free-market perspective advocating economic benefits for self-sustaining families, reforming the tax and welfare systems and increasing responsibility for fathers to pay for their children. It approves of strengthening marriage and is sympathetic and open to developing some type of marriage skills training. This is in contrast to the Labour government and think tanks like the IPPR which argue for better access to child care, improved parental leave and flexible working conditions. Constructions of the family forms in the UK are complex, but policies reinventing nuclear families or subsidizing marriage are not on the political agenda. For this reason, the current UK marriage policies would appear to provide at best ambiguous evidence regarding the claim that modern liberal democracies fundamentally seek to strengthen the institution of marriage. The lack of emphasis on 'marriage' and the greater acceptance of cohabitation, single parenthood and same-sex unions appear to provide explicit support for different forms of relationships. In doing so, government policies tend to hold the contention that liberal conceptions of relationships will be inclined to undermine orthodox notions of marriage.

Marriage and relationship support remains a highly contentious issue within the broader British context of families, parenting and children. Despite the policy interest in marriage and relationship support in the late 1990s and early 2000s, more recent resistance illustrates the shift in government policies. The main priority is on parenting and protecting children's interests; this confirms the enduring political challenges for the UK government as it tackles the complexities of modern relationships.

The main goal for the Labour government concerns how to support families, particularly those with children, regardless of marital status. An ongoing dilemma is how to encourage stable adult relationships without being seen as interfering in people's lives. It is clear that at risk populations are not a single homogeneous group; therefore a combination of policies developed for different sub-groups may be more effective than blanket policies. Nevertheless, the uneasy privileging of the status of marriage remains; the continuing ambivalence towards alternative family forms is part of the 'social problem' discourse and signifies that any genuine pursuit for social cohesion has been stalled. The Labour government's rhetoric and strategies have – at different times – either strongly endorsed or strongly opposed policies that encourage strengthening marriage. How to improve children's welfare absorbs a great deal of the debate, rather than how or whether marriage initiatives like those being attempted in the US should be considered more seriously on the policy agenda.

Upon closer inspection, however, it becomes evident that even if the UK government is reluctant to encourage marriage, its intention is to strengthen the family and protect children. In this sense, the UK government's family policies (similarly to those in the US and Australia) seem to be premised on countering the false promise of romance and the individual pursuit of self-interest. In its policy responses to strengthening marriage, Australia lies somewhere on the spectrum between the UK and the US. The next chapter examines the case of Australia and its implementation of marriage and relationship education programs in more detail.

4
Australia – Government Shifts in Supporting Marriage and Relationship Education

In Australia, there have been several shifts in policy directions as the federal government attempts to respond to the social problems of marriage breakdowns. As part of this strategy, the government has been encouraging the development of marriage education for some decades. This chapter demonstrates the role of government policies in facilitating the provision of relationship advice and skills to marrying couples. On the one hand, in a bid to address the problem of 'marital decline', for decades the government has supported marital education programs that target heterosexual women and men intending to marry. The goal is to strengthen marriage and families, in some ways reinforcing conservative values about 'the family' – this is evident in the fervent opposition to same-sex marriage. On the other hand, the government has not developed any specific marriage initiative, but now targets relationships and families more broadly. It has also implemented measures to assist people at the time of relationship separation and divorce. Policy is therefore also informed by the 'marital resilience' perspective.

This chapter provides a brief historical and political account of marriage support programs and how they have expanded. It reviews the latest reforms which have seen a policy shift in early prevention and intervention strategies. Rather than simply preparing people for marriage, the main objective now is to provide services for couples when their relationships are facing difficulties and/or coming to an end. The chapter discusses the activities of various participants, highlighting the role of policy makers, community groups and faith-based organizations. The chapter demonstrates that while there is political concern about the breakdown of marriage and the rise in divorce, the government now seems to be more concerned with what happens at the point of separation, rather than training people with skills to strengthen their relationships. Moreover, the changing trends and the future of marriage are not particularly important issues in policy debates – either within government, the media or the community sector. Thus, the Australian policy agenda is driven by underlying assumptions that are different from those in the US and the UK. Unlike the US, there is no explicit government support for strengthening marriage; unlike the UK, there is no great aversion to marriage either. By and large, there is not much concern about 'the marriage problem' and no development of a 'culture of marriage' like that in the US. The Australian government works with the church-based, the church-affiliated and community-based providers to deliver marriage education services, but there is no 'marriage movement' or 'marriage education movement'.

The change in the government's approach is evident in the terminology. While programs initially focused on marriage and pre-marriage preparation, there has been a shift in descriptions of the services. The more inclusive term – marriage and relationship education – is now used. This definition recognizes that marriage is changing and relationships encompass a range of different forms, which is in line with the 'marital resilience' perspective.

Political context and historical roots

Similar to other liberal democracies, the Australian federal government protects the interests of marriage, both as a public and as a private institution. It has pursued the public interest of marriage as a status under law. The Australian Commonwealth can pass laws with respect to marriage, divorce and matrimonial causes as part of section 51 of the Constitution. Nonetheless, the federal government did not ratify a national divorce law until 1959 (the *Matrimonial Causes Act*) when a divorce could be granted after five years of separation or for 'habitual cruelty'. While the idea of governments encouraging people to develop strong and healthy marriages was novel at that time in the US (although not in the UK), marriage support has appeared in various pieces of Australian legislation. The government introduced a national *Marriage Act* in 1961 with the intention of promoting marriage. In response to the newly developing model of marriage guidance at the time, the provision of funding for marriage counselling and education programs was written into this law. Thus, governments have been a party to encouraging citizens to learn about marriage. Section 9B states that

> The Minister may, from time to time, out of moneys appropriated by the Parliament for the purposes of this Part, grant to an approved organization, upon such conditions as the Minister thinks fit, such sums by way of financial assistance as the Minister determines for the conduct of programs of marriage education.

The *Family Law Act 1975* reaffirms the public character of marriage, explicitly recognizing the importance of marriage and family. In making any adjudication, the court must consider the 'need to preserve and protect the institution of marriage as the union of a man and a woman to the exclusion of all others' and 'the need to give the widest possible protection and assistance to the family as the natural and fundamental group unit of society' (*Family Law Act 1975*, s43 (a) and (b)). The Act was a landmark because it introduced no-fault divorce law, lessening the difficulty and expense of divorce proceedings. It changed 'matrimonial fault' provisions to contain a single ground – the 'irretrievable breakdown' of the marriage, not necessarily decided by mutual consent, but demonstrated by 12 months separation of the parties. One of the partners had the right to dissolve ties without public censure of private conduct within the marriage. An important aim of the Act was to support 'the institution of marriage and its reforms were to facilitate re-marriage rather than to free people from marriage altogether' (Golder and Kirkby, 1995, p. 150). The *Family Law Act* also attempts to protect the rights of the spouses by strengthening their union via funding for agencies which offer marriage education and for the Australian Institute of Family Studies, a new research centre.[1]

Financial support for marriage education has been offered (albeit in small amounts) since the 1940s when the churches focused on preventing marriage breakdown. For example, the Young Christian Workers – a Catholic youth organization concerned with social development – were pioneers in this area offering pre-marriage preparation. Harris et al. (1992) in their widely recognized study *Love, Sex and Waterskiing: The Experience of Pre-Marriage Education in Australia,* argue that the catalyst for this provision was the changing nature of society at the time. War had shattered family ties, making it difficult for mothers and fathers to convey the knowledge and skills required to be a good wife or husband. During the 1950s, the Christian churches conducted one-day conferences. By the late 1950s, priests or ministers, bankers, doctors and married couples ran classes. Holding separate discussions for men and women, lecture topics included courtship and engagement, masculine and feminine physiology and the morals of marriage. These church-sponsored classes promoted Christian values as a solution to the increasing incidence of marital breakdown. Courses were eventually offered in every capital city and many provincial centres. By the mid 1960s independent marriage agencies like Marriage Guidance Councils were expanding (1992, pp. 11–12). Concurrently, government sponsored marriage services were increasing. Due to public recognition and financial assistance, organizations began using professionally trained staff for counselling and tutoring couples contemplating marriage (1992, p. 11).

Government funding for marriage education was provided via the Family Services Program which was established in the 1960s. In fact this program was an aspect of national family policy which included taxation and a universal health scheme (House of Representatives Standing Committee on Legal and Constitutional Affairs (HRSCLCA), 1998, p. 77). Grants went to Christian churches and secular organizations offering marriage counselling. Accordingly, a partnership developed between the government and community and faith-based organizations. The program involved three main areas: preventive programs offering services such as marriage preparation and family skills training and parenting; programs such as marriage counselling to support marriage where problems had arisen; and programs aimed at harmonious separation offered via Family Court counselling and family mediation (HRSCLCA, 1998). Government policies tended to focus on the third matter because it deals with the most difficult problems and has the highest demand for government services, involving high-conflict situations and families in distress.

Nevertheless, funding for marriage education programs gradually increased, pursuant to provisions in the *Family Law Act 1975*. Harris et al. argue that 1976 was a 'landmark year for the development of pre-marriage education' because the Attorney-General increased funding for pre-marriage education as a preventive approach to the growing rates of marital breakdown. Consequently, it became possible to employ trained, professional staff, heralding 'the government as a new and active influence on the programs' (1992, p. 13). By the 1980s there was a significant change in the content of the subject matter and a greater focus on the paradigm of adult education. Besides assisting couples to reflect on themselves and marriage, courses began teaching marital communication and conflict resolution. Pre-marital education was developing into an instructive practice in its own right responding to increasing community, church and government concern for marrying couples (Harris et al., 1992, 12–13). Inventories such as FOCCUS and PREPARE were introduced.

The mid-1980s saw a more commercial approach to marriage education because of the increase in user pay policies, emphasis on training standards accreditation and academic studies of counselling and education. However, public funding of the programs was not particularly generous. For instance, in 1989–1990, the federal Labor government provided $248,000 to 24 agencies; this increased to $500,000 by 1991–1992 (Andrews and Andrews, 1997, p. 111).[2] Kevin Andrews was elected to Parliament in 1991; as a chief supporter of marriage education, this allowed him to influence the policy agenda. Impetus for government recognition has come largely from people like Andrews who were personally involved in delivering programs and convinced of the benefits of marriage education (1997, p. 112). In 1994–1995, 28,173 people, three-quarters of whom were couples attended over 17,000 sessions in marriage education agencies (1997, 113).

By the 1990s, the divorce rate had increased, fewer couples were marrying and more were cohabitating. A number of reviews of marriage education programs and services during the Labor government's rule advocated improving services. For example, the 1992 Joint Select Committee on Certain Aspects of the Operation and Interpretation of the Family Law Act (para 4.97) stated that

> there is a compelling cost benefit argument in favour of more funding for preventative education, which might help reduce the number of marriages which reach the stage of breakdown. Successive governments have given this field far too low a priority for funding, and the Committee believes that immediate actions should be taken to rectify this situation.

The Labor government increased funding for marriage education in 1995, but the federal Opposition promised to double funding in their 1996 election platform.

When the Liberal National Coalition government came to power in 1996, it acted on its concern about the consequences of marriage breakdown and the escalating rates of divorce. As Kevin Andrews explained it: 'I had to push for the inquiry' (interview, 2003) that was consequently established to examine the government's role in providing aspects of family services. Chaired by Andrews, the House of Representatives Standing Committee on Legal and Constitutional Affairs (HRSCLCA) produced its report *To Have and to Hold: Strategies to Strengthen Marriage and Relationships* in 1998. The report acknowledges that unemployed and work-related problems and a redefinition of gender roles and the feminist agenda of equality are factors contributing to marriage and relationship breakdown (1998, p. xv). However, rather than addressing specific ways to deal with these issues, the committee advocated preventive action to promote strong and healthy marital relationships which would benefit not only adults but also children. It recommended educational programs for couples intending to marry, suggesting that the government should increase financial support for relationship advice and skills. It argued that marriage education is a valuable service to the community and that preventive strategies offer a pragmatic way of coaching people about marriage practices, far removed from the romantic messages of many cultural representations (1998, p. 67).

To Have and to Hold reasoned that the government should promote the benefits that can accrue to adults and children (in terms of enhanced educational, mental and physical health outcomes) by encouraging satisfying and stable marriage and family life (1998, p. 141). Preventive programs suffer by association with therapy and counselling, reinforcing two powerful social taboos: relationships are entirely private and natural. In its objectives and funding mechanisms, the report distinguished marriage education programs from therapy, counselling and mediation which are generally offered to already distressed couples. The report supported reforms that encompass pre-marital education and it deliberately emphasized the importance of prevention to foster functional relationships. While there are different approaches to strengthening marriage, the common theme of many education programs is for couples to understand the positive ways in which couples work out their differences (1998, p. 142).

The distinction between marriage education and relationship education was discussed in *To Have and to Hold* by Michele Simons who co-authored two Australian studies about marriage education.[3] She informed the Committee that the terms should not be used synonymously because they may be targeted towards different things. Marriage education, she says, is about promoting and enhancing the stability of marriage, which is different from the general promotion of broad relationship skills (cited in HRSCLCA, 1998, pp. 145–146). The goal should be to promote personal responsibility through an educative process. Nonetheless, the committee recommended that the primary emphasis should be on the marital relationship (whether *de jure* or *de facto*). In this way, couples could ascertain whether their relationship was satisfactory – and if so – they could progress to marriage and children. Moreover, the committee recommended that marriage and relationship education should relate to three major life transitions – marriage, the birth of the first child and separation or re-partnering (1998, p. 146). This recognized the benefits of education programs at different phases of life, moving beyond marriage as the primary focus.

In response to this report, the government delivered a clear policy statement. It declared that it would develop a national strategy 'to strengthen and support families' and that it was 'strongly committed to preventive approaches for supporting family relationships, particularly to assist people to develop marital and other relationship skills before problems arise' (Commonwealth Government, 1999, p. 4). In 1999, the federal government initiated a pre-marriage education pilot project. The then Minister for Family and Community Services, Jocelyn Newman, acknowledged the importance of educating people about conflict management and personal communication. At the launch of a pilot project which provided couples with vouchers to participate in an education course, she argued that it is important to 'teach people how to talk their problems through' and 'how to listen to each other' (1999, 1). Newman added:

> It means giving people the skills to negotiate conflicts and deal with problems in practical ways. And it means acknowledging the importance and value of their relationship, their marriage, and their family within the broader community. (1999, p. 1)

Relationship education kits were also available for couples who were unable or did not wish to attend a pre-marriage education course. They were released over a four month period in 2000. Senator Newman stated that these support measures helped to prevent family break-ups and were therefore are a 'very effective investment in family well-being' (2000, p. 1). She articulates the tension between marriage as a 'natural' and expected condition and the idea that marriage is something for which people need training. Newman says, 'people tend to forget that it is the traditional institutions of family and community, not governments, that deliver the most effective social support' (2000, p. 2). She goes on to say that 'attitudes are changing and there seems greater acceptance of the idea that we need to acquire the skills for marriage just as we need lessons for driving a car' (2000, p. 3). The vouchers were discontinued after the first trial period, according to Kevin Andrews, due to lack of funding (interview, 2003). In fact Andrews states that 'after the vouchers ended, the whole reform did too, but if you gave people $100 to do a course whenever they like, they would' (interview, 2003). This comment suggests that relationship support should be readily accessible to meet the needs of individual couples as required.

Reforms to the Civil Marriage Celebrant Program

The recent reforms to retrain marriage celebrants demonstrate another attempt by the federal government to strengthen and revive marriage. In 1973, the then Attorney-General, Senator Lionel Murphy established the Civil Marriage Celebrants Program to provide an alternative to registry office or church weddings. In 1974, civil celebrants conducted less than 3 per cent of marriages. By 1999, more than 46,000 people were married in civil ceremonies, accounting for more than half of all weddings (Williams, 2000b, p. 1). In 1996, Daryl Williams, the Attorney-General initiated a review of the Civil Marriage Celebrants Program. His 1997 discussion paper argues that celebrants play an important role in the government's objective to foster quality family relationships, particularly in their capacity to raise couples' awareness about services which would help them develop stronger relationships and reduce the risk of future relationship breakdown and divorce (1997, p. 34).

To Have and to Hold identified celebrants as an important target group because of their involvement in many wedding preparations, but discovered that they were poorly trained and often confused about the difference between marriage counselling and marriage education. The report found that approximately 20 per cent of marrying couples participated in pre-marriage education programs, with most of these getting married in a church. Referrals to marriage support from civil celebrants, however, were 'almost non-existent' (HRSCLCA, 1998, p. 184). In response, civil celebrants argued that they were not referring couples to these programs, not just because of financial costs or the fear of losing clients. It was easier for religious celebrants as they had 'certain leverage over couples' who wish to marry in their particular church. By contrast, civil celebrants did not have the 'same element of persuasion' because couples could easily approach another celebrant who did not insist on marriage education (1998, p. 185). Nevertheless, civil celebrants had the potential to raise community awareness about the available education courses and distil the myth that these programs were associated with couples facing relationship problems.

The *Marriage Act* does not provide any comprehensive guidelines for marriage celebrants. According to Williams' 2000 report *Reform of the*

Marriage Celebrants Program, 'the current system does not encourage celebrants to convey fully the intention of the Marriage Act that marriage should be understood and appreciated as a solemn and binding union for life' (2000b, p. 4). This report argues that there was a lack of clarity about the role of the civil marriage celebrant, and that the government should ensure high quality services and respecting and promoting the ideals of marriage (2000b, p. 5). The proposed strategies reinforce the importance of sustaining long, robust marriages. Consequently, the reforms contained in the *Marriage Amendment Act 2002* aimed to raise professional standards of celebrancy services and proposed that marriage celebrants should guide couples through suitable education and information services. Commencing in September 2003, new strategies included 'the promotion of pre-marriage and other relationship services which will result in stronger and healthier family relationships' (2000b, p. 6). It is now mandatory for aspiring celebrants to complete an approved competency-based training course so that they are able to plan, conduct and review a marriage ceremony. Another requirement of appointment is to meet the 'fit and proper person' test. These include attributes such as:

A commitment to marriage preparation
Adherence to the Code of Practice for Marriage Celebrants
Compliance with legislative requirements for solemnisation of marriage
Satisfaction of the necessary training competencies
Good `standing and respect within the community
The absence of any criminal conviction, history of anti-social behaviour or mental disorder which might call into question the person's ability to practice as a marriage celebrant.
(Williams, 2000b, p. 29)

Finally, at the very least, celebrants must advise couples about the availability of marriage and relationship education.

At the time of the reforms, many civil celebrants opposed the government's policy proposals. The President of the Australian Federation of Civil Marriage Celebrants claimed that celebrants probably would ignore the rules, especially if it meant couples would be sent to a church. 'They're not babies...they can make up their own minds' (cited in Kearney, 2000, p. 4). The Director of the College of Celebrancy argued that the proposal was unworkable, and that people would resent an invasion into their private lives. Couples discuss their wedding ceremony plans with a celebrant not their relationship. Moreover, relationship education is inappropriate when people approach a celebrant as they are preoccupied with wedding arrangements. The proposed reforms were meaningless unless the government enforced the plan by using 'marriage inspectors' (cited in Australian Federation of Civil Celebrants, 2000, p. 1). The Attorney-General responded that celebrants were not expected to judge whether people were suitable to marry (Williams, 2000b, p. 1).

For celebrants, the reforms presented challenges. One practitioner alleged that informing clients about marriage programs is pointless because, 'we have starry-eyed clients ... 90 per cent of couples would not do marriage education. They're just not interested and they don't think they need it' (interview, 2003). The celebrant thought that the programs were useful, but added that people have unrealistic expectations about marriage: 'they think they will become like Mum or Dad and follow what they do'. Moreover, celebrants can only suggest that clients participate in courses: 'there's no need to promote or recommend courses – the reforms are too low key' (interview, 2003). Consequently, many couples remain indifferent to the possibility of undertaking education. An educator from Centacare mentioned that for the first year to 18 months after the reforms, celebrants were keen to promote marriage and relationship education programs, but then 'lost the urge to let couples know' (interview, 2005).

Same-sex marriage

One element of a 'marital decline' perspective informing government policies has to do with opposing same-sex marriage. Prime Minister Howard has described marriage as 'a lifelong union between a man and a woman', acknowledging that this 'expresses a Judeo-Christian view' (2005, 1).[4] For that reason, he introduced legislation to prevent same-sex couples from marrying and from adopting children from overseas in the House of Representatives in 2004. The *Marriage Act Amendment Act*, supported by most of the Labor Opposition, not only states that gay or lesbian marriages are illegal but also prevents same-sex couples who marry overseas from having their marriage recognized in Australia. Gay groups argued that the legislation would enshrine discrimination in law, and send the message that same-sex couples and parents are second-class citizens. At the same time, the Government announced it would extend superannuation entitlements to same-sex couples through the creation of a new relationship category entitled 'interdependency'.

This removes death taxes on superannuation left to same-sex partners. The measure ensures that same-sex couples receive the same treatment as those in *de facto* relationships. Moreover, legislation supporting greater recognition of gay rights has been implemented via the state levels of government.

A National Marriage Forum – consisting of various religious and community groups – came together to object to same-sex marriage at the time of the discussions about this issue in 2004. Bill Muehlenberg (2004) writing for the Australian Family Association (AFA), argued that to accept homosexual marriage means effectively abolishing both the idea and meaning of marriage; the arguments used to justify same-sex marriage 'can be used to justify polygamy, incest, bestiality, group sex and so on' (2004, p. 1). Homosexuals want same-sex marriage so that society will symbolically approve and recognize the homosexual lifestyle. Most homosexuals, Muehlenberg contends, have a different understanding of relationships from heterosexuals and are willing to engage in extra-marital sexual outlets (2004, p. 2). The federal government listened to groups such as the AFA. This was evident in the decision to ban *in vitro* fertilization treatment for lesbians, a position strongly supported by the AFA and opposed by groups such as the Gay and Lesbian Community Services and the Coalition of Activist Lesbians of Australia.

While the Howard government values 'the family', its opposition to same-sex marriage highlights its preference for heterosexual families. From a 'marital resilience' perspective, the decision to oppose same-sex marriage is inconsistent, according to some scholars, because it contradicts the government's arms of strengthening and promoting marriage. As Cheal (2002) points out, some same-sex couples would like to have the equivalent legal recognition to heterosexual couples including the right to marry. They have adapted the values of the companionate marriage built on affection between equals. They aspire to similar ideals of heterosexual relationships so that 'love, friendship, sharing, communication and negotiation are all specially valued for being combined in one unique relationship' (2002, p. 77). These are the very principles that the government is trying to encourage, but clearly not for everyone.

Family relationship centres

While there has been consistent support for strategies which attempt to strengthen marriage, the government has also been concerned with what happens when marriages break down. Reforms to child support, the *Family Law Act 1975* and the Family Court have been on the political agenda for some time. A contentious issue has been the role of fatherhood, particularly when relationships do not succeed. Prime Minister John Howard announced a parliamentary enquiry into Australia's custody laws in 2003 in response to aggrieved fathers in men's groups who argued that they should parent their children 50 per cent of the time, but that judges, lawyers and social workers are biased against them (Kaye and Tolmie, 1998). Fathers' groups lobbied for more rights for men and better access to children post separation, arguing that the Family Court favoured mothers. A representative from Lone Fathers, an organization which has been operating for over 30 years, claimed that men should have better access to services such as child care and support services (interview, 2005). While various men's groups demanded equal joint custody, the government rejected this proposal and instead supported the recommendations of the House of Representative Standing Committee on Family and Community Affairs (HRSCFCA) which advocated 'equal shared parental responsibility', that is, shared decision-making in children's lives. The report, however, stressed the need for practical measures to resolve disputes and to consider what is in the best interests of the children themselves (see (HRSCFCA, 2003).

As part of the response to the HRSCFCA's report, *Every Picture Tells a Story* (2003), the federal government announced a $397.2 million investment in the family law system to support separating parents in the 2005 budget. The reform package aims to provide mothers and fathers with the opportunity of negotiating a parenting plan – it will be mandatory to obtain three hours of counselling before taking legal action in the Family Court. The purpose, the Prime Minister pointed out in a speech to Anglicare Western Australia, is to offer practical, early intervention assistance before conflict has escalated and disputes have become entrenched (Howard, 2004a, p. 2). This aims to minimize the number of conflicting couples proceeding to legal courts or tribunals.

The establishment of the 65 Family Relationship Centres (FRCs), with funding of $189 million will provide mediation, counselling and dispute resolution services for separating couples. The government, said Philip Ruddock, the Attorney General, is 'seeking a cultural change' in approaching family relationships and promoting healthy relationships. The FRCs are central to achieving this change (Attorney-General's Department, 2005). Other elements of the package include increasing the number of Contact Orders Programs, children's contact services and outreach programs for rural and indigenous communities. Funding is also available for providing people with information about preparing couples for marriage and preventing separation. Pre-marriage services would be available to 'give couples a sound start to marriage' (Howard, 2004a, p. 2). There is provision for increased funding for the Men's Line Australia, men and relationship services to assist men to manage relationship difficulties with partners and children, counselling and skills services and improving delivery of specialized family violence services. The government has also introduced a Family Relationships Online and Advice Line – a website and toll-free telephone information and advice which provide information for families to build better relationships. As part of the package, a succession of early intervention services (operating under the Family Relationships Services Program (FRSP) umbrella) commenced in mid-2007, offering family relationship education skills and training.

The package seems, therefore, to have two main policy objectives: not only making the process of separation and divorce easier but also trying to prevent relationship breakdowns and strengthen marriages. In relation to the first objective, changes to the law and courts aim to develop practical measures for resolving disputes and to consider what is in the best interests of children whose parents are separating. Mothers and fathers will receive assistance in developing a viable parenting plan to negotiate the best outcomes for their children. At the launch of one of the first FRCs, he repeated his message about 'the importance of putting children first' (Ruddock, 2006, p. 6). In relation to the second objective, establishing the FRCs has resulted in more funding for early intervention and skills development to expand marriage and relationship education services (Attorney-General's Department, 2005).

People in the field reacted in different ways to the government's proposals. A spokesperson from a fathers' group said the FRCs 'should not be recycled organizations'. He was concerned about 'who's going to run these new organizations?' and expressed some apprehension that 'the feminists' voice was heard too often at the expense of men's groups' (interview, 2005). A manager of one of the key delivery agencies was more positive, noting that if the FRCs developed 'national networking and promotion, people won't have to do the planning at the grass roots level' (interview, 2005). She added that if these new agencies were structured so that various service providers could co-locate together it would provide better services all round. This appears to be what is happening; various agencies are partnering and linking with a number of peer organizations and complementary service providers.

A number of interviewees criticized the policy shift in the relationship cycle from pre-marriage to the time of separation and breakdowns. A service provider explained:

> Preventative now means working with separating couples, rather than at the premarriage stage and with parenting programs. The government's strong interest is in post-separation programs. ... We should be pushing for normalizing relationship education and supporting families properly and early on. This (the FRCs) is 'ambulance at the bottom of the cliff' stuff. (Interview 2006)

Another organization administrator claimed that 'something was necessary between pre-marriage education and when the relationship was over – there are transitions problems in a relationship cycle' (interview, 2006). A common observation was the need for the Department of FaCS to avoid 'being seen as setting up divorce shops. We want a referral centre with one assessor who would refer people to existing organizations' (interview, 2005). Many of the interviewees maintained that the FRCs would require a recruitment strategy to attract 'highly qualified and skilled' staff. Sharma (2006) writing for the Centre for Independent Studies, argues that the FRCs will duplicate services which already exist, make their money processing the simple cases and are just an example of 'symbolic politics' that will not result in any good outcomes (2006, p. 1). Moreover, 95 per cent of family law matters are resolved without court orders, so it is unclear why a new system of government sponsored services are required for the 5 per cent with difficulties (2006, p. 3). Therefore, Sharma argues that the government is confused about whether it is trying to prevent relationship breakdowns, or make them easier by making the process less adversarial (2006, p. 3).

Relationships Australia asserts that the FRCs should be a gateway rather than a single entry point to the family services system (2005, p. 6). It noted the importance of marriage celebrants who are 'in an ideal position to suggest the value of relationship education' and that it was important to promote the value of relationship education by undertaking a community education campaign, using mediums such as community radio and television, community health groups and mainstream magazines (2005, pp. 25–26). Another unconvinced provider raised concern about the need to secure stable arrangements for children. She said that it was important to acknowledge that relationships are not permanent: 'we need to emphasize individual parental responsibility beyond trends of marriage' (interview, 2005).

Despite the doubts about what role the FRCs would play, anecdotal evidence suggests that there have been some positive outcomes. For example, a sector representative was enthusiastic: 'it's quite exciting. Relationship education is getting embedded into other work as people take courses in communicating or on parenting' (interview, 2007). Another advantage is that on first contact, potential clients will be able to talk to someone immediately, rather than return at a later time or make an appointment with a particular person.[5] More resources for service delivery in the area of marriage and relationship education are welcome because, as we will see below, providers have been struggling up till now.

The Family Relationships Services Program and Service Providers

From minimal beginnings in the 1960s the Family Services Program's initially modest focus on marriage guidance services has greatly expanded. Central to the government's initiatives, the contemporary-FRSP has a wide set of aims, to

> enable children, young people and adults in all their diversity to develop and sustain safe, supportive and nurturing family relationships; and minimise the emotional, social and economic costs associated with disruption to family relationships. (FRSP, 2005, p. 1)

The current Department of Families, Community Services and Indigenous Affairs (FaCSIA) and Attorney-Generals administer and fund the FRSP, which is designed to help couples to explore their relationship and develop personal skills. Services now include family relationship counselling, family relationships mediation, family relationships education, adolescent mediation and family therapy, family relationships skills training and children's contact services. The Departments also sponsor men and family relationships services, aiming to break down barriers for men in accessing relationship services. In mid-2007, FaCSIA released the *Keys to Living Together* kit which provides a DVD and information about relationships. Marriage is mentioned in the kit, but the main focus is on relationships as well as advice and tips on how to improve them. The provision of the diverse services and information packages illustrates the recognition of the changing needs of Australian families.

Programs deliverers and service providers have worked closely with governments over the past few decades to offer marriage and relationship education, many of which are funded under the FRSP rubric. Providers of various programs find it difficult to describe and classify their services using tightly defined criteria. As Simons and Parker (2002) found in their study, relationship education activities can be offered as part of a range of social and welfare services delivered by community-based health care facilities, hospitals, schools, adult and community education organizations, juvenile justice and corrections facilities, youth services, religious and specific cultural groups. The defence forces, employee assistance programs, maternal and child health centres and neighbourhood and community centres also use them. Embedded programs highlight the potential for existing providers to expand their work by forming collaborative partnerships with agencies working in related areas such as health and aged care.

The national government funds approximately 100 community organizations in approximately 400 locations to deliver marriage and relationship programs to more than 135,000 clients each year (Department of FaCS, 2003, p. 3). It spent approximately $4 million annually throughout the late 1990s and early 2000s. Clients pay for professional relationship services delivered by a range of providers who are members of the three Industry Representative Bodies (IRBs) Family Services Australia (FSA), Catholic Welfare Australia (CWA) and Relationships Australia (RA). These were established as representative bodies in the 1990s. Funded by FaCSIA and the Attorney General's Department, they provide 'representational and advocacy services to FRSP providers' and 'advice on matters significant to program policy and administration' (FaCS, 2003, p. 4). Organizations delivering programs are diverse in size and income. Government subsidies for many of these programs allow the service providers to charge inexpensive fees. Many operate on a fee for service basis, although the government's policy is that people who cannot afford to pay should not be turned away or refused access (2003, p. 3). Some agencies receive funding from state governments, churches and other benefactors. Some are linked to community legal centres, or are part of independent community organizations or in Church networks. Agencies in receipt of grants from the federal government, however, are also expected to contribute their own funds to programs and to seek some contribution from their clients (HRSCLCA, 1998, p. 98).

Centacare is part of CWA, now known as Catholic Social Services Australia (CSSA) that provides over 60 per cent of marriage and relationship education in Australia. Each diocese has a Centacare office. An educator said that before 2000, the Church's position was that 'people living together should repent and go to confession. But this turned people off' (interview, 2005). Accordingly, this view was 'thrown out' in various dioceses, although marriage as sacrament is still supported and discussed. The Catholic Church's official policy was set out in 2000 stating that couples intending to marry should participate in formal pre-marriage education. A policy template on marriage preparation was produced in 2006. As part of the preparation process, couples are expected to have interviews with the priest who will witness the marriage. They have to share time with him, either formally or informally to explore the meaning of commitment and investigate the Catholic understanding of participation in a pre-marriage education program (Australian Catholic Bishops' Conference, 2006).

In its submission to the FRSP Review (2003), CWA discussed some of the problems it faced in providing marriage and relationship education services. It argued that 'no single event, seminar, course or training will sustain relationships through all eventualities' (2003, p. 7); therefore it was necessary to promote and enable ongoing learning for relationships across the whole lifecycle. Although its staff is willing to train celebrants in the use of FOCCUS, 'there has been only limited uptake of this offer' (2003, p. 8). Radio talk back, media presentations and Internet are popular mediums to get the information out to the public. The problem according to the CWA is that FRSP data collection methods fail to give credit to media work. This type of labour becomes unattractive as it requires extra effort to develop expertise in the new mediums and then further effort in persuading the funders that this is a legitimate use of funds. Consequently, innovators in the field are in a constant state of anxiety and risk is borne by the community organization in which they work (CWA, 2003, pp. 8–9).

FSA is the largest national IRB, with over 70 members. It was established in 1994 and is funded by the FRSP and from membership fees. Its members are located in more than 250 agencies across Australia, including Anglicare, an arm of the Church of England and Uniting Care. In a 2003 interview with an FSA officer, her first response was to raise the question – 'what is a family?'. She noted that FaCS's performance framework is still pursuing families rather than relationships. FSA's position, however, is that the 'focus should be on relationships' (interview, 2003). The FSA claims that it is very diverse because it incorporates many different groups in the local community as well as the various religious divisions. This does, however, 'make it difficult to come up with a particular FSA position' (interview, 2003).

RA is a community-based organization, working in a not-for-profit capacity, but it is not aligned to any religious organization. It operates from more than 80 locations and just over half of its funding comes from the FRSP. Its objective is to provide relationship support to people regardless of age, religion, cultural background, gender, social or economic status or lifestyle choice. Almost half of its 90,000 clients are men (RA, 2003, p. 4). From RA's perspective, it is important to offer people access to services that are not affiliated with a religious organization (2003, p. 12). It acknowledges that there are some strong philosophical differences between the organizations that deliver FRSP programs (2003, p. 13). While RA recognizes that there are some inherent benefits in collaborating with other service provider organizations, it argues that this 'expectation has some limitations and should not jeopardise healthy diversity among provider organizations and the capacity of the Program to offer choices to clients' (2003, p. 13). This brief overview shows that the three IRBs have quite different structures and beliefs, but have worked quite well together. They have recently merged and been renamed Family Relationship Services Australia (FRSA). The aim of this new body is to provide a collective voice for the sector.

National organizations for marriage education

The Catholic Society for Marriage Education (CSME) was established in 1973 and the Australian Association for Marriage Education (AAME) commenced work in 1979. The aim of the CSME was to promote and support marriage and family life in the Catholic vision by encouraging marriage and relationship education for couples considering marriage and for married couples. Membership of the AAME included Christian churches and non-Church affiliated agencies. Some educators were members of both agencies, which resulted in a spirit of cooperation which still exists today. Both organizations were active in promoting marriage education and gaining funding from the government to support the development of pre-marriage education and to provide training for service providers (Harris et al., 1992, p. 12). In 1988, the government provided money for these marriage organizations to produce and expand *Threshold* – a national magazine for marriage educators. In 1989, they received funding from the Attorney-General's Department for a national trainer to provide professional development for educators, for airfares so that executive members could work together on various projects and for their first annual conference. CSME introduced the FOCUSS inventory nationally in 1990.

CSME had a larger membership than AAME which was unable to survive. The Marriage Educators Association of Australia was established as an association of individual educators whose agencies had been disenfranchized with the demise of AAME (Kerin, 2003). The name changed in 1995 and is now called the Marriage and Relationship Educators' Association of Australia (MAREAA). Kerin (2003, p. 6) explains one of the 'side effects' of the Howard government's introduction of vouchers as part of the pilot study in 1999. He cites the Catholic Engaged Encounter Perth program in Western Australia, which although run by highly trained and motivated volunteers, could not redeem the vouchers. This reduces the number of couples attending the course and could affect the attendance levels required for a sustainable economy of scale.

Collaboration occurs on a regular basis between marriage educators, resulting in important contributions to the goal of improving client outcomes. For example, the CSME and MAREAA often work closely, attempting to lobby government, sharing information, participating in a biennial national conference, as well as developing new training resources and online content. Others frequently share materials: 'we swap information and teaching manuals and review classes' (interview, 2006). However, from a more structural perspective, an important issue for MAREAA is how to link government into the specific network on a grand scale. Educators argue that networking should not just be happening among people on the ground, and that the government was not taking a leadership role. In 2003, a service deliverer explained 'this is difficult enough at state level, let alone at the national level' (interview, 2003). Three years later, similar issues were raised by another agency representative. She remarked that 'networking is fraught. Governments don't fund networking. It is expensive and underfunded. Networks work in spite of rather than because of what governments do. We network among ourselves' (interview, 2006). The larger agencies have training and professional development programs and the Marriage and Relationship Education National Conference (MARENC) is oriented towards workshops and participatory activities.

One of the distinguishing characteristics of marriage and relationship education in Australia is the focus on professionalization of the workforce. This has been developed since the mid-1990s. Educators have worked together and with the federal Attorney General's Department to develop competency standards and a qualifications framework. An explicit qualifications framework has been ratified and developed by the Community Services and Health Industry Skills

Council. This has been developed to provide a 'benchmark' for training programs for relationship educators and to assist in appropriate supervision and professional development (MAREAA, 2007). There are 11 units of competency. Assessors have to follow a set procedure if they are assessing an educator's competence. Assessment can be conducted by one educator or be peer-based; it occurs over time and involves collecting evidence about the educator's competency. Self-assessment tools are also available, divided into units which are relevant for particular forms of program delivery. For example, those working with inventories can assess how they work within an organization, how to use inventories for exploring relationships and how to participate in professional and self-development activities. For those delivering group programs, they would need to consider ways of facilitating group and couple processes to support learning (MAREAA, 2007).

While the US has a Certified Family Life Educator designation which recognizes the educational, preventive and enrichment nature of the educator's work, there are few professional requirements or training for marriage and relationship educators in the UK. In this area, therefore, Australia is at the forefront of the field. While Australian service providers face many challenges in a range of areas, the US and the UK could draw lessons from their approach to training.

Challenges in the field

Some of the difficulties include lack of time to lobby the government; lack of funding; the different values within the IRBs on issues such as same-sex marriage and cohabitation; and the difficulty of providing adequate services to 'at risk' groups. Furthermore, the CSSA – the wider Catholic Church organization – has insufficient time or resources necessary to specifically lobby for relationship education. It is, therefore, up to the CSME to lobby specifically for relationship support (Kerin, 2003). The problem is that marriage and relationship education is only a small part of the services provided by the IRBs under the wider FRSP umbrella. Their major functions include counselling, mediation, parenting, aged care and dispute resolution.

A review of the FRSP's effectiveness and appropriateness which commenced in 2003 coordinated a consultation process including forums, meetings and written submissions. I attended a meeting to discuss the review of the FRSP with representatives from MAREAA and FaCS in December 2003 in Melbourne. The service providers of marriage and relationship support were unhappy because their core work was often

not recognized due to the political focus on the well-being of children. From FaCS's perspective, it was necessary for the organizations to report their work back to the Department. One representative acknowledged that the culture within FaCS had a narrow focus and there was little interest in marriage education. She explained the need for 'credibility, you have to define outputs. You have to report real work back to FaCS. Within the Department, marriage education is the fluffy stuff – it's easy to sideline' (interview, 2003). The public servant stated that it was crucial for the service providers 'to define the process, measure outputs and outcomes and to provide qualitative information, things like quotes and accounts of people's stories. This is what the Minister wants' (interview, 2003). In response, the service providers suggested that there were plenty of stories, but that it would be difficult to measure outcomes in ways that bureaucrats wanted. One educator said 'what we do is difficult to measure, if we have a 40 minute session with a client, we have to fill out two forms for FaCS' (interview, 2003). This was labour intensive and they did not have the time or resources to complete these tasks. Listening to the debate, it became clear that there was a dilemma for both sides. The FaCS representatives were relying on the organizations to push the marriage education agenda, but the agencies were understaffed, under-funded and too busy delivering services to meet the Department's bureaucratic requirements.

The Review of the FRSP, finalized in 2004, stated that the sector faces recruitment and retention difficulties, mainly because the sector's workforce consists of lowly paid workers and volunteers. It argued that low pay levels were due to restricted funding and increasing agency costs, such as rising insurance, superannuation and occupational health and safety costs (Urbis Keys Young, 2004, p. 120). It determined that the program provides a range of valuable relationship services, but had weaknesses such as inadequate funding, limited coverage and fragmented services. In relation to marriage and relationship education more specifically, educators agreed that there were not enough facilitators and an over-reliance on volunteers. Moreover, paid volunteers received minute financial payment. Increased funding is necessary to maintain existing service levels (2004, p. 111). Staff earn 25 per cent less than people working in comparable positions in the government sector and even less, relative to the private sector. This narrows the field of candidates for FRSP positions (2004, p. 121). In addition, there are more women than men training for and working in the sector and the current workforce is ageing. One observation was that many workers 'tend to be middle class women of a certain age' (2004, p. 122). This supports my research: most of the service providers I interviewed fit this description. This may well be a problem if the sector wants to remain relevant to a younger group of potential clients. But there are challenges for younger cohorts too. As one representative pointed out,

> It is difficult to attract educators or counselors with the necessary expertise and maturity. For example, family services officers are often newly qualified social workers. They move on and become managers. They are not taken seriously as they are young, people say 'what would she know about children – she has none' or 'what would she know about marriage'. (Interview, 2005)

Recruiting staff, she continued, was 'a big difficulty for the Department' (interview, 2005). As part of the government's package of reforms, it announced a 30 per cent rise in funding to services under the FRSP in 2004 which would be maintained over the following four years at a cost of $63.1 million. However, a spokesperson for CWA pointed out that this was 'about retention of staff' and 'providing greater incentives for staff to stay' (interview, 2005). A pay rise to bring rates on par with other industries does not necessarily attract more people into the cohort.

Many of the stakeholders complained about the 'chronic underfunding of programs' (interview, 2007). One academic observer noted that 'there is vast competition for money. RA is the largest organization and gets the most; the Catholics have an extensive, informal networking system as well as small parish programs. The FSA is in danger of imploding on itself and people are not joining up' (interview, 2005). CWA praises the 'outstanding' labours of CSME and MAREAA, but notes that the program 'runs on the passion and commitment of the people involved. It is testimony to their tenacity and dedication that such enormous results have been achieved for so long with so few resources' (CWA, 2003, p. 16). For too many years, CWA contends, gains from the program have run on a deficit-funding model.

Relying on financial support from the government can restrict activities. For example, in 1995 the CSME's application for financial support for their annual conference was rejected because they were not one of the three peak bodies. According to Kerin, a previous CSME President, concerning relationship education in particular,

> the growing dependence on government funding had placed the field in an awkward position. It is true that the injection of government

funds had enabled much to be achieved, but it had also changed the environment and not just for the funded agencies. Creative writing was a sought after skill as agencies with some or all volunteer staff set about applying for funding for programs of proven value, but which had to [be] dressed up to look innovative, in a climate that had now attracted the interest of fully professional and even commercial agencies. (Kerin, 2003, pp. 4–5)

While the FaCS representative requested 'people's stories', inevitably results get translated into quantifiable figures. CWA (2003) argues that the government requires accountability and results in formats that do not keep pace with cutting-edge practice. One of the service providers agreed with this viewpoint, stating that FaCS 'wants names and addresses and whether people turned up, not qualitative data' (interview, 2006).

Other concerns have been raised. Some of the service providers made similar comments to those in the UK regarding what they perceive as marriage policies in the US. For example, one observed that:

The US model is more punitive in terms of links to welfare. Australia is not as destructive, and we don't wish to follow the US trend. I think it would be a danger to replicate it. The US has got the gurus who people listen to, but Australia is ahead on the ground in providing services and good programs. (Interview, 2006)

Another industry representative said: 'people want the Australia context – they don't want the US stuff' (interview, 2006).

With the implementation of the FRCs and the attached increases in funding, one of the service providers noted that

because there is now more money available here to fund relationship education, the area is becoming more political. Hillsong and other right wing evangelical groups are getting involved. Thirty four politicians went to their conference. And right-wing Bishops from the Catholic Church are also getting interested. (Interview, 2006)

With so many agencies competing for a relatively small pot of money, it appears inevitable that there will be some political discord amongst the various groups.

My interviews demonstrated that having to compete for funds was complicated for service providers who worked well together. As one educator put it, 'we have to go through a competitive tendering process which is difficult. It makes it difficult to go into a joint service' (interview, 2003). Another educator claimed that, 'to keep an edge, some information can't be shared. This affects trust and learning exchange' (interview, 2003). It created tensions between organizations which usually worked cooperatively. Another had a different response, 'no one begrudges money going to another organization because they'll do it well, we're devastated if others lose money. There's no envy' (interview, 2003). A member of the CSME observed that 'the government opposes the IRBs and supports individual providers. This is a way of beating down the price. It may establish for-profit organizations with the FRCs and build community and legal networks' (interview, 2005). Time will tell if this scenario is implemented. In the meantime, these various comments illustrate that while there are problems in collaborating at the wider structural levels of the FRSP, many service deliverers working on relationship education do collaborate with effective results.[6]

Various sector representatives acknowledged the different values of agencies under the RA and Catholic umbrellas, with one noting 'the fundamental differences' between them. She continued, however, by claiming that while there are 'some issues around marriage', for example, that RA and the CSSA are at

> different ends of the spectrum on issues such as same-sex marriage, it's not problematic at the moment. The (lack of) money doesn't let us fight amongst ourselves. If an agenda developed to promote marriage, that would start to divide people and you'd wonder how it would play out. (Interview, 2006)

Nonetheless, according to a sector representative, at the wider level 'some of the churches should realize that good relationships are not anti-marriage' and 'some conservatives automatically take the position that if marriage is not included, it means that programs are anti-marriage' (interview, 2007). This indicates an undercurrent of disputes about marriage, cohabitation and the rights of same-sex couples in some quarters.

As briefly mentioned, the entire FRSP has been assessed. Most significantly, the second part of the commissioned review – *FRSP: Client Input Consultancy* (2004) – found that awareness of FRSP services was 'almost non-existent among non-users' (Colmar Brunton Social Research, 2004, p. 143). The findings about public awareness – not only of the program at its wider level but also in relation to relationship education – starkly demonstrated that the benefits of programs have not been sold well. The report suggested a number of information sources and distribution channels to target both the general public and more specific audiences. It also noted that there were considerable areas of unmet need. This was particularly the case with culturally and linguistically diverse (CALD) and indigenous families and communities and services in rural and regional areas (2004). A sector representative echoed these findings: 'some of the CALD agencies and migrant groups slam services because they're designed for the mainstream, they're inflexible and don't understand their specific issues'. She noted that 'migrant agencies are hostile. They are underfunded to begin with, over-subscribed with no money for things like interpreters or training' (interview, 2007).

The report noted that indigenous users describe a real lack of appropriate and accessible services for families (2004, p. 5). They learned about their sub-program through the local community centre, but were not aware they had been using a FRSP program. Their friends and family were unlikely to access these types of services, not only because they did not know that the services existed but also because many were reluctant or suspicious of government or 'white' services particularly if it meant what they perceived to be 'external interference' with their family (2004, p. 5). The plight of indigenous families is an ongoing concern for governments and relationship support is just one area where better services are required.

Two years later, a report by CWA and the Department of FaCSIA (2006) determined that there was still insufficient funding to meet the additional operational and infrastructure costs of delivering services in remote and rural communities. Human resources are a 'scarce commodity', with less support from church agencies and volunteers. Workers in the field suffer from stress and burnout (2006, p. 4). In addition, the challenges experienced by rural and remote communities are more complex when agencies attempt to engage and assist indigenous families and communities (2006, p. 15). The various reports agree that this is a complex issue that needs particular consideration. This entails developing cultural awareness by increasing the number of indigenous workers, offering tailored education programs and different service delivery. Developing culturally sensitive programs for indigenous couples would need to begin by building trust with those going into the communities.

A beneficial development is the establishment of some networks that could be nurtured through the new development of a performance management framework. The Review of the FRSP recommended the development of a comprehensive and outcome focused performance framework. This is currently under way, with the important goal of using a partnership approach to program development (RPR Consulting, 2006, p. 5). Activities consist of consultations and one-day forums with the IRBs and service providers and data modelling workshops with the aim of developing criteria to judge the framework's success. It is anticipated that information about services and the FRSP as a whole will be not only useful in performance monitoring but could also contribute to program evaluation and research (2006, p. 5). Nevertheless, as I have indicated, many of the stakeholders are currently maintaining partnerships at the service delivery level, interacting regularly and sharing a high level of commitment to relationship education programs.

One of the reasons for good relations is that the various organizations delivering the programs agree that healthy relationships are important. Several respondents predicted that a 'huge cultural change is necessary' (interview, 2003), recommending the expansion of education and publicity campaigns, and a national strategy with national marketing. Other suggestions included developing DVDs, videos and books as 'people just want information and to be able to help themselves' (interview, 2007) and that 'there should be a suite of resources about relationships for different groups such as CALD etc' (interview, 2006). RA recommends that pre-marriage education should begin at home and then in primary school; and that governments should undertake a community educating campaign promoting the value of education as a positive and useful tool (2005, p. 25). Many of the interviews mentioned the importance of providing relationship education in high schools. This could consequently convey a firm basis of knowledge for further adult relationship education. Representatives from all three IRBs emphasize that much work still needs to be done.

Conclusion

In some ways, public policy seeks to privilege certain types of relationships such as marriage, but it does not oppose supporting *de facto* relationships. The federal government, does, however, oppose same-sex marriage. Thus both the 'marital resilience' perspective and the 'marital decline' perspective are appropriate in explaining the Australian situation. Governments have continued developing a preventive role to protect marriage since the 1960s. Well aware of the challenges that the institution of marriage faces, the government has implemented a range of strategies in attempts to strengthen relationships. Early intervention and prevention remain key themes in the government's national family strategy, but a vital part of the long-term policy framework focuses on families and children at the other end of the spectrum – at the critical point of family breakdown. While the government has established FRCs, it does not simply want to intervene in a remedial role when marriages dissolve. Marriage and relationship education still receives some attention and funding, although there are areas of unmet need. Customized programs may be necessary to assist those at risk of relationship difficulties.

The various findings from the Review of the FRSP, reports from the IRBs and my interviews suggest that there are ongoing difficulties in delivering marriage and relationship programs. Providers have struggled with insufficient funds to facilitate expansion and delivery of programs across a wider sector. Resources are overstretched and even with increased government funding over the past few years, it has been difficult to provide adequate services. Some of the agencies rely on volunteers and there is little capacity to expand service delivery. These are some of the problems faced by people at the coalface. The federal government also confronts many challenges in developing and implementing marriage education programs. Chapter 6 turns to these challenges, but the next chapter examines the US where the federal government has developed a 'healthy marriage initiative'.

5
The US – Governments Promoting 'Healthy' Marriage

Of the three countries discussed in this book, the US has been the most active in developing policies that promote stable marriage through various marital education programs and services. This chapter provides a broad overview of the US federal government's marriage initiatives and investigates the successes and the difficulties. While there is growing support for developing these policies, political involvement in promoting marriage has sparked controversy in some quarters (and probably indifference in others). There is no consensus about what can or should be done to endorse marriage – this contributes to the complexity of this policy area. Although many politicians, policy makers and stakeholders contend that marriage is an important rock of stability in a time of rapid change and argue that it should be protected, others disagree. What is significant here is the tension played out between the perspectives as set out in Chapter 1. Some actors perceive marriage as a social institution in decline which should be revived, while others view marriage as resilient, adaptable and a matter of personal choice. These two perspectives are not necessarily mutually exclusive, but have led to policy challenges for the government.

A well-rehearsed statistic is that 90 per cent of Americans want to marry and expect to stay married. Coontz (2005) argues that Americans greatly value marriage and still marry at greater rates than in most other industrial countries. It 'is the highest expression of commitment they can imagine' (Coontz, 2005, p. 278).[1] This wide level of support for marriage intimates that sustaining the institution of marriage would be a non-partisan issue. However, this is not the case. On the political spectrum, views about marriage policy range from the libertarian perspective that governments should stay out of people's intimate affairs to the view that governments should be making divorce more difficult. The

US federal government has regulated the institution of marriage in various ways and its encouragement of marriage is not new. Cott's (2000) history of marriage as a public institution illustrates how marriage has been subject to the will of the state which changed regulations as it saw fit. For example, government policies supported marriage for freed slaves and Indians and polygamy in Utah. Cott (2000) argues that assumptions about the importance of marriage and its appropriate form have been deeply implanted in public policy. Political authorities expected monogamy on a Christian model to prevail, not only because of widespread Christian faith and social practice but also because of government policy choices and laws (2000, pp. 25–26). Political and legal authorities endorsed marriage, aiming to perpetuate it as lifelong and monogamous, and formed by the mutual consent of a man and a woman.

This chapter provides a brief historical and political overview of the development of marriage policies before discussing the various players. This includes policy makers, participants from the marriage movement, community and religious organizations, think tanks and research centres. The chapter continues by providing examples of some of the most ambitious and successful initiatives which are designed to tackle the breakdown of marriage and the rise in divorce, cohabitation and bearing children out-of-wedlock. It then examines some of the opposition to the government's marriage policies.

Political context and historical roots

The effects on marriage of government welfare and tax policies have been a subject of concern and debate for several decades. However, marriage education programs have only reached the policy agenda within the past decade. Marriage education had roots in the 1960s and 1970s when mental health counsellors, drawing upon research, developed educational programs designed to prepare couples for marriage and prevent divorce. The hope was to provide help early on and thus avoid the need for personalized counselling and treatment of marital distress and breakdown. Among the early pioneers of this new preventive approach were David and Vera Mace – clinical psychologists – who established the Association for Couples in Marriage Enrichment in the early 1970s and developed couple peer support and education programs that were not tied to professionally provided services. A similar development in the religious sector was the establishment of the non-professional Marriage Encounter programs (now available around the world) which provided marriage renewal sponsored by the Catholic Church. It too offered an alternative to therapy or focusing on professional marriage or family services and hundreds of thousands of couples attended. The aim of the weekend retreat programs was marital renewal in the context of spiritual renewal. Thus, Doherty and Anderson (2004, p. 425) contend that there was enormous potential for lay-led community-based programs. Pre-marital courses such as PREPARE and Catholic Pre-Cana (before the wedding feast) began to be offered widely in the Catholic Church. Indeed, increasingly engaged couples were required by their pastors to attend (2004, p. 425).

Meanwhile, secular-based pre-marital education and marriage enrichment programs expanded. For example, the Center for Marital and Family Studies at the University of Denver, funded in part by the National Institute of Mental Health, designed the PREP. Its co-directors, Howard Markman and Scott Stanley have been working on this program since the 1980s. These psychologists succeeded in formulating a positive communication program, designed to dispel myths about marriage, teach skills and change a couple's attitudes about relationships.

In a review of family policies in the 1990s, Bogenschneider wrote about the early government interest in marriage programs:

> policy efforts so far have been sporadic, uncoordinated, and unsupported by think tanks, foundations, or government commissions, amid concerns that marriage is a code word for an ideological agenda to de-liberate women, stigmatize single parents, or force women to remain in abusive patriarchal relationships. (2000, 1148)

Bill Coffin, a Special Assistant for Marriage Education in the federal administration, viewed the history of the evolution of marriage policy in the following way: 'over the last 20 years, we did things to counter marriage (particularly in welfare programs). We didn't talk about marriage in a good way, for example its good effects on children' (interview, 2003). In a similar vein, Robert Rector and Melissa Pardue (2004) from the Heritage Foundation in Washington DC, argue that government programs for decades sought, at best, to pick up the pieces of failed marriages. At worst, the government actively undermined marriage because public policy 'remained indifferent or hostile to marriage' (2004, p. 11). Family income is often the basis of calculating government benefits, including Temporary Assistance for Needy Families, food stamps, Medicaid (health care for those on a low income who meet specific eligibility criteria), child care subsidies, housing assistance and the Earned

Income Tax Credit. This produces a disincentive for a second wage-earner to join the family, because many of these benefits would be eliminated or cut dramatically. Rector and Pardue point out that 'means-tested welfare programs do not penalize marriage per se but, instead, implicitly penalize marriage to an employed man with earnings. The practical effect is to significantly discourage marriage among low-income couples' (2004, p. 4). This may have been an unintended consequence of policies implemented to address other concerns such as the need for income support.

Since the mid-1990s, federal policy makers have increased their interest in protecting and strengthening the institution of marriage. Theodora Ooms (2001), formerly a senior policy analyst at the Center for Law and Social Policy (CLASP), argues that the federal government had been treating marriage as the 'M-word', assuming that because of its private, contractual nature, it was 'off bounds' to government policy. As this assumption shifted, the policy agenda became primarily concerned with reducing out-of-wedlock births which was viewed as a main cause of welfare dependency and other social problems. A group of politicians, social scientists and family supporters argued for policies that increase fathers' responsibility, reduce out-of-wedlock births, encourage abstinence outside of marriage, enhance the status of marriage and boost family stability. Robert Rector's views had enormous influence with the Republicans. This is validated in an interview conducted in 2003 with his colleague Patrick Fagan, another senior analyst, from the Heritage Foundation. He explained that his organization, 'prepared the national debate – we prepare, provoke. There's gradual consensus now that marriage is a good thing. Ten years ago, a politician would have been stupid to talk about marriage preparation' (interview, 2003). This activism was successful in generating ideas for new policy initiatives.

As a spokesperson for a progressive perspective on these issues, Ooms, now a couples and marriage policy consultant, described the numerous challenges of trying to convince politicians and policy makers about the value of marriage programs in the late 1990s. For example, there were fears that government would bribe or encourage poor women to enter or remain in violent marital relationships. She informed me that one less discussed barrier is that

> there is no issue in public policy so personal and so sensitive. As I presented the statistics and research and discussed the programs at meetings I could see people's eyes would glaze over as they were thinking about their own personal and family situations. (Interview, 2003)

But the discussions continued: 'We would have to talk again and again, trying to help people understand the decline in marriage as "a public health issue"'. She notes that 'a few years ago, people working in the government or outside would have laughed at, or were actively hostile to the notion of marriage preparation. They were looking at the issues too narrowly – eventually they "got it"'. Ooms explained that gradually many of their fears diminished as they began to understand what the proposed government programs entailed. However 'we need to remember that the field is still in its infancy. Many challenges lie ahead as policy makers get to know the service providers and vice versa, so they are all on a huge learning curve' (interview, 2003).

A major policy goal in the mid-1990s was to enact reform of the welfare system to decrease the dependency of recipients on welfare (mostly single mothers and children). In the long drawn out debate that ensued, marriage promotion and support as a policy issue reached the national political agenda through the Personal Responsibility and Work Opportunity Reconciliation Act (PRWORA) finally enacted in 1996.[2] The Act initiated a new welfare program, replacing the Aid to Families with Dependent Children (AFDC) program, the main federal-state program assisting poor families, with the Temporary Assistance for Needy Families (TANF) program. This welfare reform package provides each state with a block grant to provide financial assistance to needy families. The key elements of this reform – which attracted the most interest and controversy – were to require TANF recipients to work and provide only time-limited assistance. Much less noticed was the inclusion in the Act of provisions that encouraged two parent families and marriage. Indeed, TANF's preamble states, 'marriage is the essential foundation of a successful society' and is 'an essential institution of a successful society which promotes the interests of children'. The legislation put forward broad policy goals: the promotion of job preparation, work and marriage; the prevention and reduction of out-of-wedlock pregnancies; and the encouragement of forming and maintaining two-parent families. The package was the first federal law to provide the funds, the mandate and the flexibility to states to strengthen the institution of marriage. However the 1996 welfare reforms provided no dedicated funding stream for marriage programs. This would not occur for another decade.

President Bush listened to child advocates such as Dr Wade Horn, whom Bush appointed as the Assistant Secretary for Children and Families in the Administration for Children and Families (ACF).[3] A clinical psychologist and fatherhood specialist, Horn has argued consistently for policies that support marriage because both adults and children benefit from healthy and stable marriages. He was described by a number of interviewees as 'the key guy', 'the main instigator' or 'the man who drove the ideas' concerning marriage education programs. In 2002, President Bush began to focus on marriage as an important issue, demonstrating the federal government's interest in marriage and initiated federal policies promoting healthy and stable marriage by announcing the Healthy Marriage Initiative (HMI), which is administered by the ACF within the Department of Health and Human Services (DHHS).[4] To avoid criticisms from the academic community and domestic violence advocates that it is naïve and potentially harmful to support marriage *per se* and to assume that marriage automatically insures healthy family relationships, the focus shifted to building 'healthy' marriages. This is now recognized as a legitimate goal of public policy, at least by the current Administration. George W. Bush declared:

> To encourage marriage and promote the well-being of children, I have proposed a healthy marriage initiative to help couples develop the skills and knowledge to form and sustain healthy marriages. Research has shown that, on average, children raised in households headed by married parents fare better than children who grow up in other family structures. Through education and counselling programs, faith-based, community, and government organizations promote healthy marriages and a better quality of life for children. By supporting responsible child-rearing and strong families, my Administration is seeking to ensure that every child can grow up in a safe and loving home. (Cited in ACF, 2002)

This statement clearly supports 'healthy' marriages as a stable place for children and as being 'mutually enriching and satisfying'.

At the time that the initiative was created, it did not receive much public attention because the main focus of public debate and controversy was triggered by proposals to establish a Constitutional amendment banning same-sex marriage. This was as a consequence of another attempt to restore traditional (that is, heterosexual) marriage which occurred in 1996, when the Republican Congress passed the Defense of Marriage Act (DOMA) which defined 'marriage' and 'spouse' in federal law as concerning one man and one woman. Many Democrats voted to support DOMA and President Bill Clinton signed it into law. This law also upheld that no state would be required to honour a same-sex marriage contracted in another state. The government listed more than 1040 ways in which married people receive special status under law.[5]

Nonetheless, the ACF's HMI did receive attention. Its mission position clearly illustrates a defence of political intervention into the personal sphere of relationships at a time when many couples view their relationships as a matter of private choice. The ACF states that the HMI is not encouraging marriage for its own sake or telling single people that they should get married. Neither is the federal government attempting to run a dating service. Participating in programs should be voluntary and designed to meet the diverse needs of different groups. The goal is to support making marriages better, and the ACF stipulates that it is not attempting to make it more difficult to get out of a bad marriage, for instance, where domestic violence occurs (ACF, 2004). The ACF administers a variety of programs that promote child and family well-being, drawing on pre-existing marriage education services because this has the advantage that service providers have developed programs that meet the local needs of their communities. It is charged with the task of transforming directions from Congress into working policies and proposals that must be developed to benefit particular populations.

As part of the reauthorization of the 1996 welfare reform Act, President Bush requested a $300 million package to promote child well-being and healthy marriages in 2002. This would provide, for the first time, some funding specifically dedicated to marriage programs.[6] This would reassign money from the out-of-wedlock 'bonus' award funds which were available for the states which lowered the rates.[7] Consequently, H.R. 4737, the *Personal Responsibility, Work and Family Promotion Act* passed the House of Representatives in 2002. This Act asked for substantial funds of $1.6 billion over five years to ensure that promoting marriage as set out in the 1996 legislation would be implemented. It included a DHHS program entitled 'Healthy Marriage Promotion Grants' and an initiative for marriage research and demonstration funds. It also provided for the promotion and support of responsible fatherhood programs.

Various versions of the bill were voted on and rejected over the next few years, but the reauthorization bill passed the House of Representatives for the fourth time in 2005 and President Bush signed the *Deficit Reduction Act of 2005* in 2006. The legislation included public funding for community and faith-based organizations, as well as federal, state and local governments, over the next five years to strengthen marriage. This reauthorization included $500 million ($100 million for the next five years) to support marriage strengthening programs, with a further

$250 million available for programs to encourage responsible father-hood ($50 million for the next five years). As part of the reauthorization of the TANF Act, funding would provide a range of programs and activities including public advertising campaigns on the value of marriage, marriage education and skills training for those planning marriage and married couples and marriage mentoring.

While marriage advocates welcomed what seemed to them a large infusion of federal money, this is in fact a very minute amount of the total DHHS budget. Moreover, it was not 'new' money, as it draws on redirected funds from the existing budget. Currently, there is a push from a small handful of lobbyists at the state level to increase state spending on marriage to 1 percent of all TANF funds which would bring the amount up to $400 million per year (Wetzstein, 2006).[8] Therefore, funding for the various programs remains relatively low – what Diane Sollee, one of the well-known marriage education protagonists – describes as 'this little pittance of money – I'm appalled at how small it is. It's a colossal joke when you realize the cost to the poor of family breakdowns and the emotional cost' (interview, 2007). Another way of understanding the amount was provided by Wade Horn: 'one needs to keep in mind that that amount is in the context of a 2 *trillion* dollar federal budget' (interview, 2003).

The DHHS funded healthy marriage programs via several discretionary funding streams within ACF for a few years until the reauthorization funding stream was mandated. Consequently, from 2002 to 2005 the ACF awarded more than 170 grants totalling over $61 million. This included support for programs within ACF such as the Administration for Native Americans, the Children's Bureau, the Office of Community Services and the Office of Child Support Enforcement. African American Healthy Marriage and Hispanic Healthy Marriage promote and support programs to their respective populations. The Office of Family Assistance operates TANF and awarded more than 200 new grants in 2006. The ACF also provides technical assistance to state and local agencies through contracted resources and staff. More federal funding has been made available to target diverse groups such as low-income families, military families, adoptive and foster families, refugee and migrant families, high school students and prisoners.

An interesting outcome from the reauthorization process was that although the complex and difficult issue of domestic violence had not been initially discussed by federal officials, it has now been incorporated as part of the policy. Agencies applying for federal funds now have to consult with experts or coalitions involved with domestic violence in developing program design and activities such as intake and referral procedures and staff training.[9] ACF has gone further to require all their healthy marriage grantees to develop site-specific protocols describing how they plan to address the concerns of domestic violence advocates. Hence, domestic violence is now recognized as an important factor in education programs and screening processes are being incorporated into the programs.[10] Ooms noted that, 'no one had talked about DV in the past, so this was a big shift in rhetoric' (interview, 2006). Most domestic violence agencies, while still not totally convinced about marriage education programs, 'now feel a bit more at ease – some level of comfort' with the new procedures (Coffin, interview, 2007).

The government has a clear awareness that there are constraints in what it can actually do or how far policies can go in influencing people to make choices about marriage and their personal relationships. As Horn explained it to me,

> this is not 'an ideological crusade', we'll build on existing communities, federal bureaucracies and organizations. The healthy marriage initiative is not about setting up a new, categorical program, but rather an attempt to integrate an additional service – marriage education – into existing public sector social service programs. As such, they should be affordable and accessible, especially for low-income populations. (Interview, 2003)

Horn acknowledged that

> there are limits to what the government can do, even in the name of doing good. Government should not get involved in the personal decision making, as to whether or not a couple should get married. But once the couples has made the decision to get married, government can play a role in helping that couple achieve the aspiration they have set out for themselves: a healthy marriage. (Interview, 2003)

Nonetheless, the value of the programs was made clear by Horn: 'at worst, healthy marriage education programs will do no harm, as it is difficult to imagine how teaching someone the ability to communicate effectively and listen with respect to others would result in negative effects' (interview, 2003). Therefore, HMI proponents do not seek to limit or govern individual choice. Indeed, there is a clear recognition that if they did, policy would suffer.

While this chapter focuses primarily on developments at the federal level, policy initiatives to strengthen marriage have also occurred at the state level. The US constitution gives the states the power to regulate marriage and divorce (that is, it determines the conditions of entrance and exit). Some states have also passed specific marriage legislation seeking to strengthen the institution of marriage and reduce divorce. For example, in 1997 Louisiana adopted a covenant marriage law. This law offers marrying couples a choice: if they choose covenant marriage, they agree that their marriage is a 'lifelong relationship'. They have to undertake pre-marital preparation and sign a 'Declaration of Intent to Form a Covenant Marriage' which makes them legally accountable for their promises. A marriage can only be dissolved after a two-year waiting period or proof of fault, including adultery, felony conviction, abandonment, abuse, or after a specified period, following a judgment of separation from 'bed and board' with a judicial declaration that the couple were separated (Louisiana Session Law Service Act 1380). Arizona enacted a covenant marriage law in 1998 as did Arkansas in 2001.[11] Couples in other states, however, are not choosing covenants (Hawkins et al., 2002). Moreover, there is little evidence that these 'fault' divorce bills have had any significant effect as the divorce rate has not reduced.

Another example of a state-wide marriage initiative is the 1998 Florida Marriage Preparation and Preservation Act which stipulated that high-school students must take a course in marriage and relationship education. Engaged couples who complete a four-hour course receive a reduction in the cost of their marriage license and can marry upon application, waiving the three-day wait. In Arizona, Florida, Texas and Utah, marriage handbooks or manuals set out rights and responsibilities for couples when they apply for marriage licenses (Brotherson and Duncan, 2004, p. 462). These books provide information about building strong marriages, the effects of divorce and the availability of community resources. In Utah, marrying couples are given a video and website about marriage (Parke and Ooms, 2002).

The Center for Law and Social Policy (CLASP) produced a report *Beyond Marriage Licenses* which illustrated that every state has commenced at least one activity or introduced at least one policy change intended to strengthen marriage and/or two-parent families since the mid-1990s (Ooms et al., 2004, p. 10). Many of these strategies have been modest, however, with limited funding and small numbers of participants. The report reveals that state policy makers are realizing that strengthening marriage is a complicated issue and multi-faceted strategies may be required. It identifies three main trends: increased attention to prevention; expanded efforts to reach low-income couples in different settings; and interest in economic and other indirect strategies (2004, 17). The report illustrates that Arizona, Florida, Louisiana, Michigan, Oklahoma, Utah and Virginia are the most active in offering marriage programs (p. 23). This is still, however, a fairly small number of participating states that are attempting to strengthen marriage. Nonetheless, healthy marriage programs are increasingly becoming available in all states and spreading as a result of the infusion of federal funds.[12] An active marriage movement is also contributing to the expansion of programs.

The marriage movement

Over the past few decades, attempts to place the goal of strengthening marriage on to the policy agenda have increasingly become an issue not only for the public sector but for the private sector, grassroots groups, academics and religious communities. Apart from supporting and providing marriage programs, many professional groups and individuals who believe that marriage is in decline have been involved in contributing to the policy agenda. Brotherson and Duncan (2004) convey the historical advance of efforts to strengthen marriage, describing the numerous players behind the emergence of a broad cultural trend to work together to 'revive the institution of marriage' (2004, p. 425). As they depict it, the 'marriage movement' refers to a 'growing social awareness of marriage, its role in society, and a loose-knit coalition of multiple social sectors that are interested in strengthening marital relationships' (2004, p. 461). Brotherson and Duncan contend that although the marriage movement is based on a grassroots combination of private organizations, faith-based groups and educational programs, the addition of significant public-sector initiatives provides a new impetus and focus (2004, p. 465). Doherty and Anderson (2004) agree, asserting that since the mid-1990s, activism in connection with marriage education has experienced 'a remarkable renaissance' and that 'the current energy and impetus for change comes from the growing marriage movement' (2004, p. 426).

It is important to note here that the National Council on Family Relations (NCFR) is a professional organization of academics, advocates and practitioners who research family and marriage related topics. They have not endorsed or supported the government's HMI. In partnership with five universities and the Child Trends organization, the NCFR won an annual $900,000 ACF grant to establish a National Healthy Marriage

Resource Center in 2004. However the NCFR withdrew from the project in 2005 because the government-funded clearinghouse would not include issues such as same-sex marriages and because the project planned to place President and Mrs Bush's photo and a presidential statement on its website. The NCFR decided that it did not want to risk its image and tax-exempt status as an education and policy organization. Despite this resistance, other groups, while coming from a rather small base, are increasing their activism in relation to marriage programs, some of which receive government funding in some form.

Critical scrutiny has exposed a strong religious connection between the Christian right, the fatherhood groups, the marriage movement, conservative academics and conservative think tanks and foundations (Coltrane, 2001, p. 388). Many conservative and religious groups lobbied for DOMA. This frames the debate about marriage in moral terms and these policies promote a particular type of family. According to Coltrane, this abuses the principle of liberty by not respecting the right of the individual to choose with whom they associate. It also violates equality for those who choose to live in non-traditional households, as they do not receive the same rights and resources as those enjoyed by traditional families. Coltrane (2001, p. 388) claims that,

> These proposed policies favor married heterosexual couples over other family types and hold the promise of fulfilling evangelical Christian goals of promoting premarital sexual abstinence, male family headship, and female family identification while resisting what is seen as the growth of secular humanism, exemplified by feminism, homosexuality, cohabitation, abortion, and the like.

The President of the Family Research Council, Tony Perkins, strongly advocates traditional marriage and opposes same-sex marriage. This conservative religious organization contends that policy makers should uphold the institution of marriage and that 'marriage should be privileged in public policy' (Perkins, 2004; Maher, 2004). This group continues actively opposing same-sex marriage and does not lobby for HMI provisions.

Marriage matters. So say 113 leading American social science researchers who supported this proclamation, signing 'The Marriage Movement: A Statement of Principles' in 2000. Following the 'marital decline' line, they declare that marriage 'is an important social good, associated with an impressively broad array of positive outcomes for children and adults alike' (2000, p. 1). Under the umbrella of the Institute for American

Values (2000), an organization that researches and contributes to debates about marriage and family life, the researchers elaborate on the statement.

> We are teachers and scholars, marriage counsellors and marriage educators. We are judges, divorce lawyers, and legal reformers. We are clinicians, service providers, policy analysts, social workers, women's leaders, religious leaders, and advocates for responsible fatherhood. We are people of faith, asking God's blessing in the great task before us. We are agnostics and humanists, committed to moral and spiritual progress. We are women and men, liberals and conservatives, of different races and ethnic groups. We come together to pursue a common goal. We come together for a marriage movement. (2000, p. 1)

The declaration asks the question 'is strengthening marriage a legitimate public goal'? The answer, unsurprisingly, is a resounding 'yes'. Marriage, the signatories of the statement say, protects children and is a unique generator of social and human capital. As activists, the members of the movement appeal to America's community, religious, professional, political and intellectual leaders to work together to renew a marriage culture (Institute for American Values, 2000). They provide explicit principles that support marriage as a primary policy goal rather than settling for policies that are neutral about marriage. The special status of marriage should be respected, they argue, and the benefits of marriage should not be extended to couples who could marry, but choose not to. Marriage and childbearing should be reconnected and the ideal of marital permanence and satisfying marriages should be promoted (2000).

David Blankenhorn is founder and President of the Institute for American Values. His 2007 publication *The Future of Marriage* strongly opposes same-sex marriage because this correlates with the deinstitutionalization of marriage. Heterosexual marriage, he argues, should remain the main protector of children. Many participants in the marriage movement are opposed not only to same-sex marriage but also to cohabitation and they support abstinence before marriage. The Institute's website has established its Center for Marriage and Families, citing the work of Linda Waite and Maggie Gallagher (2000) who provide evidence that marriage is good for people's finances and their mental and physical health and Elizabeth Marquardt (2005) who argues that children of divorced parents experience a great deal of inner struggle and confusion.

Other participants in the marriage movement include the National Marriage Project, established in 1997. On its website, the project describes its involvement as a 'nonpartisan, non-sectarian and interdisciplinary initiative'. With many well-known academics on its advisory board, it actively seeks to strengthen marriage through research and analysis to inform public policy and the media, emphasizing the link between marriage and child well-being as a matter of public concern. It publishes an annual report, *The State of Our Unions: The Social Health of Marriage in America*. David Popenoe and Barbara Dafoe Whitehead, the leaders of the project and the researchers who produce this report, argue that assuming there is no domestic violence, major conflicts or unhappiness, marriage has benefits not only for adults but also for children who tend to be better off, financially and emotionally when their parents are married to each other.[13]

The Institute for American Values released a new statement in December 2004, declaring its intention to 'lead a marriage renaissance' (2004, p. 1). This objective illustrates part of the wider marriage movement's concerns that marriage as a legal and social institution is in decline and needs to be protected. It has listed shared goals including working with state legislators to push for new state laws offering financial incentives such as lower marriage license fees for those who take a marriage education class and tax credits. It also aims to work with members of Congress to increase federal funding for marriage education for low-income communities. Other goals include expanding marriage and relationship education to schools, reforming divorce laws and creating public forums to discuss the issue of same-sex unions. Finally, it intended to establish a Task Force on Marriage and work to expand the number of people in the marriage movement (2004, pp. 5–6). Another 86 goals targeting the various sectors of the marriage movement were also formulated, but are still forthcoming.[14]

Apart from the religious faction and the research arm of the marriage movement, a very active and more pragmatic grassroots organization deserves attention. An influential stakeholder is the Coalition for Marriage, Family and Couples Education (CMFCE), an umbrella organization whose mission is the promotion of marriage education. Diane Sollee is the founder and director of both the Coalition and SmartMarriages.com. A former marriage therapist, she clarifies: 'I'm not part of the marriage movement, but the marriage education movement' (interview, 2007). Bill Coffin suggested that Ms Sollee 'has worked hard at this stuff; she's a one person show'. He added: 'she is the centre, the hub of the whole thing. She has been the mover and the shaker for the last 12 years' (interview, 2007). Working in the marital counselling and therapy field, she was frustrated with the high rates of divorce and family breakdown and aware of a growing body of new research about what made marriage succeed or fail. Sollee believed that there must be a better model to help marriages. She elaborated:

> There was not only a lack of accurate information about marriage, but so much misinformation. My goal was to get the new research-based information out of the labs and to couples. The theory being that if they know better, they'll be able to do better in their marriage. I was also determined to get this new information to policy makers and the media. (Interview, 2007)

She actively galvanizes support to improve people's access to useful information about marriage so that they can apply it to their particular situation. She explained it in the following way:

> therapy is the medical model – a therapist is trained to diagnose and 'fix' (treat) an underlying disorder and voila! Your marriage is supposed to work. A marriage education approach is focused on giving couples the tools and information you need to build and sustain a marriage or whatever kind of relationship is their choice. It is not a choice to have a successful marriage if you don't know how to do it. (Interview, 2007)

Although Sollee maintains that the same skills will work for any relationship including dating and cohabiting, she named her organization Smart Marriages rather than Smart 'Relationships' or Smart 'Couples' which many people in the field wanted. 'The problems we were facing were with the breakdown of marriage' she says, and she wanted to call attention to the fact that there was a new way to approach this problem – through education. Sollee continues:

> it's affordable, research-based and something the government could do and in fact should do. It's the government's job to get information to its citizens about how they can best take care of their own health, wealth and well being. Not to mention their own children. An educational approach is not intrusive, not counselling. And especially when they've paid for the research done in their universities and paid for by their tax dollars. Imagine if the government sat on research information about smoking or seat

belts or other behaviours that predict health and well being. (Interview, 2007)

Describing herself as a 'liberal feminist Democrat', Sollee experienced much resistance to her 'crusade'. She explains: 'I lost a lot of friends in the therapy field who felt I was a turncoat and I lost friends among liberals who thought that I had sold out to the right wing and the Republicans' (interview, 2007). However, she continued:

> I never say to people 'you should get married' – that is not our problem. People get married. And, when they fail, they rush out and remarry. I say 'let me show you the research that will help you create and maintain a satisfying marriage and let me show you the benefits of marriage'. (Interview, 2007)

SmartMarriages.com is an independent, non-partisan, non-denominational, non-sectarian organization. It encourages networking and collaboration among groups working to strengthen marriage and does not rely on any public funding or support from foundations. It lists a range of marriage education courses in its web-based directory for couples at any stage from youth to dating, engaged to new parents, stepfamilies, empty nesters and couples in deep distress. Sollee explains that the most exciting aspect of marriage education is that courses work well with even the most troubled couples.[15]

The Smart Marriages website provides information on a range of issues concerning marriage to thousands of subscribers. Marriage educators, community groups, policy makers and the public can access this information and provide feedback which is communicated via the Smart Marriages email list. Information is available about a range of profit-based marriage workshops, programs, books, DVDs and other resources. Sollee has provided information to policy makers and government agencies at the federal, state and local levels. She explains that 'we need to invest resources upstream on helping educate the public about how to have strong, stable, satisfying relationships rather than continuing to focus all our resources downstream trying to pull drowning parents and their children from the river after their families have collapsed and fallen in' (interview, 2007). The website has actively encouraged people to organize state and community initiatives to lobby politicians. For example, when the reauthorization of the TANF Bill went to the Senate in 2005, Sollee pressed supporters to write, visit or telephone their Senators and inform them about marriage education in their state.

Because Smart Marriages receives no support grants or money from any source, the sole supply of funding is the annual conference. Sollee pronounced, 'this is necessary so I can stay cutting edge and do what is needed' (interview, 2007). I attended the 10th anniversary of the Smart Marriages Conference which was held in Atlanta, Georgia in 2006. While a few hundred people attended the first conference in 1997, more than 2,200 people attended in June 2006. The conference featured the 'who's who' and the 'what's what' of the marriage-strengthening, marriage education field. Participants included marriage educators, therapists, psychologists, lawyers, welfare workers, community organizers, the clergy and government representatives. Unlike a traditional 'mental health' conference, Sollee says, the general public is also invited to attend. This is possible because presenters are not talking about their 'patients' and because the public is encouraged to take the training and become marriage educators. She adds: 'research shows that lay educators get results that are as good as, or better than, instructors with mental health degrees' (interview, 2007). Representatives came from religious groups as well as secular organizations; there were people with a Republican or Democrat leaning; others with no particular political leaning, all ostensibly leaving their ideologies behind. There were attendees of all races, economic classes and from 26 countries. These delegates from a range of diverse areas share a commitment to supporting marriage education rather than old-style therapy.

Wade Horn spoke at the Smart Marriages conference in Georgia, describing the reauthorization of TANF as 'an extraordinary public policy moment'. While not everyone would be successful in gaining funds, Horn emphasized that 'we can't let money divide us as a group' and that 'the worst thing that could happen is if people fight over money'. Those in the movement had done the work without government funds up till now and this should continue. He suggested that 'a lot of people want to see this fail', so that it was important to produce good results. His appeal that people should continue to work together was couched in terms of everyone being dedicated to one thing – strengthening marriage. This plea illustrates the importance of cooperation within the movement.

A range of workshop presenters attempted to convince participants that their program held the key to family stability and successful marriages. Different subjects included interfaith marriage of different persuasions, stepfamilies, strengthening marriage in the black community, active parenting, internet sex addiction, rekindling desire, recovering from an affair and children of divorce. Sessions dealt with domestic violence, discussing screening clients for any warning signs of domestic violence, gender and cultural matters and maintaining safety. Some of the attendees told me that at previous conferences it had been decided that people would 'agree to disagree' on the issue of same-sex marriage, and that it was best not to raise it. In response to these claims, however, Sollee noted that 'same-sex is not our issue. Neither are abortion laws or gun control laws, or stem cell or any number of legal battles. We're narrow in our focus on research about marriage skills and information' (interview, 2007). This position illustrates why SmartMarriages.com does not accept public funding. The *Defense of Marriage Act 1996* (DOMA) opposes same-sex marriage. As pointed out to me in a later interview with a representative from the ACF (interview, 2006), from the federal government's point of view, this Act precludes spending funds on programs that do not target 'a man and a woman'. Nevertheless, Wade Horn argued that DOMA requirements and definitions for the purposes of legal benefits and services are

> quite a different matter from who receives services. Indeed I consistently – and emphatically – directed that if anyone wanted access to marriage education under the federal program, the only appropriate response was 'welcome'. That included married couples, unmarried couples, individuals, heterosexual couples and gay couples. No one was to be excluded from the delivery of the service. (Interview, 2003)

The Smart Marriages conference offered individuals the opportunity to complete various programs and courses which allow them to teach in their practice, community or church. This includes lay educators. A range of training programs are available: PREP, PAIRS, Couples Communication, 10 Great Dates, Family Wellness, Skills for Fragile Families, Basic Training, Love's Cradle, Marriage Links and the Power of Two. These programs raise issues about the variability in training and the anticipated capacity of the learners who were expected to go back to their communities and conduct the courses. This is particularly significant for the new 'teach-out-of-the-box' programs. These kits put the training on DVDs, including demonstrations of working with couples in a classroom setting. When I asked Sollee about the importance of teaching experience for class presenters and how new educators would deal with couples in class who were resistant, disbelieving or aggressive, she responded:

> resistance is old therapy talk. This is not therapy. We're not diagnosing and analyzing. Marriage education does not examine childhood

wounds and analyse motivations. It's about teaching basic skills to manage disagreements and conflicts so you can work as a team – understand how to work together for life. (Interview, 2007)

This is the main message of the marriage education movement.

Faith-based organizations

Historically, religious organizations have provided marriage education services. Faith-based organizations – groups of individuals united on the basis of religious or spiritual beliefs, including churches, synagogues, temples and mosques – have been supporting marriage in different ways for many years. By the late 1990s, many community and faith-based initiatives had been developed with some government funding. Millions of dollars in child-support funds were provided to 11 projects that offered not only child support but also marriage education services. These Special Improvement Projects were given to faith-based and community-based providers as well as state, local and tribal governments (ACF, 2005). Policy actors like Wade Horn claim that it is reasonable for faith-based organizations to play a role and be a partner in helping couples form and sustain healthy marriages, because most Americans marry in a place of worship (cited in Kotlowitz, 2002, p. 9). Nonetheless, Horn adds the following caveat: 'But government's ability to work directly with faith-based organizations, if the faith-based organization is going to use the delivery of those services to proselytize, is quite limited, and ought to be' (cited in Kotlowitz, 2002, p. 9). In fact, one of the conditions of receiving federal money is that they cannot be used to support religious activities such as holy instruction. Moreover, materials produced with federal resources or used in federally funded classes must be neutral in relation to religious beliefs and any religious activities must be offered at a different time and location.

However, some of the advocates for the government's HMI like Bill Coffin argue that 'promoting marriage got a bad rap. It was mistakenly seen as being about right wing men and Christians wanting to return to the 50s. There was a misbelief that generations of men and women would go back to traditional marriage – you cannot go back to the 50s, even if you wanted to. But it's more difficult for couples today – the norm, their expectations were clearer in the 50s, but people need more skills today' (interview, 2006). Here, traditional marriage conjures images of the male breadwinner and female carer in the home.

A spokesperson from the Center for Faith-Based and Community Initiatives within the DHSS posed the rhetorical question 'who would be the best people for teaching couples'? His answer was 'the churches, it should be clergy rather than secular' (interview, 2003). He advocated a voucher system similar to that used for child care, where clients accessed the local institutions of their choice. He explained that there were already existing marriage support programs in various neighbourhoods delivered by pastors. He gave the example of people with a substance-abuse problem also receiving marriage support as 'the components working together'. Funding mechanisms for programs to flourish were now available which empowered groups, particularly those on welfare. He said that many 'pre-marital groups already have a child, and various services are required – jobs, health, housing. We need to put marriage programs into the list of benefits' (interview, 2003).

The spokesperson from the Center for Faith-Based and Community Initiatives acknowledged that while 'the idea of the church and state working together, when money's involved, makes some people nervous', many churches are participating.[16] He cited the Pre-Cana Catholic Training, Marriage Encounter and the Mormons which all provide mandatory programs. He said that the Baptist Church did not want government funds, and provides free training for Pastors, therefore no government contracts are necessary (interview, 2003). The Roman Catholic Church is involved in marriage preparation, particularly in issues such as family planning (see United States Conference of Catholic Bishops, 1998). The Catholic Church takes an active role in preparing couples for marriage. Five components include a six-month minimum preparation period; the administration of a pre-marriage questionnaire (either PREPARE or FOCCUS); the use of lay leadership and 'mentoring couples' with the engaged and newly married; the use of marriage instruction classes and engagement ceremonies held before the entire congregation (Browning, 2003, p. 193). These components may differ depending on the particular diocese or parish, but complement marriage education.

A senior policy analyst from a research centre explained the development of community partnerships: 'people are now accepting, shape it, getting over personal stumbling blocks, and see that it is relevant to their communities' (interview, 2003). A variety of stakeholders, including religious, business and government representatives are involved. It is important, however, to keep in mind that as a researcher pointed out, 'what Washington thinks about a program or how it should be run is different to what actually happens in local communities' (interview, 2007).

President Bush approves of church-based programs using 'mentor couples' who counsel couples intending to marry. Mike and Harriet McManus have been promoting this concept of mentoring along with the development of Community Marriage Policies (CMPs) since 1986. Mike McManus, a Presbyterian layman, established Marriage Savers in 1996. A national non-profit organization that works with local communities and the clergy, he based Marriage Savers on the premise that religious leaders could contribute more to strengthening marriage than others because 86 per cent of marriages occur in churches. Founded on a ministry that works with local congregations, the aim is to help couples and train mentor couples to become 'Marriage Savers', working with engaged and young married couples, promoting marriage enrichment and supporting troubled marriages. Mentors are chosen by local religious leaders and complete the McManus' couple training for 12 hours over two days. Congregations consist of diverse denominations including Baptist, Lutheran, United Methodist, Presbyterian and Evangelical. Overall, Marriage Savers has assisted clergy in more than 220 cities and towns by 2007 (Marriage Savers, 2007). Couples take an inventory – such as FOCCUS – and then they meet with a mentor couple to discuss the results (2003).

The Institute for Research and Evaluation assessed McManus's program involving 114 cities and counties. These were compared with similar cities and counties which did not employ CMPs. The final study by Birch et al. (2004) found that divorce rates declined, translating into a two per cent difference annually in favour of counties which used CMPs. While there are limitations in the analysis because it remains unclear how the CMPs were actually implemented, Doherty and Anderson argue that 'the study gives the first scientific support for the possible efficacy of community marriage initiatives' (2004, p. 427). According to McManus's own report, the marriage rate has plunged by 37 per cent since 1970; in 1960, 88 per cent of Americans aged between 35 and 44 were married. By 1999, that figure fell to 70 per cent (2003, p. 20). A major reason why there are so few marriages is that millions of adult children of divorce are fearful that if they marry they too will divorce. Marriage Savers accordingly adopts a religious perspective on marriage and as part of the program, couples are taught subjects from a biblical standpoint and complete a work book which researches Scripture on marriage. A strongly articulated view is the 'common myth of marriage' – that it is founded on love:

> No one can promise to love another person always, although they can vow to always seek the other's welfare, happiness, well-being

etc...to be determined to love, while possibly not being in love....
The reason we need these vows is because we are inadequate to keep
these big promises.... It is not so much that we keep the vows, but
that the vows keep us – they form a wall around our marriage...they
protect us. (2003, p. 12)

Therefore, lasting marriages are founded on the vows and the commitment of couples to remain together. In 2005, the McManuses produced
DVDs which instructed mentors couples on how to administer and discuss the results of the FOCCUS pre-marital inventory and provided
exercises to help pre-marital couples to improve, among other things,
communication and conflict resolution skills. The organization won a
federal grant of $49,000 through an intermediate agency – the Institute
for Youth Development – to reach unwed couples.

While Marriage Savers appears to have some success, the CMPs have
been criticized. Kotlowitz (2002, p. 3) disapproves of McManus's
approach because he is 'given to moralizing, some of which can be
alienating' for couples, for example, when he suggests that the collapse
of marriage 'creates monsters' because it leads to the possibility of childhood drop outs and delinquents. In an interview conducted in 2003, a
policy researcher commented to me that 'McManus has a great passion
for his mentoring programs, he inspires people and gets them enthusiastic. The mentor is a good idea, but there is 'no follow up', and 'more
training is necessary, there's no proper infrastructure' (interview,
2003).

Community-based initiatives

Other community marriage initiatives such as First Things First (FTF)
aim to strengthen the institution of the family. Established in 1997 in
Chattanooga, Tennessee, FTF was concerned about the low rates of marriage and the high rates of divorce. A group of community leaders
formed FTF to 'rebuild, renew and revitalize our city, beginning with
the family' (FTF, 2006). A secular, non-profit organization, it has contributed to the establishment of a divorce education pilot project,
launched marriage public service campaigns, and trained hundreds of
professionals through marriage enrichment seminars and sponsored
pre-marital classes. FTF works with local churches in community marriage programs; approximately 20 per cent of its work is with the faith
community. While a policy analyst from a think tank commented that
FTF is 'led by idiosyncratic leadership and the way it gets its resources
has its own wrinkles' (interview, 2003), FTF is regarded as a template

and a training ground for the development of further initiatives around the US (Doherty and Anderson, 2004, p. 427).

The ACF has brought interested community leaders to FTF so that they can see and utilize the FTF model and the organization recently received over $1,000,000 from the Healthy Marriages program. Ulrich (ndp) claims that 145 churches now require pre-marital preparation before marrying couples and that more than 6,000 people have attended FTF's marriage education seminars. Ulrich (ndp) emphasizes the importance of relationships between people in the community and that the programs sometimes require partnering with people or programs with different views. He suggests participating actively in the system because this allows for networking and having an impact on setting the agenda that will shape public policy (2007, p. 12). FTF has partnerships and collaborative relationships with more than 100 organizations. Not all of the activities focus purely on marriage, but cover a range of issues to do with the law, health, parenting, teen pregnancies and domestic violence. As evidence of FTF's success, Julie Baumgardner, FTF's President and Executive Director claims that the divorce rate is down 20 per cent and teen out-of-wedlock births are down 23 per cent since 1997 (email, 2007).

Another example of government participating in a community initiative is the Greater Grand Rapids Community Marriage Policy. Established in 1996, the project is now known as the Healthy Marriages Grand Rapids (HMGR). Working in partnership with City Vision and the West Michigan Christian Foundation, the initiative also promotes CMPs. These agencies are collaborating to improve couple relationships and reduce the potential for domestic violence. This is part of a five-year project with the main aim of improving child-support enforcement and the financial well-being of children from low-income families. The project received $990,000 over five years in federal funding under a waiver from the office of Child Support Enforcement in ACF in May 2003. Local businesses are urged to become involved and include marriage education as an Employee Assistance Program benefit. This is considered to be more cost-effective in preventing marital distress than incurring the costs of counselling and lost productivity involved when workers' marriages break up (Mettler, 2003: 1).

HMGR mobilizes the resources of many sectors of the community. Its distinctive strategy involves collaboration between government, education bodies, legal service providers, faith-based organizations, businesses and the media in attempting to create a more marriage-supportive culture. Social workers from the Department of Human Services, psychologists and education facilitators have been partially funded to promote the virtues of marriage to clients, students and armed services personnel and to teach classes. Public service announcements highlighting the benefits of marriage and the necessary skills for successful marriages have been shown on television and billboards, in newspapers and announced on radio. The coalition developed through HMGR supports Healthy Marriages Health Relationships (HMHR) an initiative which includes ten faith-based organizations. HMHR provides relationship and marriage education to low-income parents with the goal of improving the lives of children. Since its establishment in 2003, the project has delivered at least one class to 2000 participants. The curricula includes programs such as Family Wellness, How to Avoid Marrying a Jerk(ette) and Parenting Wisely (Bir et al., 2005). The project was featured as one of 12 programs in a best practice brochure produced by the ACF.

In 1999, the first statewide comprehensive model to generate and provide marriage service began in Oklahoma. An extensive experiment began between community, faith-based and business groups, when Republican Governor Frank Keating announced his goal of reducing his state's divorce rate (which was the second highest divorce rate in the US at that time) by one-third within ten years. This led to the establishment of the Oklahoma Marriage Initiative (OMI). In 2000, the state used $10 million of unspent TANF funds for marriage programs. The OMI is a female owned and operated public relations for-profit firm. Both public and private groups are working together to develop strategies for supporting strong marriages. The aim is to lower the state's divorce rate, strengthen families and reduce dependence on government support. The OMI argues that despite a growing divorce rate and larger numbers of cohabiting couples, 75 per cent of first marriages are conducted in a church, synagogue or mosque with a religious leader performing the ceremony (OMI, 2003). Therefore, faith sector leaders have been leading partners of the initiative.

The OMI provides a clear rationale for why public organizations are becoming involved with private organizations in marriage support. It says,

> Some may wonder why government should get involved in something as personal a decision as marriage. First, the OMI does not penalize the couple that chooses divorce, nor does it encourage people to remain in violent or unhealthy relationships. What it does encourage is a positive way for government to support healthy marriages. The government's current role as it relates to our families

usually occurs after a crisis event or when the family has reached unbearable circumstances. Does a healthy family require child support collections, welfare and food stamp allocations, foster care, court actions, etc? These are all ways that government intervenes in our personal lives, wouldn't it be better to have that interaction on a positive note and before the crisis occurs rather than after? (2003, p. 3)

Thus government support of early intervention programs to strengthen marriage is viewed as an acceptable measure. In the early development stages, the OMI formed a research advisory group to provide research-based input into the development of the initiative. The group included sociologists, psychologists, social workers and representatives from Oklahoma's Department of Human Services and its State University's Bureau of Social Research. Oklahoma is training state workers, community groups and pastors to deliver PREP, the skill-based marriage educational program. The OMI has provided approximately 100,000 people with at least 12 hours of marriage education between 2001 and 2006. It prioritized building capacity to deliver services which aim to improve the quality of relationships. The curriculum is delivered in different formats by trained workshop leaders, either from public organizations or private individuals. Public agencies have the advantage of gaining public assistance for the initiative's goals and they tend to serve low-income clients who would otherwise be difficult to reach. Moreover, these agencies have statewide infrastructure and networks (Dion, 2006, p. 5). Volunteers in local communities can receive free workshop training in PREP and in exchange, agree to provide at least four free workshops. While the majority of these independent workshop leaders are not paid for delivering the OMI services, some have incorporated PREP into their private professional practices. Many are members of the faith community but others represent law enforcement, businesses and family services.

An example of a small community group carrying out effective work is the East Capitol Center for Change on the outskirts of Washington DC. This family-centred, non-profit organization offers marriage education workshops to low-income African Americans.[17] This Center also provides various programs such as Life Starts, fatherhood programs, abstinence programs and mentor programs for troubled youths. It receives funding from a range of federal, state and county agencies as well as from foundations. A government official acknowledged that it is difficult to manage such small organizations because they receive 'so many different money streams – it's a jigsaw puzzle of funding. ... Even in DC, the left and the right hand don't know what the other is doing' (interview, 2007).

The East Capitol Center for Change's 'Together is Better' campaign aims to strengthen families, marriages and communities. Through funding from the ACF's HMI, relationship classes are offered over eight or nine sessions. According to a representative, the classes work via 'word of mouth recruitment' (interview, 2007). The Center contracted Nisa Muhammad, who operates the Wedded Bliss Foundation and is the Founder of Black Marriage Day, to deliver the workshops. She wrote a specifically designed curriculum for African Americans with Rozario Slack, who is the Director of Urban Initiatives at FTF. Drawing on a mix of programs such as PREP and PAIRS, they adapted them for low-income black populations in their Basic Training for Couples. Hence the courses are set in the context of racism, discrimination and cultural phenomena which are specific to the black community. Muhammad teaches some of the classes, and has trained approximately 100 facilitators around the US to deliver the program. She monitors classes when she can and provides feedback to facilitators. As Muhammad expressed it, her organization is trying 'to reach people at the bottom of the barrel. They are the poorest of the poor. ... People are struggling to find a job, keep a job, look after their children. It's rough being black, it's hard' (interview, 2007). She argues while black marriage was strong in past, the sexual revolution and the civil rights movement changed that: 'People bought into the hype that marriage doesn't matter.' Furthermore, she maintains that 'the welfare system has wrecked marriage for blacks. When white marriage has a cold, black marriage has pneumonia'. Thus, in relation to problems in the black community, marriage support, Muhammad contends, is 'not the answer, it's a part of the answer' and should be connected to the 'availability of social services, paying for living expenses such as rent and gas and finding jobs etc' (interview, 2007).

I attended marriage education classes conducted by the East Capitol Center for Change in March 2007. Held in a community hall, the program supplied child care, dinner and $100 on completion of the course. These incentives are provided because couple recruitment and retention are difficult, but necessary because programs receiving federal grants have to meet particular participation targets as specified in the grant application. It is particularly difficult to recruit men, but male facilitators and married couples run the classes and have been effective in dealing with this resistance. The couples attend a graduation dinner and are encouraged to stay in contact with each other, maintain friendships and provide support. The couples (some married, others not) clearly enjoyed the course and told me that they found the classes very helpful for their relationships.

These diverse community and faith-based initiatives provide just a small sample of activities in grassroots communities. Doherty and Anderson (2004, p. 431) contend that although community initiatives are in their infancy, their strategies 'reflect community organizing principles in which traditional marriage education approaches are built in after the community is organized, rather than determined in advance by professionals'. However, others are attempting to introduce new programs into different communities. The main goal is to spread the message about the value of marriage. Coffin argues that 'facilitators should not be therapists. ... Lay people who show empathy and compassion are important' (interview, 2006). There are clearly a plethora of programs and different approaches to marriage education, raising issues of quality control and evaluation which will be addressed in chapter 6.

Think tanks and research centres

An entirely new and influential development is that several of the most prestigious and respected policy research centres across the political continuum such as the Urban Institute and Mathematica now conduct federally funded research, evaluation and analysis of marriage-related policies and programs. This has resulted in the generation of new knowledge and helped to garner stronger support for the federal HMI. The Heritage Foundation formulates and promotes conservative public policies, adopting a robust policy approach and a strong public-relations campaign supporting traditional family values. One of its policy analysts, Patrick Fagan, supports the government's policy of providing funds to educate people on the benefits of marriage and encouraging unwed parents to acquire the skills for stable marriages. He argues that Congress can jump start the process of rebuilding a culture of marriage in America and improve the prospects for millions of America's most fragile families (2002, p. 2). He cites the case of Wisconsin, where reforms tied welfare benefits to work via TANF funding and, consequently, caseloads were reduced by about one-third. Fagan recommends that a similar approach should be adopted for restoring a 'culture of marriage among unwed parents in fragile families, most of whom are likely to be receiving some government benefits' (2002, p. 5). Fagan said that 'we are building a culture of shepherding people towards strong marriage, we're able to pull together disparate parts' (interview, 2003). Fagan supports the goals of marriage education programs, highlighting the influence of the Heritage Foundation in drawing attention to their value: 'you do the rhetoric before you do the legislation' (interview, 2003). He approves of President Bush's initiative focusing on marriage as a way of dealing with the underlying causes of child poverty and welfare dependence. While the government's million dollar marriage initiative cannot restore a culture of marriage, it represents a critical first step (interview, 2003).

The Fragile Families and Child Wellbeing Study is a joint project of Columbia and Princeton Universities. The study follows approximately 5,000 children born in the late 1990s in 20 cities with a population of more than 200,000. Romantically involved, low-income couples are being studied in more depth. The study found that women are sceptical of 'marriage for marriage's sake' and point out that men who do not have good jobs, or have drug or alcohol related problems do not offer much as potential husbands. Initial findings are that greater benefits are positively associated with couples staying together (McLanahan et al., 2003). The Fragile Families Survey found that most unwed mothers wanted to marry the father of their child. It found that one-half of unmarried parents are living together, and another third are romantically attached but not cohabiting when their child is born. The researchers suggest that the time around a child's birth might offer a window of opportunity, a 'magic moment' for sending a strong message about the value of marriage to the parents. Nonetheless, the study showed that three years after birth, there was no initial evidence that marriage has significant positive effects on children.

The Brookings Institution is involved in programs in Baltimore with disadvantaged communities and low-income families sponsored by the Casey Foundation. A spokesperson said that through his work, he saw the value of marriage for the poor. The HMI, he said, is operating 'exactly the way public policy should be done' (interview, 2006). He also acknowledged that people within the marriage movement are sensitive about not using compulsion in getting poor people to participate in marriage programs.

Few advocacy organizations that are positioned on the more 'liberal' end of the political spectrum champion marriage policies and initiatives. One that does is CLASP – a non-profit organization aiming to promote a progressive agenda in family policy and to improve life for those on low incomes. While CLASP supports marriage and relationship education, during the welfare reform debate it argued that too much funding was being proposed for the programs given that so little was known about whether they work and while funding for basic economic necessities and services for poor families was being reduced. CLASP has proposed an approach dubbed Marriage Plus, arguing for a wider set of goals for the HMI that acknowledges the needs and circumstances of low-income families. First, public policies and programs should aim to help more children grow up with their two biological parents in a healthy, stable relationship. However, marriage may not be a feasible or desirable option for all parents. Therefore, the second goal is to help those parents who are never-married, separated, divorced or remarried to be financially capable and responsible and to cooperate in raising their children (Ooms, 2002).

Marriage Plus is guided by the following principles. 'Healthy' marriage is not about encouraging marriage for its own sake. Participating in marriage-related programs should be voluntary and designed to meet the diverse needs of different groups. Programs should be evaluated and evidence-based. Ooms (2002, pp. 4–7) argues for a package of services to offer young families a combination of 'soft' services. This would include relationship skills and marriage education workshops, financial management classes and peer support groups and 'hard' services – job training and placement, housing, medical coverage and substance-abuse treatment if necessary. She claims that 'Marriage Plus is becoming more acceptable. People realize that you can't just look at marriage in isolation without looking at the context' (interview, 2006). When I asked her about the importance of program evaluation, she said 'while well designed evaluations using random assignments are important and underway, it is difficult and expensive to evaluate the effects long term'. Meanwhile, she added that it is more important to improve and redevelop existing programs based on implementation studies. Activities should focus on marriage, but may feature different strategies that indirectly have positive effects on marriage. This includes increasing income and employment, reducing work stress, preventing teen pregnancy and out-of-wedlock births. Not just governments, but the legal, education, health, business, faith and media sectors should work in partnership with policy makers to pursue these goals.

Opposition to marriage promotion

When the healthy marriage initiative was first debated over a decade ago, there was vocal opposition from several quarters including women's groups, researchers and the social justice wing of the churches. Coming from a 'marital resilience' perspective, major critical responses include that there is too much concentration on morality, family structure and pro-marriage programs at the expense of other public policies such as addressing unemployment and providing good access to child care, education and health services. The 1996 legislation received criticism, for example, from academics like Nancy Cott (2000, p. 222), who argues that supporters of the PRWORA linked issues such as 'increases in welfare caseloads, births out-of-wedlock and female-headed households in poverty' to 'male irresponsibility', 'female profligacy' and 'marital failure'. While Cott acknowledges that female-headed households with children are poorer on average than married-couple households, she criticizes proponents of the Act for assuming that the marriage ceremony itself 'magically solves the problem of poverty' (2000, p. 222).

There have been some vocal critics of the Bush Administration's HMI. For example, the Council on Contemporary Families and the National Women's Organization (NOW) opposes providing TANF funds to married families ahead of single-parent families, and rejects demands for repealing or modifying no-fault divorce. The Council on Contemporary Families argues that marriage education may be useful for couples, but should not be implemented at the expense of other support such as education or child care. Two of its well-known spokespeople, Coontz and Folbre, (2002) advocate that:

> Public policies should not penalize marriage. Neither should they provide an economic bonus or financial incentive to individuals to marry, especially at the cost of lowering the resources available to children living with single mothers. Such a diversion of resources from public assistance programs penalizes the children of unmarried parents without guaranteeing good outcomes for the children of people who are married. A variety of public policies could help strengthen families and reduce poverty among all children, including a broadening of the Earned Income Tax Credit, expansion of publicly subsidized child care, efforts to promote responsible fatherhood, improvements in public education and job training, and efforts to reduce income inequality and pay discrimination. Unlike some of the pro-marriage policies now under consideration, these policies would benefit couples who wish to marry but would not pressure women to enter or remain in intimate relationships they would not otherwise choose. (2002, p. 11)

Coontz and Folbre call for wider economic reforms to reduce poverty, improve education and job training, regardless of marital status and income support.

The NOW Legal Defense and Education Fund has produced a statement titled 'Looking for Love in All the Wrong Places: The Case Against Government Marriage Promotion' which criticized the government's marriage support programs for many reasons. First, the programs divert funds way from the battle to defeat poverty and to create jobs.[18] The NOW statement asserts that 'no advocate of marriage promotion can point to a single, audited marriage promotion program that has helped alleviate poverty, let alone improved the rate of healthy marriages' (ndp, p. 1). Second, it argues that approximately 60 per cent of women on welfare are survivors of domestic violence and the government's marriage promotion includes no provisions to ensure that it would detect couples in abusive relationships (ndp, p. 2). Third, it argues that the programs hamstring the states that are forced to spend TANF funds on marriage promotion when the money could 'be better put to use in programs that directly combat poverty' (ndp, p. 3). Fourth, marriage programs encourage poor women to be dependent on men, sending the message that

> it's more important to find a good man than a good job. To leave poor women without job skills, and treat marriage as some sort of elixir to poverty, takes away from those women any control over their own economic security. Marriage promotion is not just outmoded thinking, it's dangerous policy. (ndp, p. 3)

The issue of marriage education was raised at various committee hearings, and many people have criticized welfare reform reauthorization. As NOW's Senior Staff Attorney, Sherry Leiwant's 2003 testimony to the Senate Finance Committee strongly criticized welfare reform reauthorization. Apart from mentioning the issues discussed above, she argued that 'at a time of huge budget deficits and high unemployment it is irresponsible to focus over a billion dollars on untested unproven marriage promotion programs' (2003, p. 1). Moreover, Leiwant states that polls indicate that most Americans oppose the government's involvement in personal decisions concerning marriage and do not support using scarce public resources to promote marriage for the poor. She cites the 2002 PEW Forum on Religion and Public Life poll which found that 79 per cent of respondents oppose government programs aimed at encouraging marriage, with only 18 per cent supporting marriage programs (2003, p. 4). Leiwant suggests that:

> This is not surprising as Americans value their personal privacy and their right to make personal decisions free of government intrusion,

and most adults who have experience with intimate relationships are rightfully sceptical that the government can or should try to influence them. Opposing use of scare public dollars for this purpose is not the same as being 'anti-marriage', but rather recognizing that there are some issues that should not involve government'. (2003, p. 2)

Instead, NOW (2002) argues, governments should aim to move families out of poverty and into self-sufficiency by ensuring that all families have adequate resources to meet their basic needs of food, clothing, shelter and health care. This goal can be accomplished by supporting caregivers, promoting education and training for jobs that pay a self-supporting wage and safeguarding access to other public supports while respecting family privacy and women's autonomy in family choices. States must ensure equitable treatment of all needy families and should not discriminate among families on the basis of marital status, race, gender, disability, recipient status, legal immigrant status, and language barriers, ethnicity, national origin, or sexual orientation. NOW and Legal Momentum, another advocacy group oppose the Promoting Responsible Fatherhood Initiative, arguing it illegal because the program intends to serve only men (Lee, 2007). The groups allege sex discrimination and that the program should be open to women. This is despite the fact that the ACF, which oversees the grants, aims to help men to become better fathers.

Other activists have additional criticisms to make. They have argued that the current marriage policy puts 'governmental pressure on women's intimate decisions', 'fails to support women's family choices and caregiving work' and 'wastes taxpayers' money on conservative anti-feminist, anti-choice, and anti-lesbian-and-gay organizations that promote marriage' (Fineman et al., 2003, pp. 1, 7). They are alarmed about the treatment of women of colour, arguing that those on welfare receive discriminatory treatment and are subjected to extra pressures to participate in marriage preparation classes (2003, pp. 1, 7). They disapprove of policies which narrowly target marriage, but do not consider wider issues such as sex discrimination in the workplace, or that the number of single parent families and the decline in marriage may be explained by something other than welfare dependency.

Marriage support ignores structural causes and economic circumstances of relationship breakdowns. The lack of resources, so the criticisms go, puts strain on both men and women in their roles as income providers, partners and parents. In fact, intervention into the private sphere via the provision of marriage programs is an easier solution than providing some of the wider public services which would improve people's economic prospects. A representative from Catholic NETWORK criticized social conservatives for confusing marriage policy with welfare – they would like to replace welfare with marriage policy. This, she described as the 'get married and stay married and you won't need welfare' argument (interview, 2006). She contends that these types of programs stigmatize single mothers and risk being dismissive of children who happen to find themselves in single-parent families.

Marriage education programs in the US developed from studies on middle and upper-income white couples and have mostly been offered to these populations. Recent studies of marriage support for disadvantaged couples recommend that couples should be assisted in understanding and dealing with external factors that influence their relationships (Fein and Ooms, 2005; Ooms, 2007). Accordingly, governments need to examine ways of adapting these programs to meet the needs of low-income populations. This not only includes health, education, employment, social supports, finances and housing but also requires improving more general conditions such as the economy, societal norms and racial and ethnic discrimination (2005, pp. 5–6).

Avis Jones-DeWeever, a Director from the Institute for Women's Policy Research told me that the marriage policies are coming from a perspective of ignorance about African Americans and that they do not understand the dynamics of what goes on in the communities. She was disappointed that more was not being demanded of government and that some in the community seemed to be 'settling for this marriage diversion' (interview, 2006). Jones-De-Weever adds that a lot of contextual issues often get glossed over. For example, continuing discrimination means that a white man with a felony has a slightly better chance of being called back after a job interview than a black man with no criminal record. Furthermore, there are three women for every eligible man, because of high rates of drug abuse, unemployment and imprisonment. In addition to these difficulties, a black woman is less likely to marry outside of her race (interview, 2006). An ACF spokeswoman who is involved with the African American HMI acknowledged the problems of 'out-of-wedlock births and issues such as incarcerated men. It is a precarious situation – there are not enough men to marry, there's a multiple partner fertility issue. Women have complex lives and it gets very difficult'. She asserted, however, that a different value is now placed on marriage. 'White women follow the sequence of getting married, then having children. Black women have children and don't get married. It may take the next generation to turn that around' (interview, 2007).

As Edin and Kefalas (2005) argue, while relationship skills are useful for resolving daily conflicts, this may not be the case when there are more serious problems in the relationship.

> It's harder to see how these tools will be of as much use when the quarrels result from chronic infidelity, physical abuse, alcoholism and drug addiction, criminal activity, and incarceration. Indeed, it is hard to envision any type of social program that would, or even should, motivate couples to wed in the light of such serious problems. (2005, p. 214)

Nonetheless, Kathryn Edin has become a supporter of the healthy marriage programs and has been involved in revising the PREP curriculum for single mothers.

Some of the women in the marriage education movement disagree with these criticisms. For example, Nisa Muhammad argues that if black women were asked would they rather be married or a single parent, they would choose to be married. She asks 'how many people want their daughter to be a single mum or their son to be chased by child support? Nobody wants that for their children'. She adds 'It's white feminists, not black women who are saying that marriage is bad for black women' (interview, 2007). Diane Sollee noted that when she created SmartMarriages. com, 'feminist organizations were not supportive – especially in the beginning. ... Many would literally cross the street, saying that marriage programs encouraged domestic violence and trapped women'. She continued: 'it is really sad that women's activists aren't on board. It puzzles and amazes me. Marriage is one of the biggest civil rights issues for women and blacks and it should be a leading issue' (interview, 2007).

A few of the interviewees claimed that women's organizations are less vocal about marriage policies as they have shifted their focus to the Iraq war. Moreover, now that the TANF funds have been reauthorized, women's groups are less resistant. The following comment was also made by a policy analyst in reference to the Democrats. 'As far as the HMI goes, the Democrats publicly won't say anything bad about marriage. Four years ago, marriage was controversial, but the Democrats are on the losing side on this issue, so they have kept quiet' (interview, 2007). Time will tell if a new Administration – whether it is run by Republicans or Democrats – maintains support and wider acceptance for the healthy marriage agenda.

A criticism coming from a different perspective is given by groups such as the Cato Institute which argues for limited government and individual liberty. From a libertarian perspective, marriage programs are nothing but a form of social engineering and too invasive. Government attempts are 'intrusive meddling in people's most intimate relations'. Zeigler (2005) argues that while Congress's marriage initiative is 'a good idea', she disagrees that it should be federally funded. These type of initiatives should be a matter of private choice, rather than forced onto society by the government. In addition, promoting marriage as a solution to poverty is an insult to those who are struggling to escape poverty. She cites studies indicating that many fathers of children born out-of-wedlock did not finish high school, were unemployed, had low incomes and criminal records. She argues that:

> If Congress wants to encourage marriage, it should start by removing the disincentives to marriage. The current welfare system, as well as our tax code, erect barriers to marriage by reducing benefits and/or increasing tax liability if a couple weds. Before the government starts spending new money on incentives, it should fix current programs to reflect its pro-marriage agenda. Additionally, research shows that financial difficulty is one of the leading causes of divorce. Congress should focus its resources on encouraging a dynamic economy, through lower taxes and less regulation of business. Job security, higher wages, and a lighter tax burden would go a long way toward securing marital stability. (Zeigler, 2005)

There are therefore, several reasons for misgivings about the government's marriage education policies, ranging from the effects for women to the right to privacy and the need for improved economic structures as a way of alleviating poverty.

Conclusion

Since the 1990s, political activism has been successful in generating ideas for new policy initiatives and marriage education programs. At the tenth anniversary of the PROW Act, government officials, social scientists and welfare beneficiaries assessed the results. One goal of the 1996 legislation was to reduce the level of teen pregnancies. according to Hymowetz (2006) this goal has been accomplished. However, as indicated by Dafoe Whitehead, 'the unfinished business of welfare reform is marriage' (cited in Marshall et al., p. 4). Nonetheless, marriage policies are in place and many programs are available in the communities and on the ground. If we consider the symbolic message sent by the government, the rhetoric offers strong signals about the value of marriage. There are now many different marriage activities with many more receiving interest and gaining momentum in communities across the country.

In the US, marriage education programs are currently on the policy agenda. Major developments are continuing such as the launching of the revamped National Healthy Marriage Resource Centre – a national resource and clearinghouse for healthy marriage – and a national media campaign on healthy marriage sponsored by the ACF.[19] The progress of marriage education provides a very clear example of the tensions between the arguments that marriage is in decline or that marriage is resilient. Policy makers, researchers and activists argue that marriage is good for the community, children, couples, the poor and those on welfare. The marriage movement strongly supports and encourages government facilitation of marriage policies and programs. Those who oppose this stance argue that marriage support is not necessarily beneficial for women, especially for poor women and women of colour. There has also been fervent opposition because they argue that public money could be better spent on improving the lot of the poor. Furthermore, marriage is a matter of private choice which is based on the individual couple's decisions. Consequently, there are many disagreements about the optimum route to strengthening families and there are still many challenges ahead. Perhaps the best way forward is to view marriage and relationship education as one important element of policy that deserves further consideration. Clearly, creating robust marriages matter to the government and to the public.

Part III

Challenges for Governments

6
Individualism and the Private Sphere

The cultural, legal and religious meanings of marriage remain important in the twenty-first century, despite the fact that individualism reigns supreme. We have seen that the 'marital decline' perspective wishes to revive marriage as a stable, committed and functional form; while for those celebrating marriage's resilience, personal satisfaction overrides any traditional considerations. Both sides of the debate would agree, however, that the key is how to strengthen and rejuvenate relationships. This chapter, along with Chapter 7, analyses my research findings and argues that governments face many challenges in their attempts to facilitate marriage and relationship education. While strengthening marriage has gained attention as a public policy issue – particularly in the US – there is no single cure or magic potion which offers a panacea for dealing with the changes in people's personal relationships. Neither public policy nor private institutions can revive marriage as *the* socially sanctioned institution for love, sex and reproduction.

This chapter highlights the difficulties that governments confront in their attempts to enhance the stability of relationships and families. This is in many ways a tough assignment as they must consider marriage not only as a political institution but also as a social one, with particular cultural meanings. As Chapter 2 demonstrated, marriage has been shaped by different ideals according to local, historical, religious, economic and social aspirations. In new governance arrangements policy makers are moving into the private sphere as they respond to demands from many different actors. Accordingly, this chapter argues that governments must handle challenges revolving around factors such as religion, romance, feminist views of diverse families, privacy and divorce reforms when addressing marriage and relationship education.

As the previous chapters have demonstrated, a variety of multifaceted and intertwined perspectives and factors frame the debate – deliberations about whether and how to protect marriage remain contested. Conservatives focus on marriage as the central institution of society and aim to restore its strengths by returning to the traditional culture of heterosexual relationships and parenthood. Thus they view the absence of fathers, divorce and out-of-wedlock births as evidence of moral weakening and a lenient society. They lament the increase in individualism and the loss of religious faith. Progressives and liberals consider the importance of economic structures, advocating that poverty needs to be addressed so that all citizens have access to good housing, employment and education. These advancements not only improve people's economic well-being, but are linked to people's personal well-being and relationships. Therefore, workers need better working conditions, while higher income earners need better access to ways of managing family life and work balance. Some liberals and communitarians support marriage because of evidence that it has health benefits – consequently, their position at times becomes indistinguishable from the religious and conservatives in supporting marriage education programs. Feminists argue that a gender perspective should inform the debate so that socialization of the family is paramount: marriage is not the solution. Some feminists have argued that marriage education programs could trap women in abusive relationships; others argue that they do little to alleviate poverty for women. Libertarians argue that governments should not be interfering in the private sphere, because this is not the proper role of government. Moreover, some conservatives agree, arguing that government funds should not be wasted on marriage education. Many gays and lesbians argue that they are discriminated against because they are not legally permitted to marry. Clearly, governments have to contend with – and often attempt to appease – these conflicting views and political positions.

More nuanced insights concerning the role of government demonstrate the challenges ahead: as the nature and purpose of marriage has changed and become more complex, it is increasingly difficult for policy makers to find solutions to the problems facing couples in their family lives. Should governments explicitly favour marriage over other family forms? Should governments leave it to individuals to choose? Should governments be playing Cupid? While these questions are difficult to answer, governments of all political hues must deal with the changes in the institution of marriage, both in its public form and in its private capacity.

Given the complexity of intimate relationships, it is doubtful that governments can pinpoint any specific factor to explain more than a small proportion of any aggregate-level changes in the institution of marriage. The debate about the purpose of marriage is in many ways a debate over symbolism and marriage's importance in creating a stable, happy and functioning society. According to the 'marital decline' perspective, it is necessary to restore and revitalize marriage which has been weakened by various social forces. Marriage gains political mileage among traditionalists by not including same-sex couples single parents, or cohabitating partners. While marriage has many different purposes which many people continue to value highly, the increase in cohabitation suggests ambivalence as well as a lack of knowledge or confidence about how to embrace marriage.

In spite of these shortcomings, marriage is an institution which many people will continue to enter. While the significance of marriage has declined, it has symbolic importance in terms of enhancing trust and as a marker of prestige (Cherlin, 2004, pp. 854–855). In the US, most Americans continue to value marriage and nearly 90 per cent will eventually marry (2004, p. 853). Similarly, in Australia a majority of people will be married at some time and the institution is perceived as relevant to contemporary society (de Vaus, 2004, p. 163). In the UK, there is also strong support for marriage, despite the growth of cohabitation (One Plus One, ndp). And as Cherlin reasons, marriage still entails a public commitment to a long-term, possibly permanent relationship even if it occurs within an individualist society.

For all governments, a defining characteristic of many marriages is the presence of children and how to attend to their well-being. The US government sponsors marriage over other family types, because marriage is favoured as a way of contributing to the solution of welfare dependency, with the rationale that married two-parent families offer the best life opportunities for children. Moreover, the more number of married people, the less of a burden on the welfare system. The policy agenda in the US has developed a clear pro-marriage strategy, although this occurs to a lesser extent in Australia and even less so in the UK. In these two countries, the interests of children are important, but are not perceived as closely linked to strong marriages. Marriage promotion is thus significant as a declaration of how governments view the family, rather than just a policy matter concerning particular programs.

The paradox of religion

The links between religion and marriage remain strong. For many people of faith, marriage is a sacred reality, or clear sign of God's love which strengthens the union of marriage. Religiosity may protect marriage indirectly by influencing the quality of marriage, and directly by increasing the stigma attached to leaving it. The problem, however, is that those who are not religious may not have this protection. Moreover, my interviews suggested that non-religious people may not attend classes because they do not want to participate in activities run by or located in a religious organization.

The US is the most religious country of the three and it is here that religion plays the most influential role. Ninety per cent of adults acknowledge some sort of religious preference, while a majority of Americans have stated that religion is important in their lives, that they belong to religious organizations and take part in religious services at least occasionally (Amato et al., 2007, pp. 29, 190). Religious groups call for public vows of unconditional love and commitment to marriage as a lifelong relationship (Hawkins et al., 2002, p. 167). In contrast, the 2006 Australian census found that 19 per cent of Australians claimed that they had no religion. It is compulsory for those marrying in the Catholic Church to complete a marriage course, but not for other marrying couples. Therefore, attendance is much higher for couples marrying in a church and very low for those married in a civil service. More than half of all Australian couples are married by civil celebrants and as Chapter 4 discussed, it is very difficult to entice these couples to participate in marriage education. Similar to the UK, Australian policy makers do not perceive cohabitation as a particular social threat or social problem – as is more the case in the US (Barlow and Probert, 2004, p. 6). For this reason, Barlow and Probert argue that it may be easier to impose pro-marriage legal norms founded in Christianity in the US, as these may coincide widely with expressed social values. This is not to say that the UK and Australia have a uniform approach or the same social values; for example, they have implemented different legislation regarding same-sex marriage.

The funding criteria for marriage education in US religious organizations are very different from criteria for religious groups in the other two countries. While potential clients do not have to hold particular religious beliefs, for example, they do not have to be Catholic to attend Catholic marriage classes, funding requirements from the US federal government explicitly state that organizations are not permitted to include any religious teachings in their classes. This is striking because many marriage advocates are motivated by deep religious convictions, yet are unable to use religion to frame or inform discussion of the programs. However, given the separation between state and church, the government does not – and cannot – fund religious-based programs. Thus, for example, Protestants, Catholics, the Presbyterians or Mormons can espouse their religious beliefs in their education programs but are ineligible for any public funding. The government's guidelines state that faith-based organizations cannot 'use any part of a direct federal grant to fund religious worship, instruction, or proselytization. Instead, organizations may only use government money to support non-religious social services' (White House, ndp, p. 10). Although they can conduct classes in their church or school, they must present programs in a secular format. Consequently, a program such as Marriage Encounters – a Catholic program which has been operating for decades – is disqualified from funding. As a representative from the ACF pointed out, many people want religious information because they are religious. However, while the churches are able to mention that they will be, for example, teaching a scriptures class, this class must be conducted at a different time and location, so that it is separate from marriage education.

Organizations such as the American Civil Liberties Union and the Freedom from Religion Foundation (FFRF) monitor the websites and activities of faith-based providers to ensure that they are not 'crossing the line' between government and religion. These groups work to defend the constitutional principle of the separation of state and church. The FFRF won a federal lawsuit against Marriage Savers, the organization overseen by Michael McManus, because it was openly promoting the use of HMI funds to promote its religious ideas about marriage. The FFRF also 'exposed' Maggie Gallagher, a strong advocate for marriage, for receiving funding from Health and Human Services (HHS) to promote President Bush's initiative and for receiving funds to write a report for the National Fatherhood Initiative which appeared under the by-line of Wade Horn in *Crisis* (Catholic) magazine (FFRF, 2005). The ACF has, consequently, deliberately kept the programs separate from religion and goes nowhere near the line.

Bradford Wilcox (2002) addresses some of the challenges for governments that are attempting to strengthen marriage, but are unable to draw on religious principles. He argues that US public officials are reluctant to introduce religious or explicitly moral discourse into public policy discussions regarding marriage for two reasons. First, many religious conservatives believe that the US is now in a post-Christian society and are fearful of being branded as intolerant members of the religious right. 'God talk' would interfere with their efforts to win support from their colleagues. Second, the cultural turn towards an expansive view of tolerance has meant that there is a reluctance to make strong arguments in public about moral obligations (2002, p. 5). Wilcox claims that the government is advancing 'normative marriage policies that seek to directly reform the meaning and practice of marriage' (2002, p. 31). These policies draw on utilitarian and therapeutic understandings of the nature of marriage, rather than explicit moral conceptions of marriage embedded in a religious or secular view of the good life. This, says Wilcox, raises difficulties for governments. First, the 'pragmatic problem' is that such polices may not succeed. Public efforts encouraging virtue 'are notoriously unreliable' because they cannot instil virtue into the community's vision or commit couples to this vision (2002, p. 31). Marriage is depicted as an institution that is useful insofar as it promotes a healthy relationship that secures the emotional well-being of adults. Second, the 'principled problem' is that

> the religious meanings of marriage – from its connection to procreation to its capacity to engender self-sacrifice even in the midst of marital unhappiness – are obscured by the expressive focus and therapeutic-utilitarian assumptions embodied in most marriage policies. (Wilcox, 2002, p. 31)

The dilemma, according to Wilcox, is that when the state tries to reform the practice of marriage it shies away from addressing the religious and moral dimensions of marriage. He argues that the public purposes of marriage are effective when wedding vows imbue 'a sense of sacredness' derived from both religious and secular sources. But the paradox of the US experiment is that it is difficult for the government 'to directly cultivate this sense of sacredness' (2002, p. 32). Thus, Wilcox declares that civic society should be more pro-active in assisting people to secure the public goods guaranteed by virtuous and stable marriages. Although this is a substantial burden the emergence of the marriage movement and civic-oriented public policies suggest that society may rise to the challenge (2002, p. 32).

In response to Wilcox, Wade Horn (cited in the Pew Forum on Religion and Public Life, 2002) argues that it is possible for someone to be motivated by a personal faith perspective, to be grounded in a religious view about the importance of the institution of marriage, while also making utilitarian arguments, particularly in the public sphere. He therefore supports the advancement of both utilitarian arguments and an understanding about marriage from a broader religious and moral perspective. Horn argues that the government's healthy marriage initiative is not just about developing skills – people need to be motivated to apply those skills. Therefore, a broader understanding of the wider context of marriage is necessary. The idea of commitment to the institution of marriage is very important: the obligation and responsibility to others and from certain faith perspectives, a responsibility to God. Wilcox, states Horn, sets up an artificial distinction that views marriage from a secular and utilitarian function or from a faith-based and moral perspective. It is possible, Horn maintains, to do both (2002, pp. 37–39). This is evident in such programs as Christian PREP.

While organizations such as the Institute for American Values and SmartMarriages.com consist of an ideologically diverse group without any explicit religious mission, there are religious influences. Much of the US marriage movement is situated within religious communities (Hawkins et al., 2002, p. 167). According to Wilcox, the religious diversity of the movement at the national level obscures the fact that it is an outgrowth of the largely evangelical Protestant movements associated with institutions like Focus on the Family and the Family Research Council (2002, p. 7). At the state and local levels, religion plays a central role in motivating public officials and clergy to push a range of public policies and civic efforts on behalf of marriage (Wilcox, 2002, p. 8). This does not necessarily mean that religion plays a vital role in promoting marital virtue, but it does mean that 'some religious institutions and individuals are attempting to reform the *laissez faire* attitude to family formation and divorce that is so deeply entrenched' in US life (Wilcox, 2002, p. 11). At any rate, the conviction of President Bush that same-sex marriage should be prohibited by constitutional amendment reveals the strength of the religious right in his constituency (Barlow and Probert, 2004, p. 5). Like his counterpart in America, the Australian leader, John Howard, privileges religious values in debates over same-sex marriage. He argues that such marriages are incompatible with Australian values, including religious ones (Howard, 2004b).

A recent US study suggests that community marriage initiatives may be more successful if they include a religious component. Hughes (2004) argues that several pastors have stated that the church, rather than the government should adopt the lead in discussion about healthy marriages. The challenge is that religious leaders do not have the capacity to address out-of-wedlock births and high divorce rates (2004, p. 8). Some churchgoers are reluctant to receive marriage education through their local church because they wish to protect their privacy. This concern could also apply to religious followers in Australia and Britain. In addition, there are many faith-based organizations, which differ from group to group, community to community drawing on different resources, people, expertise and public awareness. It is therefore difficult for governments to monitor the programs and to assess or maintain quality control.

In all three countries, religious agencies may not discriminate against a person seeking a particular program, but must serve all clients, whether they profess a certain faith or participate in religious activities or not. In Australia and the UK, non-government and non-profit organizations that receive public funding have a fair amount of autonomy to conduct programs as they see fit. Perhaps there is a perception that there is something akin to 'big brother' about public agencies telling religious organizations how best to offer marriage and relationship skills training. More to the point, religious agencies have provided marriage support for many decades and religious content is available for those couples who want it. For example, the Catholic marriage programs include topics such as the sacrament of marriage and draw lessons from the Bible. Not all programs, however, are delivered from a religious perspective. Indeed, couples who complete an inventory may not focus on religious issues at all. Couples can choose from classes offering a religious or secular perspective. Either way, a variety of religious organizations have received British or Australian government funding to assist in delivering their programs at different times.

Many of the people I interviewed for this book agreed that local churches offer stability and are esteemed as enduring and trusted organizations. Several noted the importance of the connection between strong marriages and strong religion. A US researcher provided the example of African American churches which are able to draw their community together. There was much praise for the ministries and church-based community groups that provided friendships and networks support. A common remark was that the role of religion was becoming increasingly important as individuals became more isolated. There were more buffers for couples in the past if they experienced relationship problems, because they had close connections with their extended families and local community. Now, however, there were huge strains on individual couples and too much demanded of their marriage in terms of support, commitment and expectations. Religion continues to be a significant factor in shaping government policies concerning marriage education.

Romantic illusions

The challenge of romance for government reforms supporting marriage education deserves more attention. This is because for many couples, romance plays a vital part when choosing a partner. Romantic love influences people's expectations of marriage, placing different demands on relationships than in previous times. Marriage is now commonly based on and linked to romantic love and on the perception that romance is necessary for marriage (Jackson, 1999, p. 96). Yet the concept of 'romance' is complex and there are many different interpretations and experiences of romantic love in modern Western societies. Class, ethnicity, gender, religion and education are important factors that may influence people's experiences in personal relations (Sarsby, 1983; Illouz, 1997). Collins (2003, p. 219) argues that, in an odd way, individualism has also enhanced the attraction of partnerships, even as it reduced its likelihood. The vulnerability of modern relationships provides enduring ones with a certain scarcity value. A thirst for self-gratification leaves the individual all the more dependent on their partner for its satisfaction. The loosening of wider family networks has made career women reliant on their husbands and unwilling to countenance juggling work and family without considerable spousal support. Romance and emotional attachment are important ingredients in this mix and contribute to heightened expectations about relationships.

In response to my question about the importance of romance for marriage, the different perspectives were evident. For example, one US government official clearly refuted romance's relevance; instead his perception of marriage was situated within the traditional context. This raised the necessity of asking questions such as: 'what's going to sustain marriage?', 'is this good for the kids?', 'is this economic unit more viable?' rather than 'do I still have good feelings about this person?', 'what are my feelings for this person?' which is a weaker foundation for marriage. This line of argument defends the idea of marriage as a responsible and long-term commitment involving sacrifice and responsibility.

The interview responses highlight that, at the very least, romance remains a fraught area not only for couples but also for governments attempting to instil values about the significance of marriage. Service providers acknowledged some of the problems that couples face. These included practical matters such as a lack of time to nurture relationships and do things together to keep romance alive. Another challenge is maintaining a good work/family balance. The impact of mortgages and financial commitments was also mentioned as a concern which undermined romance. Couples who face economic difficulties and other pressing demands quickly lose the romance in their relationship. An Australian educator commented that cohabiting couples particularly struggle to preserve romance. After they marry they expect the romance to return, and when it does not, it leads to a cooling of the relationship, frustration and can ultimately lead to separation. For some, however, this fading of romance was not perceived as a problem. Indeed, one observation from a UK researcher was that romance was not an important variable for a strong, successful marriage. From this perspective, the answer to the question 'what's love got to do with it?' is 'very little'. Romance is only about personal commitment, not moral or structural commitment, and so was perceived as a thin and unstable reed of affection which would not last.

The issue of commitment is crucial for successful marriages. The concept of marital commitment can be separated into three dimensions – this idea draws on Johnson's commitment framework (1999). First, structural commitment is where one has to continue a relationship because of constraints from external pressure and censure from others. Second, moral commitment is where one ought to continue a relationship in terms of one's own value system; because it feels right to do so. Third, personal commitment is where one wants to continue a relationship because it is satisfying and pleasurable. In the past, structural commitment ensured stability through constraint and public censure. In terms of prevailing values, to stay for those reasons alone would be disingenuous. Contemporary relationships are forged on personal commitment. This is based on the perception of 'I love you so I want to stay with you'. Such a basis for commitment, however, is inherently insecure as satisfaction waxes and wanes over time. Moral commitment is central in achieving a sense of security. For the religiously observant, their beliefs can supply the basis of such commitment. Scott Stanley (2005) provides a useful overview in *The Power of Commitment*. In his 'guide to active, lifelong love', Stanley argues that 'the road to lasting love takes dedication and determination' (2005, p. 12). Therefore, Stanley maintains that it is important to understand the nature of commitment and to dispel some of the myths surrounding it. This includes myths such as the notion that you can have it all; that the grass is greener; that love is all about the self and what a person can get from their mate; and that a soul mate exists for each and everyone of us (2005, p. 13). Commitment is thus about making deliberate choices.

Putting it in a different context, one of the interviewees suggested that romantic love changed gender relations in a positive way: more women and men had developed relationships on the basis of consent and mutual commitment. Compromise is still necessary in relationships, yet people value their independence which is particularly empowering for women. Others commented on the need for romantic love to be transformed into 'grown up' love, acknowledging that the initial spark and the chemistry had to be built on for a robust relationship. Indeed, one comment was that the romantic phase in partnering was an immature stage in any relationship and to get stuck at that point was dysfunctional. The problem, it was generally agreed, was that romance played such a central role in Western culture and the celebration of individualism. The goal of marriage education is that as more people are becoming aware of the importance of self-awareness, and exploring their relationships in a mature way, they will be able to move beyond the romantic stage. Some of the civil servants admitted that they did not discuss romance; perhaps this reluctance was because romance is a mystery which is less served by rational policies. If government-funded programs were to consider romance in more depth, this might give people a sense of political intrusion. Yet – first and foremost – governments wish to avoid being accused of meddling in people's private lives.

I raised the issue of romance and how it fits with marriage and relationship education in the interviews. The key issue for the programs is giving couples the information and the tools to enjoy their relationship and to understand how marriage works. Here, the goal is to dispel the myth that a successful relationship is about meeting the right person – 'the one'. Nor is it about the cultural stereotype of 'being in the right place at the right time' – a good relationship is not based on chance and luck. Nonetheless, it is important to cherish what romance has to offer and many service providers agreed that classes should discuss how to maintain it in relationships. In fact, many of the programs acknowledge the importance of appreciating romance in relationships and include materials such as 'ten romantic tips' on their web pages or in their class notes. Examples of gestures and ways to keep romance alive include the usual strategies such as sending flowers, ringing or texting the partner, cleaning their car or some other small acknowledgement that they are valued.[1] The problem, though, is that if the programs are strongly promoting marriage, they may inadvertently be reinforcing the myths of romance. Part of the message in this promotion is 'get married and all will be well'. Diane Sollee, from SmartMarriages.com does not, therefore, support the use of an inventory, because the danger is that

it keeps the emphasis on the romantic, soul-mate myth that it's all about matching couples up – 'then they'll work'. We need to change that expectation – 'no matter how well you court and no matter how carefully you match up and no matter how many inventories you take' you still need to expect differences along the marital path and you must learn how to manage them in a loving, empathic, sexy way that strengthens, rather than erodes, your love. (Sollee, email 2007)

Thus, the importance of honouring romance needs to be considered in marriage and relationship education, particularly in our cultures where the allure of meeting one's soul mate who will fulfil all our needs is so powerful.

Advocates of marriage education argue for making information about the importance of marriage available to the general population. This is necessary to challenge the popular assumption of romantic love that relationships do not take much effort if the couple really love one another. Some of the strategies to counteract the cultural representa-tions of romance that send messages about living 'happily ever after' are to teach relationship skills and emotional literacy throughout life phases. Many of the service providers commented that high school stu-dents in particular want more information about relationships, love and marriage. A service provider from the UK argues that clever market-ing is important, echoing comments from other educators that getting marriage preparation into big-budget films or television comedies would assist in normalizing the problems of relationship difficulties, the ups and downs and renegotiation of daily life.[2] There was broad agreement that advertising campaigns should articulate the message – 'this is the way marriage actually is'. Similarly, there was concern about couples who spend a great deal of money on lavish weddings, make grand vows but find that their marriage is in trouble a few years later. Thus it was crucial to challenge the false expectations about marriage. Other suggestions – assuming that there was a market – included making rela-tionship education via DVDs cheaply available in supermarkets and department stores so that they were widely accessible.

A major challenge for governments and those in the field is how to introduce the cultural shift that is necessary not only to make the idea of relationship education more widely acceptable but also to convince the public of its benefits. How to implement these strategies without moralizing or being 'preachy' is also difficult, especially when targeting diverse cultural groups, or those who are not religious. Nonetheless, there was agreement in the interviews that it is important to publicize information about the 'reality' of relationships. While there are some activities supporting public advertising campaigns, marketing, videos and other materials, they are not widespread in the UK, Australia or the US. Moreover, increasing public awareness about the actual benefits of the marriage education programs receives little public attention. Both governments and the public understand that romance 'gone wrong' leads to much distress and heartache. Romantic love, relationships and marriages tend to be captivated by the promise of individual happiness. If this can be used as a starting point, it may be a positive way to obtain not only government support but also to increase interest and positive responses from the public at large.

Feminist recognition of diverse families

Feminists argue that the family should be protected, but that this should include diverse family forms – regardless of marital status – in order to develop more freedom and equality for women and children. They wish to avoid any privileging of two-parent, married families and to value 'the family' in its widest meaning. In this way, all families would be respected for their unique capacity to provide financial and emotional support. Many feminists focus on the lack of institutional supports for families, whether they are headed by single parents or have dual earners.

Sex equality is important for feminists who challenge gender role assumptions. For example, McLain (2006) makes a strong case for governments embracing sex equality in policies that attempt to strengthen marriage. While she does not suggest that marriage and family life are private matters and none of the government's business, she does argue that marriage promotion efforts

insufficiently attend to the fact that marriage still benefits men more than women and to the connection between sex equality and marriage quality. These efforts – especially when combined with arguments about marriage's role in taming men – risk perpetuating historic and contemporary forms of inequality within marriage, which themselves have contributed to the supposed contemporary 'marriage crisis'. (2006, p. 127)

Thus, government support should explicitly highlight the gendered division of labour and challenge traditional gender roles that lead to women's deference and to men's power to make decisions within the home and at work. McLain advocates fostering a more egalitarian model of marriage, linking marriage quality with sex equality. An equal partnership, she says, may be a way to deal with some of the contemporary problems facing families who juggle home, work and other responsibilities (2006, p. 152). She also questions whether faith-based groups will teach skills in a 'neutral' way without reinforcing values based on the provider/caregiver model (2006, p. 149).

Opposing marriage promotion in the US, Jones-DeWeever argues that for low-income women, economic factors play a key role in whether to marry or not. In a briefing paper published in 2002, she offers the following policy prescriptions to increase women's economic security. These include education and training; non-traditional employment opportunities to open up work in new areas; earned income tax credit and earned-income disregards so that those on welfare benefits could keep more of their benefits when working; and total funding of child care subsidies (2002, p. 4). If a single mother finds a mate who has good economic prospects, she may then decide to marry, 'but neither she nor her children should have to wait for that day' (2002, p. 4). Therefore, social and family policies at the broad level need to protect women and children by providing good working conditions, access to good quality child care and health care and housing subsidies.

From a different perspective, the issue for women is to make sound life decisions in a particular sequence. As Barbara Dafoe Whitehead, a strong supporter of the marriage policies in the US put it, if women can avoid unwed pregnancy at a young age, complete their education and obtain work with good conditions, 'they are likely to find themselves situated in a better marriage market than if they were single mothers socially isolated in a low-income community' (cited in Marshall et al., 2006, p. 5). Nevertheless, as Pateman (2005) observes, women – whether married or not – do most of the caring work and also bear the brunt of casual, low-wage employment. This also applies to the UK (Dean and Coulter, 2006; Equal Opportunities Commission, 2006) and Australia (Pocock, 2007; Human Rights and Equal Opportunity Commission, 2007).

For feminists, the division of labour in the domestic sphere is an ongoing concern. Marriage sanctions domestic work and care giving; this includes housecleaning, caring for children and the elderly, providing emotional support for the family (particularly husbands) and deference and sacrifice (Bernstein, 2003, p. 185). This multitude of tasks is often concealed and women 'often feel irked by their diminished status' (2003, p. 186). If divorce ensues, legal procedures may not necessarily take account of a woman's contributions to the household through domestic, unpaid work and child care, as well as her loss of income, forgone earnings and earning potential. Rather than making divorce more difficult, which would probably discourage marriage, it should be possible, some feminists say, to define simpler, more flexible partnerships that set some guidelines for people who choose to live together (Shanley, 2004). This should protect both parties as well as any children they have.

Another relevant gender issue concerns the rights of gays and lesbians to marry. In the US and Australia, the federal governments sponsor traditional marriage as between 'a man and a woman' and oppose same-sex marriages, although some of the states have acknowledged and legislated support for gay and lesbian couples. Both federal governments' rhetoric leads a retreat into past ideals about the family, while the changes in the community are not conservative at all, pointing instead to increasingly diverse lifestyles.

Finally, in relation to acknowledging the diversity of families, some feminists question marriage's legal status (Bernstein, 2006). In fact, some make a case for its abolition. For example, Fineman (2004) argues that the caregiving work within the family that women do leads to dependency and lists the advantages of abolishing marriage as a legal category. Denying marriage would 'make policy conform to our modern aspirations. On an individual level, abolishing legal marriage and the special rules associated with it would mean that we are taking gender equality seriously' (2004, p. 134). Formerly labelled husband and wife, a man and a woman would regulate the terms of an individualized agreement. This would not just be about private ordering, but protecting the economically weaker party. Abolishing marriage would also mean that single motherhood would be unregulated. Consequently, the stigma against single mothers in policy would be eliminated. While not advocating the end of marriage, Folbre (2001, p. 229) claims that the state should be less concerned with the regulation of relationships between consenting adults, and more concerned with strengthening obligations to dependents such as young children and the elderly. Rethinking the definition of the responsibilities of kinship may pose difficulties for some parents, but joint custody of children in the absence of marriage or after divorce is far superior to an arrangement in which one parent cares, while the other parent pays. This leads to the recommendation of devising new ways of promoting active and engaged fatherhood (2001, p. 228). These suggestions of course assume that relationships are not experiencing problems such as violence and substance abuse and that couples are able to negotiate on an equal footing.

The privacy of relationships

Liberal democracies value a domain outside the reach of government to defend the sanctity of the private sphere. Most people consider marriage, divorce and bearing children as intensely private matters; matters that should be protected from the prying eyes of the political world. Thus, it is challenging for governments to attempt to enter this intimate space. In relation to the US, Ooms (2002) illustrates that this had led to a controversy about values. 'Any policy proposals that hint at coercing people to marry, reinforcing Victorian conceptions of gender roles, or limiting the right to end bad marriages are viewed as counter to US values of individual autonomy and privacy' (2002, p. 3). Jones-DeWeever argues that marriage is 'one of the most private, personal, and critical decisions one makes in life' and that it appears the 'ultimate in big government, if not social engineering, to have public policy anywhere near these critical, life-altering decisions' (2002, p. 1). Certainly these arguments also apply in Australia and the UK.

Findings from Australia suggest that many people may resist government intervention into that most personal zone of relationships, as it is *too* private. Increasing the number of participants in education programs before they marry is therefore a difficult policy objective. As the HRSCLCA (1998) report acknowledges,

> Many consider marriage a natural, voluntary relationship based on the ideal of romantic love. Love is the cement that binds the couple together and is either present or it isn't. The notion that programs and policies might have anything to do with improving the quality of a couple's relationships or their decision to divorce is viewed with scepticism [sic]. (1998, p. 67)

Because many people regard their relationships as private, a common perception is that there is no need to discuss them publicly or openly, except in a very general sense. Marriage, people maintain, is a natural state and people know automatically and innately how to 'do it'. For that reason, education is not required (HRSCLCA, 1998, p. 155). This view is significant, given that one of the barriers to consumers' participation is that marriage education invades their privacy. Governments are careful to avoid being seen as interfering in people's private relationships. Many service providers argued that couples often believe that they know why they are choosing their partner and therefore regard relationships courses as an invasion into their personal lives. Nonetheless,

Relationships Australia found that 69 per cent of women and 52 per cent of men agreed that if they had problems in their relationship, they would not hesitate in seeking professional help (2006, p. 24). The challenge, however, is to encourage people to acquire relationship education before they face any particular problems.[3]

The perception that relationship education is a form of therapy still exists. Policy analysts in the three countries noted that it was important to publicize the fact that marriage education was not therapy. In addition, couples needed to be reassured that they will not be forced to disclose any intimate details. While resistance to public discussion is understandable, it can be difficult not to reveal any personal information because this is precisely what the programs are attempting to do. From the classes that I attended and from talking to service providers, it appears that couples may be asked to share experiences about their relationship. The key is that they are not compelled to disclose anything or participate in ways in which they feel uncomfortable. Nevertheless, some facilitators adopt a more 'private' approach: each couple works alone on completing the various tasks and activities. This is less confronting than conducting the sessions with all participants sharing personal stories in public. The resistance of men to participating in education programs was another common theme – it seemed that men, generally speaking, were more sceptical and resistant than women. Some of the service providers were more familiar with working with women than men and found it challenging to broaden the focus of support to include both sexes. A government official from the US confirmed that people on the front line were cynical and reluctant at first to get involved with programs where they would have to deal with men. However, this reluctance may be diminishing. Anecdotal evidence from service providers intimates that men have become more enthusiastic and open to the idea of working on their relationships with their partners.

Many hurdles are still ahead for a range of reasons. A collective concern that was frequently raised in the interviews was the challenge of 'getting people through the door'. Apart from viewing their relationship as a private issue or thinking that marriage support is for those with problems, people may not attend classes because of the cost. Typically, as many educators revealed to me, couples regard classes solely as another expense which receives low priority in their bridal budget. That is, people were willing to spend substantial amounts of money on the wedding dress and ring, reception, honeymoon and other items, but did not want to spend any money on marriage education.

Programs were not perceived as a great investment in their relationship that could provide long-term benefits. This is despite the fact that the classes cost a small amount of money (and are often free for those on low incomes). Furthermore, even if the cost of the programs was minimal – or free – other barriers remain. Couples maintain that they are too busy planning their weddings to attend classes. Partners with children from previous relationships, those who live together before marriage and those who are not religious are less likely to attend education programs. Others do not find it convenient to attend several group sessions (Simons et al., 1994).

Both civil servants and service providers noted people's unrealistic expectations about relationships and the fact that many couples do not think that they need help. An English service provider said that some of his clients believe that programs would make no difference to them. This was especially the case for couples who were already living together. But, many educators pointed out, living together was very different to being married and sometimes cohabitating couples were unprepared for marriage and unaware of the commitment that it entailed. Cohabiting, they believe, is a 'trial run' for marriage and a good way to test their relationships, but studies show that this is not the case. There is no clear evidence that cohabitants lower their risks of relationship problems via the pathway of living together before getting married, especially for those who 'slide' rather than 'decide' to cohabitate (Stanley et al., 2006b). A widespread goal is therefore to attempt to get people to become more 'curious' about long-term relationships – whether living together or not. Interviewees maintain that once people attend the classes, they enjoy the learning experience. In particular, their reluctance diminishes once they realize that their privacy is not being invaded. This correlates with studies which show that service providers are also more comfortable with providing marriage and relationship education after discovering that participants are enthusiastic about it (Dion and Strong, 2004). Dealing with these various forms of resistance provides further challenges not only for service providers but also for governments.

Governments supporting marriage education policies have been criticized for promoting a nanny state, as being paternalistic, involved in social engineering and telling people what to do (McLanahan et al., 2005). In a climate where it is expected that liberal democratic governments should be less interventionist and removed from personal matters, this is not surprising. To avoid these negative perceptions, the three governments emphasize that participation is purely voluntary.

While public money is available for a variety of services, governments do not endorse any particular program. A shared theme in my interviews with a wide variety of stakeholders was that couples have a choice of programs, conducted by a mixture of community and church groups. It is possible, therefore to 'shop around' and find a class or an educational approach which best suits the individual couple.

Divorce reforms

Another issue of concern for the 'marital decline' perspective – that was raised by a number of people – was the ease of divorce. Reflecting the growing individualism within society, divorce law has been loosened in the past few decades, so that it is now easier and less expensive to escape from unsatisfactory marriages. Consequently, people 'give up' on their marriages because they are no longer committed to their partner and no longer love them. Moreover, these couples who are eager to go their separate ways have not been taught the basic skills to deal with the disenchantments and disagreements of married life. A comment from a US stakeholder was that because no-fault divorce does not blame anyone for the relationship breakdown, it implies that people have 'just been unlucky' in their relationships. This sends the message that they just married the wrong person, that it was simply fate or destiny and 'not meant to be'. In this scenario, the person may remarry and continue to be unsuccessful in their ensuing relationship because they have not learned the necessary skills about how to partake in a healthy marriage.

Whitehead (1997) challenges the popular assumption that divorce is an individual right and that people should be free to pursue it without considering other stakeholders in the marriage, particularly children. Strategies to reduce the harmful impact of divorce on children include collecting child support at the federal level, enforcing tougher child support, mandatory counselling for divorcing parents and reforming no-fault divorce laws (1997, p. 10). Whitehead argues that it is important to bear in mind the duties and obligations imposed by social bonds, the reasons for dissolving them and the differences between voluntary and coercive obligations. If these issues are not considered, 'the effort to change behaviour by changing a few public policies is likely to flounder' (1997, p. 10). She argues that while there is a collective attempt to protect children, this 'cannot be detached from the goal of strengthening the individual ethic of commitment to children' (1997, p. 10). Whitehead says bluntly, 'many of the ideas we have come to believe and vigorously defend about adult prerogatives and freedoms in family life are undermining the foundations of altruism and support for children' (1997, p. 11).

The US has implemented the more-difficult-to-exit covenant marriage in some states. These laws generally stipulate more limited grounds for divorce and longer waiting periods before being permitted to divorce. They may also include the requirement to complete marriage education before marrying and to seek counselling before divorcing. It remains unclear, however, whether these laws will be effective because the couples who sign up for covenant marriages tend to be religious and well prepared for marriage in the first place (Hawkins et al., 2002). They have thought carefully about marriage and made a deliberate decision to remain together, regardless of any struggles and challenges they may go through.

In Australia, 'no-fault' divorce laws were introduced in the *Family Law Act* 1975 and in the UK in 1996. A shared criticism among some of the interviewees was that divorce provides people with an easy option when experiencing trouble in their relationship, when in fact these problems could be fixed. Education was held up as the solution. An Australian who represented a father's group argued that it was too easy for people to get out of marriage because they knew that they could rely on government support and maintenance from their ex-partner. He recommended that there should be some penalty for the person who breaks up the marriage. Many women's groups would resist this suggestion, however, because if women are leaving a relationship where there was physical violence or substance or emotional abuse, afflicting them with a penalty would be unwarranted.

Many service providers argue that the focus should be on sustaining the adult relationship so that divorce becomes less likely. One perspective from the UK in 2003 was that Margaret Hodge, the new Minister for Children at the time, was pouring money into children's services, but without any strategy or long-term view about what was happening with the couple. Thus, the government's attitude was – if couples divorce – so be it. In the UK, divorce is not necessarily seen as a negative outcome of relationship breakdowns. The fundamental issue is how divorce is handled. Margo and Dixon (2006) reveal that while divorce in itself may not always be difficult, conflict can be detrimental to children's well-being. Frequent family clashes appear to deter fathers' positive engagement with their offspring. Children exposed to regular disputes are more likely to perform poorly at school, and may experience mental health problems including aggressive and anti-social behaviour, or depression and withdrawal. Nevertheless, Margo and Dixon (2006) propose that conflict can be constructive when children are encouraged to learn about negotiation and resolution. For example, research on post-divorce family life has shown that people can learn how to manage divorce and move on to facilitate rather than constrain their family relationships (2006, p. 100). Therefore, it is more important to consider what support people need to weather the process of divorce, rather than attempting to make divorce difficult or focusing solely on preventing it. This is what the Australian government is attempting to do with the establishment of the FRC, discussed in Chapter 4.

The merits of marriage

Family values discourse, based on the moral panic of 'marital decline' argues that governments should promote marriage. As we have seen in previous chapters, Waite and Gallagher's *The Case for Marriage* has become a leading manifesto for the marriage movement. According to further American research, marriage leads to advantages for children – a higher standard of living, more effective and cooperative parenting and less stress or disruption. The affluent marry and tend to stay married, while the poor are less likely to marry and more likely to divorce. Low-income women want economic stability before marrying a partner and men want wives who earn good wages. Clear policy implications emerge. More people should get married in the US – and in other Western societies – because married people do better.

Not everybody embraces 'family values' in the way that proponents of marriage do; many scholars have disputed Waite and Gallagher's and other proponents' arguments. Bernstein (2003), for instance, argues that health and wealth are not independent variables: people with money can afford health insurance and good quality health care; they live in safe areas and work in safe occupations (2003, p. 160). She is unconvinced about the benefits of marriage *per se*, arguing that the law extends benefits to married people, citing advantages in the tax system such as the joint income tax return, access to health and life insurance and other privileges that deliver wealth to married people. Bernstein contends that

> If marriage leaves us better off with respect to sex, health, wealth, and children, then, we have laws – which can be changed to take away privileged treatment – to thank for at least some of this largesse. One might speak of the 'case for being privileged'. ... Policymakers

must acknowledge that legal favouritism is an artifice, a construct that new artifices can supersede' (2003, pp. 162–163). ... The utilitarian 'case for marriage' – marriage is good because it makes people healthy, wealthy and happy – reduces to tautology. (2003, p. 200)

In the instance of Australia, Penman (2005) challenges Waite and Gallagher's arguments on a number of points. For example, she argues that the Australia evidence does not show that women benefit as much from marriage as the US authors suggest. Penman draws on evidence to show that marriage benefits men more than women in terms of the distribution of domestic labour. Further, people live together or get married for different reasons and are not a homogenous group. Penman argues that Waite and Gallagher have not been able to show any causative mechanism for the act of marriage itself and have approached the case for marriage in an overly simple way (2005, p. 34). Moreover, Relationships Australia's survey found that married and *de facto* couples were equally satisfied with life (2006).

From the chapter on the UK, it is clear that there are limitations to the evidence and complexities concerning whether children do best in an intact, two-parent family. Margo and Dixon (2006) found that marital status is not as important as many other factors in influencing whether couples stay together. Another factor to consider is age: the chances of a couple in their teens and twenties splitting up are twice that of a couple in their thirties (2006, p. 96). The Millennium Cohort Study demonstrates that the richest 20 percent of cohabiting couples are more likely to stay together than the poorest 20 percent of married couples.

Evidently, ideological demands have played an important role in influencing political and social opinion about the value of marriage. Those citing the benefits of marriage and the ill effects of other family forms often cite each other's work, so that a set of claims is presented as 'uncontested' (McLain, 2006, p. 128). Many liberal scholars accuse conservatives who espouse 'family values' as attempting to restore the 1950s model that pushes women back in the traditional home (Marshall and Sawhill, 2004, p. 198). Accordingly, any moral push to do so is ill-founded and if marriage breakdowns occur, governments and the community need to deal with the practical consequences. From the perspective that marriage is resilient, the argument is not that marriage is irrelevant, but that the form of relationship between parents is less important than its quality. Promoting children's well-being is an important justification for government interest in strong, nurturing families, but marriage is not the only alternative for family forms that lead to improved child outcomes.

Conclusion

Marriage education policies are being reshaped by many factors such as the shifting cultural norms and attitudes, the impact of religion, the allure of romance and the politics of gender. Governments in the UK, Australia and the US confront a complex range of interrelated challenges. The struggle between social changes in marriage and political objectives is overlain by a tension within the governments' goal of protecting this oldest of institutions. While progress has been made in the US, there is still much to be done. In Australia, the Howard government has seemed unsure about the best way to organize marriage, or how much to intervene. It has adopted neo-liberal strategies, viewing marriage as a personal matter for the individual to manage. But it is taking a more active role – this stance is visible in changes made to family law and the establishment of the FRCs. It has actively intervened, providing assistance and endeavouring to inculcate its moral and political ideals on to people's relationship choices and decisions. By contrast, the UK government supports civil partnerships for same-sex couples and seeks to protect children in diverse family forms. Social policies do not necessarily privilege marriage and the Labour government has been criticized for recognizing non-marital relationships and for abandoning marriage by the Tories. Here there is little conviction at present that targeting people's skills in relationships may overcome the problems entrenched within marriage. Indeed, political efforts to strengthen relationships highlight precisely the fact that people's relationships are based on diverse values, norms and expectations.

Marriage education offers an alternative and distinctive policy tool in an arena where it is very difficult to influence the changing cultural and social norms. Nevertheless, for all their efforts, governments find themselves in the grip of fluid trends in relationships. The marriage in decline perspective promotes the idea of 'when you are planning marriage' – public policies should support skills training so that all marriages will survive. The marriage is resilient perspective promotes the idea of 'when you are in a committed relationship' – public policies should not denigrate other forms of relationships but should support them as much as marriage. Whether marriage education succeeds is not primarily related to the programs themselves. To be more exact, the choices people make and their expectations of relationships are often quite different to those that the government and service providers would like them to hold.

It is difficult for governments to steer the course of adult relationships and marriages, particularly in an individualistic society. In policy terms, therefore, emphasizing marriage does not seem to correspond with people's outlooks about the practicalities of life as partners and parents. Given this complicated context, it is easier said than done for governments to promote the importance or relevance of marriage and relationship education. Many people view marriage as an intimate relationship between freely consenting adults that does not merit the development of public policies. Intruding into the private domain of marriage may be offensive to some, but governments will inevitably intervene through the divorce courts and child support agencies. Therefore, building policy capacity to deliver early intervention and prevention programs is worth attempting, but will have a better chance of success if the effects of marriage and relationship education are evaluated. Success is also more likely if governments adopt a 'whole-of-government' approach to matters such as alleviating poverty and other issues which impact on people's well-being and relationships. The next chapter examines these policy issues.

7
Managing the Public Policy Process

The emergence of marriage and relationships skills programs on the policy agenda has led to a flurry of contentious political responses at different times, receiving various amounts of public funding and attention in the three Anglophone countries. While there appears to be some common ground in the marriage education programs themselves, the way they are translated into policies demonstrates particular variations. Marriage education has become a tool of public policy, designed to assist couples develop and sustain healthy marriages. As we have seen, however, this is a diffuse and challenging process which remains highly contested. Marriage and personal relationships are complicated arrangements that demand understanding from multiple perspectives and raise many challenges for public policy. The manner and form in which problems and issues appear on a government's agenda is part of a complex policy process. We have observed that government resolution of relationship problems can be initiated by politicians and policy makers or by the private and voluntary sectors – adding to the demanding political scenario.

This chapter provides some analysis of whether governments should become involved in marriage education and how they should do so. It endeavours to understand how effectively governments can facilitate success in intimate relationships from a broader policy perspective. One of the major challenges for the three liberal democracies is how to effectively wrestle with the problem of family breakdown. This chapter analyses the problems of poverty and addressing the needs of 'at risk' couples. It also considers the difficulties of balancing work and family, which impact on the policy objective of strengthening marriage and relationships. The chapter then examines the capacity to deliver marriage and relationship education programs by non-government organizations. A range of difficulties concern coordination because policy capacity is dispersed across and located in numerous organizations. Initiatives to strengthen marriage are premised on bringing service providers into government to improve policy capacity. This is a challenging aspect of marriage and relationship education service delivery, because no 'one size fits all'. Just to complicate the mix even further, the approach to implementation and service delivery depends on the needs of the groups, the available resources and the training of the educators. If the programs are to be successful, expenditure will be required to raise publicity and awareness, increase capacity in the field and improve services for at risk groups. The chapter argues that evaluation is imperative to ascertain whether the programs are an effective use of public funds. If marriage education proves to be ineffective, governments will face criticisms, particularly from quarters which argue that too much money is already being spent on these programs. Despite this plethora of challenges, governments continue attempting to implement policies that offer people opportunities to improve their marriages and relationships.

Marriage support programs and services share many similarities in the three countries; however, there are major differences in the government policies themselves. This chapter briefly discusses the policy implications of these differences. Clearly, the definition of a problem and how it is perceived will stimulate different proposals for policy solutions. Policy formulation has involved gauging possible solutions to the problem of declining rates of marriage and increasing rates of divorce. The proposals may originate in the agenda-setting process itself, as problems and solutions are positioned onto the government agenda (Kingdon, 1995), or they may be developed after an issue has moved onto the official agenda. Available options are considered and narrowed down to those that policy makers can accept. Thus marriage education has made the agenda in the US, where the problem of family breakdown has been presented in ways different from those in the UK and Australia. Although problem definition is vital to the policy cycle, there is no steadfast, pre-arranged way to proceed. As Bridgman and Davis (2004) put it, there are no 'neatly defined rules and ready solutions' (2004, p. 45). Remedies become connected to problems and both are contingent upon favourable political forces such as support from the wider community. This is likely with policy windows which provide advocates of proposals with opportunities 'to push their pet solutions, or to push attention to their special problems' (Kingdon, 1995, p. 165). Agenda-setting – defining and interpreting a problem – is a highly nebulous process that does not always lead to clear or agreed-upon definitions of problems. Indeed, as Kingdon notes, some 'items may not rise on the agenda because of the financial cost, the lack of acceptance by the public, the opposition of powerful interests, or simply because they are less pressing than other items in the competition for attention' (1995, p. 18). This analysis may assist in explaining the lack of support for marriage education in the UK.

Marriage education raises an interesting set of questions about the meanings that are attached to what governments actually do and how they go about doing it. Is government too blunt an instrument to improve couples' relationships? How should governments work with providers of marriage education programs and services? Are particular programs an appropriate use of taxpayers' money? Some may well argue that marriage education should be left to churches and other community groups.

Differences in the problem definition and the policy process help to explain variations in how governments are involved in the three countries. For example, marriage education programs in Australia are not connected to welfare policy as they are in the US. Moreover, there is no particular focus on encouraging the poor to marry as a means of decreasing welfare dependency in the UK or Australia. There has been more focused attention on meeting the needs of different racial and ethnic groups in the US than in Australia or the UK. Australia is investing proportionately more public funds in providing services for those who are on the road to divorce rather than on preventive measures for those in the pre-marriage or marriage phases. The UK is more inclusive, acknowledging same-sex unions. Further, it has been focusing attention on the legal rights of those who cohabitate, but has not been encouraging these couples to marry. In the UK, the main objective is to create stable families and maintain them, whether they are married, cohabiting or same-sex. The US government is funding the facilitation and ongoing conduct of research and evaluation, but there is a lack of evaluation in the UK and Australia. Evaluation is an important part of the policy cycle and is critical in uncovering whether the programs meet their objectives of preventing relationship difficulties and creating healthy stable relationships.

The UK's negligible support for healthy marriage initiatives is a pragmatic recognition that the government operates in a climate different from that of the US and has been reluctant to implement policies which might be viewed as 'pushing' marriage. However, as Smeeding et al. (2004, p. 14) argue, 'changes in the family' are now so deeply entrenched that 'there is no turning back'. While public policy institutions have attempted to adapt to these changes, they have not overtly backed them. They continue:

> indeed, public institutions are often ignorant of secular changes until they are well underway. And in most countries public policy and institutions are slow to change in any case, particularly on issues as emotionally and culturally volatile as family change and out-of-wedlock births. (2004, p. 14)

Governments carry on with the aim of conquering social problems and improving policies that strengthen the family.

A 'whole-of-government' approach

Combating poverty

Two enormous challenges for governments exemplify the lack of a 'whole-of-government' approach in relation to marriage education. The first is the lack of coordination between marriage education and tackling poverty and the needs of 'at risk' groups. A major criticism of the programs – particularly in the US – is that by focusing on marriage education, the government is ignoring structural causes of poverty that underlie social problems such as unemployment, low education and training and poor housing and health services. Addressing these problems is, after all, far more critical than funding marriage education. Moreover, marriage *per se* is too simplistic a solution to the complex problems of the poor. Marriage guidance will not miraculously rescue families on low incomes when the parents have no skills, no jobs, poor housing, and may be struggling with depression, substance abuse or domestic violence (Fineman et al., 2003, p. 8). Put simply, marriage programs are not enough: effective relationship policies do not develop in a vacuum. In order for marriage education to have the best possible chances of success, governments must do more to alleviate poverty for low-income couples.

Problem definition has examined particular indicators such as lower rates of marriage, high divorce and cohabitation and, consequently, created the elements for policy change. In the process, the underlying structural problems of poverty have not been adequately tackled as causes of poor relationships or marriage breakdown. On the contrary, family breakdown is claimed as the cause of these forms of social deprivation. By defining failing marriages as the root cause of social problems and one of the primary routes to reform, the US government has been criticized for attempting to conceal evidence of structural material problems. For example, proffering marriage as the ideal blames single mothers. Smith (2001) argues that the Personal Responsibility Act in the US stipulates that

> A poor single mother is explicitly expected to marry her way out of poverty, both for her own sake and for that of her children. In this manner, patriarchal heterosexual marriage is more than a moral category; it is an institution that is supposed to replace the state's obligations towards the poor. (2001, p. 315)

Poverty is a chronic problem in specific sectors of American society according to some activists. For instance, Jones-DeWeever from the Institute for Women's Policy Research, argues that the African American community has a poverty rate that is nearly double the rate of the nation as a whole. There are few jobs, particularly good jobs that provide above poverty level wages and the school system is substandard. Given the problems faced by this community, she is disappointed that 'marriage promotion is the best idea that we can come up with' (cited in Brookings Institution, 2006, p. 53). She goes on to say that the US should 'acknowledge marriage promotion for what it is, a diversion away from a true policy agenda meant to attack poverty' (2006, p. 56). In addition, Pateman (2005) argues that single mothers on welfare payments are not dependent on men's wages, allowing them, if necessary, to leave an abusive or unsatisfactory relationship (2005, p. 41).

As we have seen, the emotive discourse of the marriage crisis and what to do about it has a rich history, and has become quite persuasive – predominantly in the US. It has, however, also become more fractious – especially in the UK.[1] British studies have found that couples who are poor face greater risk of relationship breakdown. If their relationship does end, they are likely to experience more poverty (Kiernan and Mueller, 1999). As Hughes and Cooke succinctly put it: 'poverty is a cause of fractured families as well as being its consequence' (2007, p. 250). Providing relationship education that recognizes diversity and is culturally appropriate and is available at different times for at risk couples will be challenging for any government. The difficulties of forming and sustaining stable and healthy marriages are particularly acute in poor communities because marriage education programs have not been specifically designed nor tested for disadvantaged populations. Despite the typical struggles and distinctive circumstances of at risk groups, marriage programs designed specifically to address the needs of low-income families are lacking (Dion and Devaney 2003; Ooms, 2007).

Service providers in all three countries commented that in some cases, community groups were trying to assist people in meeting their basic needs such as food, shelter and work. When particular communities are facing chronic poverty and other pressing problems, therefore, marriage has to be 'low on the totem pole', as one American researcher succinctly put it. A service provider working in an Australian city explained that her organization was reluctant to discuss marriage with low-income clients as this could be perceived as ignoring the difficulties of their economic situation. In Australia, there is a dearth of education programs to support couples during life transitions, such as becoming parents, formation of step-families, relocation and retirement and in times of crisis, such as coping with unemployment and illness (Halford, 2000, p. 66). Moreover, only about one-third of marrying couples attend some form of marriage education. Those who do not participate tend to be from non-English speaking backgrounds, indigenous people, people with less formal education, living in rural or remote areas, couples married in civil rather than religious ceremonies, couples living together and young people (Halford, 2000, p. vii).

Policy makers will face further challenges in providing marriage and relationship education that recognizes diversity and is culturally appropriate, and is available at different times in the relationship cycle. The cost of these services alone may restrict political intent, despite any potential benefits and enhancing of values that sustain healthy marriages. Therefore, governments will need to consider how best to promote the benefits that can accrue to adults and children (in terms of enhanced educational, mental and physical health outcomes) through greater awareness and sensitivity about the cultural needs of diverse groups. This may entail selecting and training workshop leaders who speak the participants' language, or employing a core curriculum more flexibly so that participants can relate to familiar ideas and scenarios. The US is advancing a range of measures to meet the needs of these diverse populations (Ooms, 2007). In Australia, several reports have raised similar concerns with regard to the indigenous population, CALD groups and those living in rural communities and remote areas (CWA and the DFCSIA, 2006).

While marriage programs provide relationship skills, governments are aware that some of the couples may have problems going back to their past relationships, or may be experiencing domestic violence or be in abusive relationships. Program facilitators may not always recognize warning signs of these deeper types of relationship difficulties. Thus, there is a need to refer couples with problems to other programs (Ooms et al., 2006). The particular challenges of step-families were also noted because couples have to adjust and deal with step-children and find harmony among their various family members.

A common thread of my interviews was the expression of interest in and need for supporting the whole family. This was echoed by many who argued that rather than focusing primarily on the adult couple, or primarily on the children, the programs should concentrate more explicitly on interactions between the two. One UK service provider gave the example of a married couple coming in for assistance because they were having problems with their child who was behaving badly. However, after some probing, it became clear that problems in their marriage were distressing the child. This theme of moving beyond marriage suggests that governments can or should be involved in different ways than at present.

Balancing work and family

Another important issue from a 'whole-of-government' perspective concerns balancing work and family – this requires access to decent paying jobs and family friendly employment policies for couples attempting to manage their work commitments. Ideally, these policies would be linked to marriage education to assist couples in sustaining their personal relationships. Many studies illustrate that while marital contentment is connected to factors such as realistic expectations and emotional maturity, adequate income and satisfaction with work and children are also important (Baker, 2001, p. 107).

If we take the case of Australia, the federal government is prescribing marriage education and relationship support services and has recently invested more funds in this area, while simultaneously introducing workplace measures which will have a detrimental impact on many families and relationships (Pocock et al., 2007) As Chapter 4 demonstrated, the Australian federal government has attempted to prepare individuals for family life at a time when relationships are becoming more complex and fluid. Marriage and relationship programs have potential, but these educational services have not been located within the context of increasing work demands and lowering protection for working families. There has been little recognition of the correlation between working patterns and family breakdowns. Yet there has been an ongoing public debate about the need to lighten the load for working families. Indeed, John Howard, the Prime Minister, famously declared in 2001 that attempting to balance work and family was a 'barbecue-stopper' – a burning issue discussed by families at social gatherings. Nonetheless, this issue has not been adequately addressed by the government or linked to its policies concerning marriage education and relationship support.

In an attempt to enhance productivity, strengthen the economy and improve international competitiveness, the latest industrial relations changes were legislated in the *Workplace Relations (WorkChoices) Amendment Act 2005*. The federal government justified the reforms as a way of simplifying and lessening the amount of regulation in the labour market, as providing greater choice for families and enhancing work–life balance. It argues that this legislation offers an improved process for setting minimum wages and conditions, guarantees minimum conditions, simplifies agreements, provides award protection and implements a national workplace relations system (Department of Employment and Workplace Relations, 2005). Ellem disagrees: despite the government's claims that its policies are about freeing up and simplifying industrial relations, the legislation is in fact long, dense, complex and prescriptive (2006, p. 211). *WorkChoices* removes basic entitlements from awards and instead establishes four minimum conditions to be known as 'Australian Fair Pay and Conditions Standards', which Waring et al. (2005) declare wither away fairness for workers. These cover annual, sick, unpaid parental (including unpaid maternity) leave and maximum (but annualized) working hours. Together with the minimum wage, this set of conditions constitutes the basic standards of employment (Jolly et al., 2006). While there have been some recent policy back flips, such as a new 'fairness test' and an improvement in some working conditions, there are still many problems.

The labour market policies have been widely criticized because workers can be put onto individual contracts that remove conditions like overtime, penalty rates and weekend rates. They will also remove workers' ability to act collectively and the yearly review of minimum wages will be abolished. These changes may affect people's families and relationships, as the stresses of the workplace spill over into the domestic sphere. According to the Australian Council of Trade Unions, 'these laws will remove basic rights for working people, cut the take home pay of workers, reduce their job security and hurt families' (2006, p. 2). Pocock and Masterman-Smith (2005) argue that the *WorkChoices* package will lead to more family unfriendly agreements, lower work and family standards for those in the federal system and offer no prospect of general advances in family friendly conditions (2005, p. 131). As they point out, provisions such as holiday leave, sick leave or long service leave have been important measures for sustaining the family. The new option of exchanging up to two weeks annual leave for cash will impact on time that 'is crucial to healthy family relationships' (2005, p. 135). Gaze (2006) contends that the changes 'remove the base-level conditions protecting vulnerable, low-paid workers and strip back conditions necessary to the resolution of conflicting work-family demands' (2006, p. 106). *WorkChoices* therefore offers little choice or alternatives for many families.

Strategies to manage the work–family balance and provide families with choice have been explored in a range of Australian policy documents. The problem is that the federal government has not considered sufficiently as to how its labour market policies have negative effects on families. Although funding relationship services and skills-based programs is useful, this learning could be well tested by the stresses and strains of balancing work and family relationships. Several recent reports have indicated the link between relationships, work and domestic responsibilities, demonstrating that managing paid work with family life generates stress (Melbourne Institute of Applied Economics, 2004; Relationships Australia 2003 and 2006). While many advocating marriage education focus on the importance of protecting children, Pocock et al. (2007) expose the detrimental effects on children whose parents are frazzled from work. The stressful demands of working life have negative consequences for children's well-being.

Similar to the US, universal maternity leave is unavailable. That the Australian government has not sufficiently acknowledged the different life stages and changes that affect people's relationships is evident in the lack of publicly funded maternity leave (let alone paternal leave) for all parents. This is necessary, however, if women, particularly those on a low income, are to participate in the paid labour market. The birth of the first baby is a challenging time for relationships, as this is a major life-transition event. Indeed, the preface of the *To Have and to Hold: Strategies to Strengthen Marriage and Relationships* report acknowledged this fact (1998, p. vi). Surely it follows that paid maternity leave would alleviate some of the stress for new parents.

The Human Rights and Equal Opportunity Commission (HREOC) has consistently argued for paid maternity leave. It published its interim paper *Valuing Parenthood: Options for Paid Maternity Leave* in 2002. In this report, Pru Goward – the Sex Discrimination Commissioner – argued that Australia's paid maternity leave arrangements were limited, haphazard and fall significantly below what could be considered a national system. At the time of the HEROC report, 38 per cent of women workers were entitled to paid maternity leave, mainly in the public sector or in large corporations. Therefore, 62 per cent of working women did not have access to paid maternity leave. A woman could take 12 months unpaid leave and their employers must protect their jobs. This also applies to part-time and casual workers who have had 12 months work. In her final report released later in 2002, Goward recommended a fully government-funded paid maternity leave scheme for women in paid work.

The government opposed paid maternity leave, as evident in 2004, when the Treasurer, Peter Costello, announced a new maternity payment. In an attempt to tackle the decline in Australia's fertility rates, the payment aimed to assist all mothers of new babies, whether at home or in paid work.[2] Costello declared that it was a 'good thing' for married couples to have children – 'one for your husband and one for your wife and one for the country'. The payment of $3,000 for each baby born after July 2004 increases to $5,000 in July 2008. The benefit is available for all families, regardless of the family's income, incorporating the existing maternity allowance and baby bonus. This is a paltry sum, however, and does not provide an adequate substitute for paid maternity leave.

In another HREOC discussion paper, Goward (2005) explores ways of providing families with choices for balancing their responsibilities, and makes a case for more flexible working hours to cater for family needs and obligations. She argues that the combination of family payments, other benefits and tax thresholds results in a complex system that influences the decisions that families make about whether a secondary earner re-enters the workforce. Her report continues:

> The costs of child care, loss of government payments and the prospect of high effective marginal tax rates will all affect these decisions. The challenge for government is to ensure policies do not unfairly promote certain family arrangements over others. (Goward, 2005, p. 106)

Thus for all families to have real choice in how they manage paid work and family responsibilities, family friendly workplaces are crucial. Particularly those in lower socio-economic groups are less likely than those in professional employment to feel that they have any choice or control over their working arrangements or hours (Families Australia, 2005, p. 7). To encourage family well-being, workplaces require, among other things, flexible working hours, paid parental leave and access to good quality child care.

A recent House of Representatives Standing Committee on Family and Human Services (2006) investigated 'Balancing Work and Family'. It argued that while paid work will not be the choice of some parents, policies should support the diversity of families and the complexity of caring arrangements (2006, p. 37). Choice and flexibility in child care is an important provision, but the report notes that for most families, the approved care category offers only group care in a centre-based environment (2006, p. 200). The report continues: 'for some parents, problems in accessing care mean that they may have to choose an imperfect option which creates stress for the family, although it allows parents to take on paid work' (2006, p. 201). The report demonstrates that working long hours can increase stress related to balancing work and family.[3] It also points out that the effects of work and family eventually impact on children's well-being. It cites a submission from Relationships Australia: 'competing commitments at home and in the workplace are significant factors in increased stress and conflict in families and in marriage and relationship breakdown. It is well known that conflict in families has a detrimental impact on children' (2006, p. 127). One of the report's recommendations is to offer relationship education programs at different stages of people's relationships through the FRSP and to produce a multimedia campaign advertising the availability and benefits of these courses (2006, p. xxiii).

The HREOC's final paper – *It's About Time: Women, Men, Work and Family* was released in 2007. Similar to earlier HREOC reports, it proposes various changes to legislation, workplace policy and practice and government policies and programs. This includes paid maternity leave for 14 weeks, addressing the gender pay gap, improving conditions for part-time work and developing community resources to assist women with workplace negotiation and individual bargaining. These various policy measures have been recommended before, but with little positive response from the government.

Obviously the debate has been going on for some time, but the government has resisted showing any commitment to implementing the raft of recommendations as a way of supporting families. Baird and Litwin (2005) claim that an estimated 40 per cent of working women still have no access to paid maternity leave. As Cass (2005, p. 204) argues, the Howard government's policies emphasise 'an apparently gender-neutral discourse of providing 'choice' to couple families', but support such as paid maternity leave is available for only a minority of employed women, entrenching inequality of access. Consequently, the government's emphasis on choice 'actually reduces choice, and does this most harshly for those with least resources' (2005, p. 222). Even couples who are relatively well off need to access affordable child care, juggle work, meet their family's needs as well as their own relationship. The Australian example illustrates the stark limitations and contradictions in policy measures: on the one hand, there are attempts to improve relationships, while on the other hand, strategies often ignore the need to balance work and family.

Building policy capacity

Capacity building means many different things from different perspectives, in both theory and practice. The prevailing ethos is that governments must become more interested in providing service to clients (Peters, 1996, p. 7). This requires new forms of public service delivery. Policy capacity includes the implementation capacity of the system, formulating clever and potentially effective policies and the political capacity to respond to changing demands from interest groups and the public (1996). Organizations and infrastructures require the capacity to think through the challenges they face. This implies encouraging the best possible utilization of knowledge during the actual policy-making process. Governments are willing to create policy capacity using other means, to draw on surrogates and external sources of policy advice, advice that in former times may have been generated by those inside government. Painter and Pierre (2005, p. 255) perceive policy capacity as 'the ability of a government to make intelligent policy choices and muster the resources needed to execute those choices'. Capacity building is a collaborative process between government and community, with each group acknowledging their roles and responsibilities (Cuthill, 2005, p. 65).

It is challenging for governments to invest in people, organizations and networks in the area of marriage education where, in many ways, policy making has become more complex, specialized and disjointed. Governments may have clear policy objectives in the area of marriage and relationship education, but the implications of capacity constraints need to be considered. First, implementation capacity is complicated because governments are attempting to facilitate people's personal relationships. It is difficult for governments to educate couples about personal relationships as this is usually considered to be a private matter. It is important, therefore, that the programs are delivered well and that clients respond positively. Second, political capacity – developing the ability to contend with conflicting interests and managing competing demands – is also fraught when dealing with a range of policy actors and complex sets of organizations drawn from the public, private and voluntary sectors. Initiatives to strengthen marriage are premised on bringing service providers into government to improve policy capacity. Like most areas of social policy, governments are confronted with numerous and diffuse stumbling blocks with the added pressure that marriage education is a fairly new area of public intervention. The risk of policy confusion tends to increase, inevitably intensifying the complexity of the policy framework.

Coordination and networking

As we have seen, in the field of marriage education there has been much rigorous discussion about the best forms of programs and what policies governments should be implementing. Governments rely on resources such as information from non-governmental actors such as marriage educators, faith-based organizations, advocacy groups, community service agencies, domestic violence experts and health-care providers. Different groups recommend different strategies and they need to be competitive because public funding is not unlimited. Contemporary governance entails a considerable degree of cooperation and collaboration between governments, service delivery and clients to make the best possible use of resources. Indeed the quality of policy outcomes often depends on productive interactions between the private, non-profit and public sectors at various stages of the policy process. This is the case not only in the UK but also in Australia and the US.

Policy making cannot be directed by government alone and networks are very important in contributing to government capacity by offering knowledge and specialized expertise. This is not to say that the voluntary sector, community groups and faith-based organizations can substitute the government's role, but that the various actors should work together as the best way of building capacity. If marriage and relationship support services are to realize their full potential to contribute to people's health and well-being, government funding alone is clearly not enough. Networks are encroaching on the consciousness of policy makers and working through partnership models of implementing programs. Chapter 4 showed that there is cooperation between service providers working together in Australia. The capacity to respond to stakeholder demands is evident in the US government's attempts to develop better links with service providers, working to maximize resources and the range of available services. Part of the reason for this is the lobbying from an active 'marriage movement' – as discussed in Chapter 5 – which has been successful in pushing marriage initiatives and setting the political agenda. In the UK, there are also some close working partnerships between various stakeholders.

Training the educators

Another capacity difficulty is that agencies often rely on volunteers or poorly trained educators. This is an issue for service delivery in the three countries. While providing marriage education is a vocation for some, it appears to be difficult to attract and reward workers with the necessary expertise and maturity as we saw in Australia. It is here, nonetheless, that training competencies have contributed to professionalizing the occupation, so this may assist in attracting more people to the field of relationship education. In the UK volunteers are trained. In the US, training occurs in different formats – a Certified Family Life Educator designation is available and those using programs such as Within My Reach or PREP are trained to use the particular programs.

The issue of training US educators was evident at the Smart Marriages conference which I attended in 2006. The conference, which is a key annual event for those in the marriage education movement, offered training 'institutes' which qualifies people to present a standardized training program. Three-day training sessions involved practical application of the programs by innovators in the field. Completion of these workshops allowed participants to qualify and teach curricula-based programs and use the teaching materials. This training is approved for continuing education credit for up to 76 hours for psychologists, social workers and family life educators. Delegates pay a fee, complete an evaluation for each session and sign a statement of attendance. Thus people can learn how to run a program in a few days at the most, but it remains unclear how successfully they are able to teach, let alone keep their own agenda and ideologies in check. There seemed to be a general consensus that educators cannot go wrong if they used the programs. Lay leaders and married couples are encouraged to conduct classes because of the belief that experience counts for more than expertise. There was agreement that people 'learn by doing'. If people use content driven programs like PREP, it is important to show empathy, to be able to reach the couples and understand the particular audience. Life experience was the key.

This approach has been supported by the Social Justice Policy Group (2007) who argues that it is necessary to stimulate capacity building in the UK by supporting local volunteers. Her report argues that lay educators can produce similar or better results than professional educators. Because marriage and relationship education entails support rather than remedial work, groups such as the BCFT – discussed in Chapter 4 – prefer to rely on volunteers to deliver the programs.

In contrast, the issue of professionalization and training is rather different in Australia. Here, educators have worked with the government for more than a decade to develop competency standards and a qualifications framework for their sector. Educators focus on continuing training needs and follow up on how newly trained instructors – whether from a professional background or not – are faring once they start conducting the education programs with their clients. The rationale is that when providing adult education; it is necessary to instil particular levels of proficiency. If course presenters have no background or training in education, they may experience some challenging situations in class. For instance, providers without adequate training may not have the capacity to deal with issues such as domestic violence or substance abuse. Even basic requirements such as dealing with reluctant or angry participants, or alternatively over-eager ones, require generic teaching skills. This is especially pertinent when delivering messages about many personal matters relating to communication, conflict and sexuality to adult learners. Therefore, how the educators are trained and how they present the programs in the field should not remain a mystery – support for tracking their progress and assessing their class performance would add to the capacity to deliver effective programs.

While those who support marriage and relationship education programs promise good outcomes and benefits, capacity building needs to be considered with more care. Otherwise, the danger is that not only the clients and couples using the various programs but also policy makers become disillusioned. Some of the interviews suggested that stakeholders may then move on to the next 'fad', in their continuing search for solutions to marriage and relationship difficulties. A multifaceted and systemic approach may require larger amounts of public investment and resources than has been proposed in recent initiatives. At present, it is difficult to know whether this is true because of an absence of evaluation. A body of research has indicated that couples do benefit from the programs, but these benefits may be short-lived. Hence, more data is required, particularly as governments are becoming involved in funding marriage education.

Evaluation of marriage education programs

Given this plethora of fertile debates and lively views about governments and the usefulness of marriage education, the key question which must be addressed is: do these programs work? Answers to this basic question are critical for governments because they require convincing evidence that the programs actually are effective. Evaluation is important because it 'generates data for improved policy analysis and suggestions for making the program more effective. It assists policy learning' (Bridgman and Davis, 2004, p. 130). Once evaluation takes place, this can lead to policy revisions. However, as far as marriage education is concerned, evaluation is in the early stages. In short, policy makers have insubstantial data about the value of marriage education because rigorous assessment of services in the field is rare. Given the dispersed nature of the programs, policy makers have flimsy facts and figures about their long-term worth. However, the US has progressed further down the evaluation path than Australia and the UK where the capacity to appraise the programs is lacking.

The most conclusive evidence that marriage programs are effective has been demonstrated in studies of standardized training programs like Relationship Enhancement, Couples Communication and PREP which have been developed within universities. For example, the PREP curriculum has been widely distributed and used in many different settings such as US military bases, the workplace or within families (Stanley et al., 2001). Controlled trials have found that PREP has short-term effectiveness (Halford and Simons, 2005). Compared with couples who took no training, PREP participants maintained higher levels of relationship and sexual satisfaction; demonstrated greater communication skills and conflict-management skills up to 12 years after instruction and reported fewer instances of physical violence with their spouses three to five years after training (Fagan, 2002, p. 7).

There are of course, many other programs besides PREP – and these have not been sufficiently assessed. In 2007, a representative from the ACF in the US posed an important question: do the skills make a difference? Information and data would provide ACF with an assessment of potential evaluation issues to consider for a larger study and evaluation. Evidence-based programs are developed from concepts and skills that are explicitly grounded in the research findings. This includes the use of standardized training programs and teaching manuals and evaluation. Researchers from a range of US research centres are involved in various evaluation programs and support the government proposals to strengthen marriage. According to one US representative from a prominent think tank, marriage education is worth a try, because government polices have attempted to tackle poverty in different ways, but they have not worked.[4]

In the US, the Office of Planning, Research and Evaluation (OPRE) in the ACF sought information about the availability of marriage programs and began preliminary work in 2001. Until that time, people were studying single parent families rather than marriage, and there was initial scepticism about marriage education. However, as a senior civil servant pointed out, these doubts have been allayed because the ACF is investing in evaluating the effectiveness of efforts to sustain healthy marriages. It has commissioned three large-scale, multi-site, long-term evaluation projects. The major components include developing programs and selecting evaluation sites; documenting and analysing program implementation; and analysing program impact. First, Manpower Demonstration Research Corporation (MDRC) has been contracted to conduct Supporting Healthy Marriage (SHM), targeting low-income couples who are already married and already have a child or are expecting a child. This nine-year project will review and develop effective programs, provide assistance in implementation and learning which types of programs are the most effective in improving marital relationships, reducing instability and benefiting children. Second, the Building Strong Families (BSF) project aims to strengthen unwed couple relationships and assist the marital aspirations for those who choose marriage. It is developing and evaluating programs designed to assist interested unwed couples with a new-born child. This project, conducted by Mathematica Policy Research Inc. began in 2002 and will be completed in 2011. The third major OPRE project is the evaluation of the Community Healthy Marriage Initiative. This seven-year evaluation aims to develop cultural norms and values that support the institution of marriage through community-level support. Unlike the other two projects, it is non-experimental because it is difficult to conduct random-assignment evaluation at the community level.

As part of this evaluation agenda, the ACF has also funded think tanks such the Urban Institute to explore service delivery settings and evaluation options, client recruitment and retention. These projects provide the ACF with an assessment of potential evaluation issues to consider for larger studies and evaluation. A report by Macomber et al. (2005) has examined federal, state and local policies, public-funded programs and private initiatives, funded by various foundation grants and private donations. Their rigorous review conducted a systematic search of relevant studies on marriage education and counselling programs. Approximately, 500 were selected for full-text review and only 39 passed the screening test and were included in the detailed meta-analysis. Some of the report's findings are applicable to Australian and English as well as US programs, illustrating the difficulties for governments trying to solve policy problems in the area of relationships.

One obstacle that was raised time and again in interviews – not only in the US but also in the UK and Australia – is that engaged couples are preoccupied with wedding plans. The Urban Institute findings confirmed that attending classes is regarded as inconvenient, suggesting that couples are unlikely to participate in long, intensive programs. However, if classes are conducted for large groups and participants learn a few skills and collect some information in lightweight, short programs, the effects of the programs are questionable (Macomber et al., 2005, p. 20). Furthermore, it is mostly middle and upper-income couples, rather than low-income couples who take the programs. Increasing availability for low-income populations has implications for capacity building. Service agencies will have to develop capacity to apply for contracts and grants and develop more formal collaborative links (2005, p. 29).

Macomber et al. discovered that the programs are varied, using different approaches in a wide variety of settings. Providers might use well-known curriculum programs but adapt them to the local situation and client needs (2005, p. 11). For example, providers might need to reproduce particular concepts making them more understandable for clients with low literacy levels. As the government becomes more involved in providing services, the report recommended some guidance to programs on how to ensure a match between the needs of clients and the capacity of programs to address them (2005, p. 20). For example, service agencies might have clients facing problems such as domestic violence, substance abuse, mental health or low literacy levels. The report suggests that programs employ therapists or at least develop a reliable referral mechanism to deal with these issues (2005, p. 20).

The report noted that what is politically and culturally feasible in one environment may not be in another. For example, service providers are sensitive when dealing with low-income populations and appearing to tell them what to do (2005, p. 18). Large faith communities, local and state leaders sympathetic to the marriage movement and conservative political affiliations are more likely to welcome and endorse marriage services than those working in liberal environments. These tensions will influence federal funding and policy makers will have to decide what types of programs to support and what to evaluate. Nonetheless, according to a senior policy analyst, the programs are an experiment, but if they can impart some skills, they are worth attempting. And as an academic who researches in the area noted, the ACF has committed a great deal of money to develop sophisticated methodologies. This was necessary to obtain effectiveness and efficacy in the evaluation process.

Various public debates in Washington DC illustrate the ongoing disagreement about the value and use of the federal government's healthy marriage initiatives. For example, in 2006 Ron Haskins chaired a debate between various players at the Brookings Institution. A year later, in a public forum held at the Urban Institute, Bob Lerman and Avis Jones de-Weever raised similar concerns to those she raised at the Brookings Institution in the previous year. She is not persuaded by the idea that governments should promote marriage. Lerman argued that 'many people don't have a fully accurate impression' of the HMI (cited in Urban Institute, 2007). In response, Jones de-Weever disagreed, suggesting that the government does not need to insert itself in this most private area and that it is an unproven social experiment with no evidence to suggest any reduction in poverty. The HMI was 'shirking our responsibilities' and would not make a huge difference in the lives of women 'who need it most' (cited in Urban Institute 2007). A US government official argues that the government is already attempting to tackle the issue of poverty. The points raised in this ongoing debate suggest that for some concerned observers, the Bush administration's goal of improving the quality of marriage, not just increasing the amount of marriages (Horn, 2004, p. 189) has been sorely misunderstood – or just not found to be convincing.

In Australia, there are no longitudinal studies like the ones in the US, although studies have shown that couples find the programs valuable. The findings from Harris et al. (1992) indicate that participating couples view Australian programs favourably, and as a 'valuable event' (1992, p. 114). However, while pre-marital training has positive effects at the time of the classes, the effects on longer term marital stability and quality are less known. There has been little systematic evaluation of the effects of programs on couple satisfaction or stability (Halford and Simons, 2005). Therefore, the long-term benefits of the programs remain unclear at this stage and systematic evaluation of these programs is lacking (Parker, 2007, p. 6).

Parker (1999) listed a number of broad questions which nearly a decade later remain unanswered. In 1999 she asked: Do couples in pre-marriage education have better quality relationships than non-participants? How is effectiveness defined? Why is pre-marriage education ineffective for some couples? What is the best combination of program and format for particular types of couples? How long do any positive effects last? How do couples, as distinct from individuals, learn and how do they apply their skills in daily life? (1999, p. 2). The *Final Report into the Pre-Marriage Education Pilot Project* by Donovan Research (2001) evaluated the marriage and relationship education services introduced in 2000. The consultants' survey found that 25 per cent of marrying couples would not have attended these services without using a voucher. Fifty three per cent of the couples said that their relationship did not change as a result of attending classes, although 63 per cent said it had improved their communication skills. Two-thirds of the total sample of kit recipients had used one or more parts of the kit. Those who thought the kit was very useful comprise 28 per cent (2001, pp. 5–6). Although the report contains many comprehensive statistics, it does little to answer Parker's questions.

The federal government has marketed programs to promote the idea that relationship education is useful. Furthermore, it has attempted to market relationship education to civil marriage celebrants, subsidized the costs of education by accredited providers and set up web-based resource materials to promote education as socially normative and desirable (Simons and Parker, 2002). Although reviews such as the one by Simons and Parker have investigated the availability of relationship education services and provided quantitative data on location, client characteristics, cost, duration and content of courses, there is still a dearth of information about the long-term effects of the education programs.

Evaluation is important in ascertaining whether the plethora of diverse programs and providers produce any meaningful changes in addition to informing policy and the FRSP. Parker (1999, 2007) argues that agencies should be able to perform their own studies, but agrees with Halford (2000) that improved research is necessary and should be vigorous. As Parker (2007) acknowledges, while service providers have access to useful resources that would assist them in conducting research and evaluation, these tasks could create significant additional burdens. Assistance from funders, therefore, is necessary to facilitate the establishment and ongoing management of evaluation (2007, p. 6).

Service providers are convinced that marriage education programs are effective. One Australian commented that those who conducted classes were certain about the positive effects of relationship education. She asserted that because it was very expensive to evaluate programs, it might be better for governments to provide more resources on the ground. This suggestion is unconvincing however, because when public funding is involved, greater accountability is required. To date, the main source of 'evaluation' is the quantitative data collected by FaCSLink. However, service providers see this as inadequate; one informed me that this data measures the number of clients but does not show the amount of hours spent with each one. Nor does it reveal the complex issues surrounding the relationship difficulties that clients may experience. By and large, there is a dearth of evidence-based courses drawn from research findings, or systematic analysis of client outcomes. The availability of new funds for marriage support via the FRCs may offer opportunities for evaluation because programs will have to meet a particular set of criteria. These measures could assist in defining what marriage support should entail.

In the UK, when MARS organizations were being funded to provide marriage education programs, there was minimal guidance from government about ways of demonstrating the effectiveness of services (Blaisure, 2003, p. 29). With the shift in focus to the well-being of children, any prospect of evaluating marriage support programs has virtually disappeared. Programs such as Brief Encounters train people to assist parents with new-born babies and discuss relationship issues if necessary. Due to government interest in parenting, funding is available for these types of programs, but they are not evaluated in any scientific manner. Across the countries, service providers assured me in interviews that their clients found the programs helpful; indeed people who participated in various classes gave similarly positive responses. Nevertheless, an educator who conducted marriage classes admitted that there was no long-term tracking of couples from either his agency or from any government departments. At best, some of the smaller service providers communicate with their clients by acknowledging the first anniversary of their marriage, but this is not a widespread practice.

Many of the service providers agreed that there should be follow-up programs available at major life events such as having a child, losing employment, becoming ill or looking after aging parents. Many of those interviewed supported the idea of a follow-up course one year after marriage, then again three years and five years after marriage. The majority of research focuses on the short-term effects of programs in the initial stages of a relationship. Halford (2000) argues that there is less research on the medium and long-term effects of relationship education in improving relationships or reducing rates of separation. Hence, the relative effectiveness of specific components of a program remains unclear

(Larson, 2004). This is especially the case for diverse racial and economic groups and for couples forming step-families.

A US policy analyst argued that accountability was important when providing government funding for faith-based organizations. He recommended the use of outcome-based evaluations, by means of a business model with clear goals that tracked activities of various groups. However, he pointed out that administering so many diverse requests from so many groups for competing grants was challenging for policy makers. He argued that the process can still be vigorous and that the federal level can be used to get down to grassroots levels if evaluation was flexible and used a pragmatic approach. According to a policy analyst, federal funding should only be provided to groups that are allied with policy goals and this should be based on a three-year funding round. Groups should reapply competitively and the Health and Human Services Department should distribute money competitively among the voluntary, educational and non-profit organizations. He added that it was important that training was provided for faith-based communities to write grant applications and become familiar with government policies.

One of the recognizable benefits of marriage education is already evident. In 2006, Horn declared that the most important thing that the federal government did in the past five years was recapture the word 'marriage' into the culture (cited in Marshall et al., 2006, p. 10). Policies promoting healthy marriages send an important community message about how governments value the institution of marriage and the importance of families. A constructive way of thinking about marriage and relationship education is provided by Ooms (2007) who suggests that 'meta messages' may have a lasting impact. Messages are generated by the very existence of these programs and the debates surrounding them, receiving attention not only from participants but also from staff, program administrators, evaluators, people in the community and the public at large. In short, Ooms contends that these messages can create ripple effects and indirect actions that help to shift the culture in the direction of being more supportive of marriage. This includes communicating the following key points: having a healthy marriage takes work and conscious effort; it is normal to experience difficulties; there is evidence about what makes marriages and relationships work; and it is important to develop more realistic expectations about marriage (Ooms, email 2007). Communicating the idea that a good marriage goes beyond having the right chemistry therefore offers people hope. Through learning skills, the myths of romance can be dispelled. No doubt, much more debating, assessing, researching and arguing about the worthiness of marriage and relationship education will occur as governments move forward on policies over the coming years.

Conclusion

Governments face many challenges in the field of marriage and relationship education which is a very complex policy area. They are developing, funding and appraising marriage and relationship education programs and services in an environment where their policies often meet with misgiving – although doubts appear to be diminishing as more people understand what marriage education is actually about. Political leaders could also play an important role in alleviating poverty and improving work–family balance – these are important measures which impact on the well-being of couples and families. Whether governments actually do so, however, is doubtful as poverty persists in the three countries. Policy makers can assist in building the capacity of communities to provide educational and social support services to couples and public education designed to discourage hasty and ill-matched marriages, while strengthening relationships of those who are interested in participating in the various programs. There is, however, a lack of capacity in the field to meet diverse clients' needs while ensuring that programs are consistent enough to be effective. The development of government approved competency standards in Australia demonstrates that the capacity to train service providers is further advanced than in the US or the UK. Training to deal with issues such as domestic violence is another challenge for service providers, although awareness of this problem has increased. High quality evaluations of marriage and relationship programs are uncommon at present in Australia and the UK, although much encouraging progress in this area has occurred in the US.

Policy making by governments is difficult when attempting to enhance people's personal skills and knowledge; this is unavoidable when dealing with relationships between men and women, families, community groups and governments. Whichever strategies governments in the UK, Australia and the US adopt, in whatever combination, public policies have provided different forms of support for people to sustain their family lives. The utilitarian goal of improving the well-being of children is difficult to dispute. The research says that children do better – on average – if they live in married households with their parents when there is no violence, no acrimony and the parents are happy. This makes intuitive sense. If the governments have a clear function in protecting children, then they not only need to be concerned about marriage but they also need to be concerned about single parents, cohabiting parents and same-sex parents. Thus, governments should adopt a coordinated approach to marriage and relationship education, connecting it to the wider policy agenda.

Conclusions: Reinventing Marriage?

This book has studied the role of the UK, Australian and US governments in attempting to regulate marriage in a time of massive social change. Even though the rational objective is to facilitate programs which address ways of improving people's personal relationships, thereby possibly preventing marital breakdown, it has been controversial. This has been illustrated by the opposing views that marriage is either 'in decline' or 'resilient'. Moreover, I have argued that marriage education will be difficult to implement successfully unless it is linked to policies that provide access to good jobs, health and education and other services. Strengthening marriage via education programs is a novel policy area covering unfamiliar territory for governments. Negotiating and developing skills in the context of intimate relations raises public policy concerns about protecting families and about promoting the well-being of children. There are, of course, no simple solutions to the problem of relationship instability, because any policy initiative will be dealing with intricate layers of people's emotional and social lives.

Marriage can be viewed as a public institution that liberal democratic governments have an interest in nurturing, as well as a private relationship involving two individuals seeking closeness and contentment. The conviction that marriage is good for society and consequently a legitimate matter for governments lies behind the various programs and the interest in marriage and relationship education initiatives. The political predicament is that it is impossible to legislate for making and honouring personal commitments. The marriage 'crisis' has become a particular problem for governments because they have to deal with the aftermath of relationship breakdowns. The most they can do at this stage, after all, is 'honour' divorce and provide support for single-parent families. This book has demonstrated that governments can assist the delivery of programs which teach skills and provide information about relationships. This is occurring in the US much more than in Australia and the UK. But to return to the book's starting point, policymakers, researchers and educators cannot account for what sparks interest or sexual attraction between people. Obviously, partners function in different ways in their relationships and governments do not – and cannot control – the way these interactions develop. And of course it is difficult for governments to 'coerce' – however subtly – couples to develop their relationships in particular ways. Ultimately, there is only so much that governments can do.

The book has illustrated the many tensions, contradictions and paradoxes for governments as they attempt to intervene – to varying degrees – in individuals' intimate and emotionally intense decisions. The development of marriage services and programs challenges the common assumption that governments should 'stay out' of people's private business. The rationale is that this early intervention and prevention strategy can produce a public good, by building lasting, healthy relationships. Marriage's public and private values persevere: politicians wish to encourage marriage because they value its contribution to the stability of society, while couples value its personal and emotional benefits. For some, marriage is all about adults, for others it is all about children, and to some others, it is about social order and the future of society. From a religious perspective, marriage is divinely inspired and imbued with special grace. From an economic perspective, marriage is a solution to poverty. For feminists, marriage in some cases may be harmful for women. For others, marriage is nobody's business but the two people in it. The research has demonstrated that progressives and conservatives have different insights about the 'marriage problem'. I would argue, however, that solutions to this problem need to form a new synthesis that advances beyond old ideological skirmishes.

Whether it is possible to reinvent marriage remains to be seen. The increasingly secular foundation and informality of contemporary relationships create challenging issues for public policy. Factors such as the declining importance of religion, the enhanced expectations of romantic relationships, growing gender equality and the greater acceptance of cohabitation, single-parent families and gay and lesbian relationships help to explain what has been happening to marriage and how it has changed. For people who set great store by their religion, personal beliefs can provide the basis of moral commitment to their marriage. Many studies have shown that valuing religion and regularly practising it is linked to stable and satisfying marriage (Fagan, 2006). The conundrum is that not everyone is religious. As we have seen, in today's modern world, getting married has been stripped of the religious constraints, economic dependencies and family requirements of the past. Marriage is now based on passion and friendship, rather than duty and obligation. Romantic love has become the overwhelming basis for people entering into long-term relationships involving marriage. More and more, people view staying in love as the foundation for remaining married (Hendrick and Hendrick, 1992, p. 4). Popular culture is fascinated with personal growth and there is a plethora of literature which promotes ways of strengthening relationships between partners, as well as movies and television shows focusing on love, sex and marriage. Given couples' ongoing appreciation for making a public commitment and the enduring allure of weddings, marriage is important as a representation of codes depicting the happy ending.

Paradoxically, marriage is still celebrated as the road to personal fulfilment, even as people are reluctant to enter it due to their high expectations and the fear of divorce. Marriage enjoys an esteemed status – its symbolic importance remains high. Indeed, it is perceived as a prize, an accomplishment and a sign of success (Cherlin, 2004). Simultaneously, research indicates that for a range of reasons, more women and men are living together without getting married. People cohabitate in response to insecurity, unemployment, low incomes and social exclusion. Alternatively, after making the decision to marry some couples live together for the short-term before they wed (Stanley et al., 2006). Whether the three governments formalize these *de facto* relationships or not, their continued existence will redraw the boundaries of marriage (Kiernan, 2004). While marriage will not disappear, research suggests that it will never regain its monopoly over regulating sex, raising children and transmitting resources between or within families (Coontz, 2005). It may have to be reconstructed, reinvented or rethought as other forms of intimate relationships and arrangements proliferate.

Government enthusiasm for marriage and relationship programs sends a message that public involvement with the community in strengthening marriage is important – it is not simply an individual concern. If governments do not facilitate support for strengthening relationships, this sends the message that family breakdown is bound to happen, acceptable and therefore little can be done to prevent it. Governments aim to protect families from risk and harm. Political and community involvement in fraught matters such as domestic violence, divorce or child support is now taken for granted. There are many public health campaigns for anti-smoking, sun protection, dietary habits and taking daily exercise. Parenting classes and pre-natal classes are widely available. These developments suggest that the public is open to self-improvement in different areas of their lives; marriage education may be one of the last bastions to succumb to self-help strategies. As Browning (2003, p. 197) notes,

> it is a sign of the growing belief that marriage is a public as well as a private good and that government should do more than simply allow and sanction it; the state should also prepare its citizens for marriage just as it does for the responsibilities of voting, driving a car, and other life tasks.

There is however an opposing view. The claim is that marriage programs are different from campaigns promoting self-help to achieve 'the good life' because governments are using their symbolic and distributive power to send the unambiguous message that *you really should be married* (Struening, 2007, p. 254). From this perspective, marriage programs may place excessive pressure on individuals who might otherwise be wary to tie the knot.

Heralded as promising developments, especially in the US, we have witnessed the expansion of government funding over the past decade, the increase in programs that address the particular needs of at risk groups, the acknowledgement that evaluation is necessary and the wider availability of programs. Professionals and lay leaders as well as policy makers are discussing, designing and providing marriage education programs (Larson, 2004, p. 422). This is not to deny that more needs to be done, including more systematic evaluation of programs, more information about the most effective ways to work with at risk couples and how to reach those who may be most at risk for marital distress (2004, p. 422). We cannot conclude from the literature that the status of marriage and marriage education is fully understood, despite the growing research carried out by leading experts. But we can safely predict that marriage as a contested domain will continue; consequently, both the scrutiny and analysis of its transformations will endure.

The debate about whether governments should promote marriage rages on, especially in the US. Amato (2007a) repeats the claim that the US government is not promoting 'marriage for the sake of marriage', but aims to promote healthy marriage. The marriage initiative is based on the assumption that two, married, biological parents provide the best family support for children (Amato, 2007a). In response, Furstenberg (2007a) argues that if governments are genuine in their concern for children, public policies should provide support for them, regardless of whether their parents are married. Furstenberg is not convinced that education programs will have much impact on marriages or that they will increase the rate of marriage or the survival of existing marriages (2007a, p. 957). Strengthening marriage among low-income parents is another goal, but health, educational and social services are also necessary to improve family stability. Amato agrees with Furstenberg that these policies are desirable but contends that they would 'complement, rather than compete with, efforts to strengthen marriage' (2007b, p. 962). While Amato maintains that society has a practical and moral obligation to support couples and children (2007a, p. 955) Furstenberg disagrees, stating that it is 'morally indefensible for the Bush administration to privilege legal marriage over other relationships' (2007a, p. 957). Evidently, whether marriage education is a good idea or a misguided effort continues to spark ardent disputes.

Marriage and relationship education illustrates how governments develop policies to deal with a particular problem and then, depending on the political climate, seek ways of implementing solutions (Kingdon, 1995). The UK, Australia and the US have developed different programs, translating policy into a range of measures designed to achieve the objectives of strengthening the family. Service delivery to clients who may benefit, however, is still a challenge as is training, project development and management. Putting the solution into effect has occurred differently because policies are implemented depending on the national mood, public opinion, who is in power and what the administration represents. Thus, the current policy environment is much more open to supporting marriage education policies in the US than in the UK. Australia was a pioneer in the 1990s, but now the government has moved in a different direction by increasing its spending on assisting couples at the end of the relationship phase. The objective is to smooth the divorce process. Funding restrictions based on budget allocations are always a challenge for delivering programs and it is critical to discover whether programs actually work. In short, the effectiveness of programs is still waiting for the jury's verdict. As the results and findings of US evaluations come to hand, they will hopefully shed some light on whether the programs are beneficial and a constructive use of public funds. Long-term evaluation is yet to be implemented in the UK and Australia: given the current lack of political will or interest, this may not eventuate for some time.

Whether promoting marriage education becomes a government imperative in the UK and Australia or moves forward in the US remains an open question, particularly as political patronage and persuasion change. This book has shown that the major impetus for marriage stems from concerns about family breakdown and the growing social and economic inequality in society. The marital status of parents has not been studied to find whether it is a useful predictor of poverty and other poor outcomes for children. The US leads initiatives – it is here that marriage education is being designed and tested by experts and researchers in fields such as psychology, sociology and family studies. It is here that the state of marriage and its future is being explored. Further work in these areas is necessary in the UK and Australia to gain a better understanding of the specific issues faced in these countries. Finally, whatever the research discovers, government regulation of personal life will continue to be a contentious issue. Questions, misgivings and disagreements persist about how best to foster and sustain robust marriages and relationships for everybody, so that all couples have the chance to 'live happily ever after'.

Notes

Introduction: Government and Marriage: Strange Bedfellows?

1 A Labor government was voted into power in late 2007.

1 The Problem of Marriage

1 Australian evidence suggests that economic variables may be more important in explaining who marries. For example, de Vaus (2004) shows that *de facto* couples are more likely to come from a working class background and are too young to have accumulated wealth.
2 Although, see Morgan (2000, 2007) who argues the case for marriage in Britain and Maley (2001) who argues the case for marriage in Australia.
3 Popular advice books such as Laura Doyle's (2001) *The Surrendered Wife* recommend that wives obey and honour their husbands as the head of the household. Adopting traditional gender roles is the best way to achieve a successful marriage. In contrast, Pepper Schwartz's (1994) *Love between Equals: How Peer Marriage Really Works* challenges traditional gender roles as a way to a happy marriage.

2 Tensions within Marriage: Public Institution or Private Choice?

1 While there are many diverse forms of 'the family', this is not new. A study by Gilding (2001) argues that over 100 years ago, marriage was delayed and it was not the norm. In the early 1900s, some people had servants living in their house, others took in a lodger and many more had extended family living with them. So he sees the move from the nuclear family to single-parent households and blended households as part of the wider ebbs and flows of marriage. The biggest change in relationship profiles is that today the rate of divorce is much higher than it was 100 years ago.
2 Children learn romantic codes through the narratives of fairy tales which are one of the most important cultural and social influences on many young lives. It is where many children first come across the idea of meeting the prince or princess and living happily ever after (Zipes, 1983). Orenstein (2002, p. 10) argues that by reading fairy tales, boys and girls learn the social and psychological lessons that must be absorbed to reach adulthood. Adults, she asserts, believe they move beyond these tales, but in fact, they internalize their messages.
3 The analysis by Giddens (1992) that relationships are fluid can be raised here, because he does not consider gender inequalities within relationships and within the domestic sphere. While he assumes that two people in a couple

are equal and autonomous, can articulate their needs and talk about their respective rights and obligations, the number of relationship breakdowns suggests that this is not the case.

4 Amato and Booth (1997) followed couples for 12 years and found that gender equity is critical for couple stability and satisfaction. They stressed the importance of gender equity within families. They suggest that approximately two thirds of divorces stem from low-conflict, non-abusive relationships. These couples might benefit from a counselling requirement before they proceed with divorce.

5 People decide to marry for emotional reasons and form relationships on the basis of a range of factors that financial incentives may do little to appease. Similarly, economically rational decisions may not be as important as prioritizing identity and emotional well-being for women choosing to divorce. Research carried out more than two decades ago in the US by Weitzman (1985) indicate that women's income drops markedly while men's rose. Women decide that they would prefer economic hardship rather than remaining in an unhappy marriage.

3   The UK – Governments Supporting Children

1 The government has recently made breach of a domestic violence order a criminal offence.

2 The Marriage Act 1994 provided for civil marriages to be solemnised in approved premises, effective from 1 April 1995. In 2005, 160,000 civil marriage ceremonies took place in England and Wales, this proportion was 68 per cent in 2004. These marriages were performed by a government official rather than the clergy (National Statistics, 2007, p. 18).

3 The Tavistock Marital Studies Institute, founded in 1948, is based on psychoanalysis and practice and provides specialist therapeutic services to its clients. Now known as the Tavistock Centre for Couple Relationships, it does not offer pre-marriage support, but instead provides relationship counselling for any couples facing difficulties.

4 Between December 2005 and September 2006, 15,700 same-sex civil partnerships were formed in the UK (National Statistics, 2007, p. 13).

5 The law in Scotland and Northern Ireland is significantly different.

6 Thanks to the civil servant who pointed out the rights under this Act.

7 Studies have suggested that marriage itself does not necessarily bestow benefits. Two incomes help, some partners may be better adapted than others, or those with better relationships are the couples who marry (Cowan and Cowan, 2002).

8 Lone mothers head approximately nine out of ten lone-parent families (National Statistics, 2007, p. 15).

4   Australia – Government Shifts in Supporting Marriage and Relationship Education

1 The Institute has recently established the Australian Family Relationships Clearing House. This advisory unit is funded by the Department of FaCSIA and provides information about family relationships across the lifespan.

2 Commenting on the government's spending, the Chief Justice of the Family court noted 'I have seen a bill of costs for $500,000 in one family law case' (cited in HRSCLCA, 1998, p. 96).

3 These are *Love, Sex and Waterskiing: The Experience of Pre-marriage Education in Australia* (1992) and *Pathways to Marriage: Learning for Married Life in Australia* (1994).

4 Howard's social conservatism is evident in his speeches that refer to his personal values and Judeo-Christian values. For example, his 2005 Christmas message states that 'Christmas ... celebrates the birth of Jesus Christ, a man whose life and example has given us a value system which remains the greatest force for good in our community' (Howard, 2005).

5 The government opened 15 centres in mid-2006 and after five months of operation, more than 22,000 people contact the centres: approximately 18,000 telephoned and more than 4,400 virsited a centre (Karvelas, 2006b).

6 Several collaborative developments are in train. Different reference groups have been established to examine sub-programs within the FRSP which are merging partly because of the changes to the wider FRSP and partly because of the establishment of the FRCs. The role of these groups is to provide advice to government about policies and programs which strengthen family relationships. Apart from FaCSIA and AGD, members of these groups include representatives from CSME and MAREAA, the Australian Federation of Civil Celebrants, the IRBs and the research community.

5   The US – Governments Promoting 'Healthy' Marriage

1 The American Community survey released by the US Census Bureau (2006) found that less than half of households in 2005 consisted of married couples. However, this includes from 15 years onwards and it is unlikely (or legal) that people in this young group are married.

2 See Haskins (2006) for a detailed analysis of the progress of the welfare reforms.

3 Dr Horn resigned from the ACF in April 2007.

4 In 2002, President Bush also created White House Office of Faith-Based and Community Initiatives. In part, the goal was to 'strengthen the institutions of civil society and America's families' (White House, 2001).

5 Cott (2000, p. 218) argues that 'Conservative advocacy groups, intending to preempt validation of same-sex marriage by state referenda and constitutional amendments, were fashioning symbolic statements as much as pragmatic instruments'. She goes on (2000, p. 219): 'observance of Christian-model monogamy was made to stand for customary boundaries in society, morality and civilization; the nation's public backing of conventional marriage became a synecdoche for everything valued in the American way of life'. Cott (2000, p. 220) argues that opponents of the Act condemned it as a measure of Republican partisanship, an appeal to fear and bigotry and intolerance.

6 Under the 1996 law, state governments were allowed to use TANF funds to promote marriage but few did so – Oklahoma was a major exception.

7 These bonuses were unsuccessful in lowering the out-of-wedlock birth rate, which increased from 1.2 million in 1996 to 1.5 million in 2004 (Smart Marriages, 2005).

8 At present, Chris Gersten, a former ACF Deputy Assistant Secretary, is actively informing people about how to access and use state funds towards marriage and fatherhood programs.

9 A preliminary guide was developed at a conference in 2006 to build connections between healthy marriage, responsible fatherhood and domestic violence programs (Ooms et al., 2006).

10 Horn argues that the ACF began requiring that marriage grantees address the issue of domestic violence in 2002 (interview, 2003).

11 From their study of 1324 adults in Louisiana, Arizona and Minnesota, Hawkins et al. (2002) found that whether states enact a covenant law depends on factors such as the political culture of the state, the scope of the legislation, opposition to laws affecting divorce availability and the level of public support (2002). Furthermore, covenant marriage is most likely to be supported by conservative, religious people with traditional gender ideologies (2002, p. 173). There were higher levels of support for particular components such as premarital support – recognized as important for successful marriage – and for the suggestion that couples should agree in advance to seek help if problems arose (Hawkins et al., 2002).

12 The expansion of programs is evident in the ACF's map that illustrates all the federally funded programs by state on its website (www.acf.hhs.gov. healthymarriage for the comprehensive list).

13 The Alternatives to Marriage Project (2005) claims that these reports misrepresent social science research, arguing that they are a politicized attempt to maintain that marriage is the only acceptable way to form a relationship or a family.

14 The Institute raised two issues about marriage law concerning cohabitation and same-sex marriage. First, it opposes the call for changes suggested by the American Law Institute (ALI) which would blur or eliminate many of the legal distinctions between married and unmarried couples. The second concern is whether or not to allow same-sex couples to marry legally. The Director of the Institute for the Study of Marriage, Law and Culture, Daniel Cere (2005) is concerned that 'marriage is placed analytically on the same playing field with all other long-term, sexually intimate relationships. ... Marriage does not merit special consideration or attention. It's just a subcategory – one of many possible relationships' (2005, p. 80). Cere suggests that the ALI's report, *Principles of the Law of Family Dissolution* attempts to 'push family law in new directions far removed from its traditional role of supporting marriage and protecting the best interests of children' (2005, p. 78). The ALI recommends that the law should provide cohabiting, same-sex or heterosexual partners, with or without children, many of the legal and parental rights that have been available for married couples. It argues that 'close personal relationships' should be the organizing principle of family law and that this theory has increased as a model of research about intimacy, relationships and marriage (cited in Cere, 2005, p. 80).

15 However, participants do not agree on all aspects of marriage education. For example, Gottman, a well-known clinical psychologist, suggests that conflict is endemic in any relationship and that therapy can play an important role. He suggests that 'psycho-education interventions are powerful; you have to be careful about applying them. Currently, people in the marriage

movement aren't being careful. They go ahead with tremendous optimism and convince people that this is the key to family stability' (cited in Corliss and Steptoe, 2004, p. 73).

16 See Kuo (2006) for an insider's account of how this office was politicized.

17 Marital status varies greatly among race/ethnic groups. According to the survey, approximately 61 per cent of White adults, 58 per cent of Hispanic adults and 38 per cent of Black adults are married (Centers for Disease Control and Prevention, 2004).

18 In response to this charge, Bill Coffin from the ACF claims that it makes the government 'sound naïve and as if we are robbing single parents'. He also points out that the NOW objections were made in early 2001–2002 and are now 'somewhat dated' (interview, 2007).

19 Thanks to Theodora Ooms for providing this 'last minute' update.

6   Individualism and the Private Sphere

1 When I first began writing this book, a friend told me that for her, romance was 'when my husband does the ironing'. This illustrates the value that she placed on getting some help with domestic chores.

2 A good example of this is the movie, released in 2007, called *License to Wed*. In this romantic comedy, a US pastor (played by Robin Williams) will not marry an engaged couple until they have completed a marriage preparation course. The couple have to complete ridiculous tasks, but the film raises the issue about what marriage entails.

3 The National Fatherhood Initiative (NFI) released *With This Ring...A National Survey on Marriage in America* in 2005. The telephone survey of 1,503 respondents took place in December 2003 and January 2004. One of the findings was that four of the most frequently chosen reasons for divorce were 'too much arguing', 'unrealistic expectations', 'married too young' and 'inadequate preparation' for marriage. The report argues that these issues 'can be addressed quite directly by the kind of pre-marital education that is being incorporated into healthy marriage initiatives' (2005, p. 24). The problem is that the survey found that only 47 per cent of respondents agreed that couples considering marriage should be required to participate in a healthy marriage program. This was the case, even though 86 per cent thought that couples should get pre-marital preparation (2005, p. 12).

7   Managing the Public Policy Process

1 There have been calls in the UK for developing a study that is similar to the US Fragile Families and Child Wellbeing study (Kiernan, 2006). This study provided rich data about the conditions of low-income, unmarried parents, the nature of relationships between them and how children born into these families fare.

2 According to Bob Birrell, marriage offers the strongest likelihood of having a family (cited in House of Representatives Standing Committee on Family and Human Services, 2006, p. 17).

3 Data from *Australian Social Trends* (2006c) illustrates that in 1985, 22 per cent of men worked more than 50 hours per week. In 2005, this increased to 30 per cent of men working more than 50 hours per week. This supports the suggestion that families are becoming increasingly 'time poor' (although part-time workers and the unemployed may have time, but be poor).

4 Marriage education programs, Wolf (2004) contends, have the potential to assist 'some couples whose marriage might otherwise fail' and programs probably do no harm to other relationships. The problem, however, is that government-sponsored programs tend 'to adopt or endorse a far narrower range of tools, techniques, or therapies than the very heterogeneous public-at-large is prepared to find acceptable. We must be wary of a narrow set of "government approved" marital-relationship styles' (2004, p. 177).

Bibliography

Aaronovitch, D. (2006) 'You Can't Force Parents to Play Happy Families', *The Times*, 12 December, 15.

Administration for Children and Families (2005) *Healthy Marriage Initiative: Activities and Accomplishments 2002–2005*, Washington, DC: US Department of Health and Human Services.

Administration for Children and Families (2004) *Healthy Marriage Initiative*, Washington DC: US Department of Health and Human Services, retrieved at http//www.acf.hhs.gov/healthymarriage

Administration for Children and Families (2002) *Healthy Marriage Initiative*, Washington DC: US Department of Health and Human Services, retrieved at http//www.acf.hhs.gov/healthymarriage/index.html

Advisory Group on Marriage and Relationship Support (2002) *Moving Forward Together: A Proposed Strategy for Marriage and Relationship Support for 2002 and Beyond*, Lord Chancellor's Department.

Ahituv, A. and Lerman, R. (2004) 'Job Turnover, Wage Rates, and Marital Stability: How Are They Related?' retrieved at www.urban.org/publications.

Allison, L. (2005) 'Relationship Centres Quick Fix for Complex Problem', Australian Democrats, Press Release, 1 August.

Alternatives to Marriage Project (2002) 'Let Them Eat Wedding Rings Report Questions Marriage Promotion in Welfare Reform', retrieved at http://www.unmarried.org/rings.php

Alternatives to Marriage Project (ndp) 'Commentary on *The Case for Marriage*', retrieved at http://www.unmarried.org/case.html

Amato, P. (2007a) 'Strengthening Marriage is an Appropriate Social Policy Goal', *Journal of Policy Analysis and Management*, 26, 4, 952–956.

Amato, P. (2007b) 'Response to Furstenberg', *Journal of Policy Analysis and Management*, 26, 4, 961–963.

Amato, P. (2004) 'Tension between Institutional and Individual Views of Marriage', *Journal of Marriage and Family*, 66, 4, 959–965.

Amato, P. and Booth, A. (1997) *A Generation at Risk: Growing Up in an Era of Family Upheaval*, Cambridge, MA: Harvard University Press.

Amato, P., Booth, A., Johnson, D. and Rogers, S. (2007) *Alone Together: How Marriage in America is Changing*, Cambridge, MA: Harvard University Press.

American Civil Liberties Union (2006) 'Coalition Letter to the House Appropriations Labor, Health and Human Services, Education and Related Agencies Subcommittee Urging Rejection of Funding to Abstinence-Only-Until-Marriage Programs', retrieved at www.aclu.org/reproductiverights

American Civil Liberties Union (2005) 'Welfare Reform Reauthorization Proposals', submitted to the Subcommittee on Human Resources of the House Committee on Ways and Means.

Anderson, M. (2001) 'Welfare and Marriage Issues', Congressional Testimony Serial No. 107–28, 22 May.

Andrews, K. and Andrews, M. (1997) 'Strategies to Strengthen Marriage: The Australian Experience', Family Impact Seminar *Strategies to Strengthen Marriage: What Do We Know? What Do We Need to Know?* Papers presented at a Roundtable Meeting, Washington.

Attorney-General's Department (1999a) *Discussion Paper: Property and Family Law: Options for Change*, Canberra: Commonwealth of Australia.

Attorney-General's Department (1999b) *The Role and Responsibilities of Marriage Celebrants*, Canberra: Commonwealth of Australia.

Attorney-General's Department (1999c) *A Code of Practice for Marriage Celebrants*, Canberra: Commonwealth of Australia.

Attorney-General's Department (2005) *Family Relationships Centres – Information Paper*, Canberra: Commonwealth of Australia.

Australian Bureau of Statistics (2007) *2006 Census QuickStats: Australia*, Canberra: ABS.

Australian Bureau of Statistics [ABS] (2006a) *Marriages and Divorces, Australia*, Cat. No. 3306.0.55.001, Canberra: ABS.

Australian Bureau of Statistics (2006b) *Births*, Cat. No. 3301.01999, Canberra: ABS.

Australian Bureau of Statistics (2006c) *Australian Social Trends – Work*, Cat. No. 4102.0, Canberra: ABS.

Australian Bureau of Statistics (2005a) *Births*, Cat. No. 3301.01999, Canberra: ABS.

Australian Bureau of Statistics (2005b) *Year Book Australia 2005*, Cat. No. 1301.0, Canberra: ABS.

Australian Bureau of Statistics (2004) *Employee Earnings, Benefits and Trade Union Membership*, Cat. No. 6310.0, Canberra: ABS.

Australian Bureau of Statistics (2003) *Labour Force, Australia.* Cat. No. 6203.0, Canberra: ABS.

Australian Bureau of Statistics (1998) *Australian Demographic Statistics*, Cat. No. 3101.0, Canberra: ABS.

Australian Bureau of Statistics (1995) *Marriages and Divorces*, Cat. No. 3310.0, Canberra: ABS.

Australian Catholic Bishops' Conference (2006) *Marriage Preparation: A Policy Template*, Canberra: Bishops' Committee for the Family and for Life Secretariat.

Australian Council of Trade Unions (2006) 'Howard Government's IR Dream Now a Living Nightmare for Working Families', retrieved at http://www.actu.asn.au

Australian Family Relationships Clearing House (2007) 'A New Representative Body for the Family Relationship Services Program', *Family Relationships Quarterly Newsletter No. 5*, retrieved at http://www.aifs.gov.au/afrc/pubs/news letter/newsletter5.html#news

Australian Federation of Civil Celebrants (2000) 'Attorney General's Proposal for Marriage Celebrants Unworkable, Misses the Main Point, and is Invasive of Citizen Privacy', Media Release, 30 October.

Baird, M. and Litwin, A. (2005) 'Re-thinking Work and Family Policy: The Making and Taking of Parental Leave in Australia', *International Review of Psychiatry*, 17, 5, 385–401.

Baker, M. (2001) *Families, Labour and Love: Family Diversity in a Changing World*, Vancouver: University of British Columbia.

Barlow, A. and Duncan, S. (2000) 'The Rationality Mistake: New Labour's Communitarianism and Supporting Families', in P. Taylor-Gooby (ed.) *Risk, Trust and Welfare*, London: Macmillan.

Barlow, A. and Probert, R. (2004) 'Regulating Marriage and Cohabitation: Changing Family Values and Policies in Europe and North America – An Introductory Critique', *Law & Policy*, 26, 1, 1–11.

Barlow, A., Duncan, S., James G. and Park, A. (2005) *Cohabitation Marriage and the Law: Social Change and Legal Reform in the 21st Century*, Oxford: Hart.

Barlow, A., Duncan, S., James G. and Park, A. (2001) 'Just a Piece of Paper? Marriage and Cohabitation', in A. Park and K. Thomson (eds) *British Social Attitudes: The 18th Report*, London: Ashgate.

Beck, U. and Beck-Gernsheim, E. (1995) *The Normal Chaos of Love*, Cambridge: Polity Press.

Bernard, J. (1972) *The Future of Marriage*, New York: World Publishing.

Bernstein, A. (2003) 'For and Against Marriage: A Revision', *Michigan Law Journal*, 102, 129, 129–212.

Bernstein, A. (ed.) (2006) *Marriage Proposals: Questioning a Legal Status*, New York: New York University Press.

Bir, A., Greene, J., Pilkauskas, N., Root, E., Lerman, R., Castaneda, R. and Holcomb, P. (2005) *Piloting a Community Approach to Healthy Marriage Initiatives: Early Implementation of the Healthy Marriages Healthy Relationships Demonstration – Grand Rapids, Michigan*, Washington, DC: Office of Planning, Research and Evaluation.

Birch, P., Weed, S. and Olsen, J. (2004) 'Assessing the Impact of Community Marriage Policies on County Divorce Rates', *Family Relations*, 53, 5, 495–503.

Blaisure, K. (2003) *Divorce Intervention and Prevention: Comparison of Policy Initiatives*, London: Foreign and Commonwealth Office.

Blaisure, K. and Allen, K. (1995) 'Feminists and the Ideology and Practice of Marital Equality', *Journal of Marriage and the Family*, February, 57, 1, 5–19.

Blankenhorn, D. (2007) *The Future of Marriage*, New York: Encounter Books.

Blankenhorn, D., Elshtain, J. and Bayme, S. (eds) (1990) *Rebuilding the Nest: A New Commitment to the American Family*, Milwaukee, WI: Family Service America.

Boden, S. (2003) *Consumerism, Romance and the Wedding Experience*, Basingstoke: Palgrave Macmillan.

Bogenschneider, K. (2000) 'Has Family Policy Come of Age? A Decade in Review of the State of U.S. Family Policy in the 1990s', *Journal of Marriage and the Family*, 62, 1136–1159.

Bridgman, P. and Davis, G. (2004) *The Australian Policy Handbook*, Crows Nest, Australia: Allen and Unwin.

Bristol Community Family Trust (2007) E-newsletters, retrieved at http://www bcft.co.uk/

Brook, H. (2002) 'Stalemate: Rethinking the Politics of Marriage', *Feminist Theory*, 3, 1, 45–66.

Brookings Institution (2006) *Marriage and the African-American Community*, Washington, DC: Brookings Institution.

Brotherson, S. and Duncan, W. (2004) 'Rebinding the Ties that Bind: Government Efforts to Preserve and Promote Marriage', *Family Relations*, 53, 5, 459–468.

Browning, D. (2003) *Marriage and Globalization: How Globalization Threatens Marriage and What to Do About It*, Grand Rapids, MI: Eerdmans.

Browning, D. (2001) 'What is Marriage? An Explanation', in D. Mack and D. Blankenhorn (eds) *The Book of Marriage: the Wisest Answers to the Toughest Questions*, Grand Rapids, MI: Eerdmans.

Browning, D., Miller-McLemore, B., Couture, P., Lyon, B. and Franklin, R. (1997) *From Culture Wars to Common Ground: Religion and the American Family Debate*, Louisville, KY: Westminster John Knox.

Bryson, L. (2001) 'Motherhood and Gender Relations: Where to in the Twenty-First Century?' *Just Policy*, 24, 12–23.

Bush, G. (2002a) *Working toward Independence*, Washington, DC: The White House.

Bush, G. (2002b) 'President Urges Senate to Pass Compassionate Welfare Reform Bill', 29 July, retrieved at http://www.whithouse.gov/news/releases/2002/07/200207296.html

Carroll, J. S. and Doherty, W. J. (2003) 'Evaluating the Effectiveness of Premarital Prevention Programs: A Meta-analytic Review of Outcome Research', *Family Relations, 52*, 105–118.

Cass, B. (2005), 'The Contested Politics of Paid Maternity Leave in a Transforming Family Policy Regime', in P. Grimshaw, J. Murphy and B. Probert (eds) *Double Shift: Working Mothers and Social Change in Australia*, Melbourne: Circa.

Catholic Marriage Care Limited (2006) *Annual Report and Accounts*, London: Marriage Care.

Catholic Welfare Australia (2003) *Submission to the FRSP Review*, Canberra: Catholic Welfare Australia.

Catholic Welfare Australia and the Department of Families, Community Services and Indigenous Affairs (2006) *Lessons from the Field: Family Relationships Services in Rural and Remote Australia – Challenges and Good Practice*, retrieved at http://www.facsia.gov.au/internet/facsinternet.nsf/IA/frsp_review/$file/lessons from-field-frsrural&remoteaus.pdf

Centers for Disease Control and Prevention (2006a) *National Vital Statistics Reports,* 'Births: Final Data for 2004', 55, 1, Department of Health and Human Services: National Center for Health Statistics, US.

Centers for Disease Control and Prevention (2006b) *National Vital Statistics Reports,* 'Births, Marriages, Divorces, and Deaths: Provisional Data', Department of Health and Human Services: National Center for Health Statistics, US.

Centers for Disease Control and Prevention (1998) *National Vital Statistics Reports,* 'Births, Marriages, Divorces, and Deaths: Provisional Data', 47, 21. Department of Health and Human Services: National Center for Health Statistics, US.

Centers for Disease Control and Prevention (2002) 'Table 1–17 – Number and Percent of Births to Unmarried Women, by Race and Hispanic Origin', *National Vital Statistics Reports*, 55, 1; 54, 2.

Centre for Longitudinal Studies (2005) *Millennium Cohort Study*, University of London: Institute of Education.

Cere, D. (2005) *The Future of Family Law: Law and the Marriage Crisis in America*, New York: Institute for American Values.

Chambers, D. (2001) *Representing the Family*, London: Sage.

Cheal, D. (2002) *Sociology of Family Life,* Basingstoke: Palgrave Macmillan.

Cherlin, A. (2004) 'The Deinstitutionalization of American Marriage', *Journal of Marriage and Family*, 66, 4, 848–861.

Clancy, R. (2001) 'Richer and Smaller Households Dominate British Society', *The Times*, 20 September.

Clulow, C. (2000) 'Supporting Marriage in the Theatre of Divorce', in Rt Hon Lord Justice Thorpe and E. Clarke (eds) *No Fault or Flaw: The Future of the Family Law Act 1996*, paper delivered to the *Third Inter-Disciplinary Conference on Family Law*, Bristol: Family Law, 20–25.

Clulow, C. (2005) 'Couples and Parenting: Missing the Links?' *Sexual and Relationship Therapy*, 20, 3, 265–267.

Collins, M. (2003) *Modern Love: An Intimate History of Men and Women in Twentieth Century Britain*, London: Atlantic Books.

Colmar Brunton Social Research (2004) *Family Relationships Services Program: Client Input Consultancy*, Canberra: Department of Family and Community Services.

Coltrane, S. (2001) 'Marketing the Marriage "Solution": Misplaced Simplicity in the Politics of Fatherhood', *Sociological Perspectives*, 44, 4, 387–418.

Commonwealth Department of Family and Community Services (2000a) 'Fact Sheet: What is the Pre-Marriage Education Voucher Pilot?' Canberra: Commonwealth of Australia.

Commonwealth Department of Family and Community Services (2000b) *To Have and To Hold: Final Response*, Canberra: Commonwealth of Australia.

Commonwealth Government (1999) *Government Response to the House of Representatives Standing Committee on Legal and Constitutional Affairs: To Have and to Hold*, Canberra: Commonwealth of Australia.

Cooke, B. (2001) 'Christian Marriage: Basic Sacrament', in K. Scott and M. Warren (eds) *Perspectives on Marriage: A Reader*, 2nd ed., New York: Oxford University Press, 47–58.

Coontz, S. (2005) *Marriage, A History: From Obedience to Intimacy or How Love Conquered Marriage*, New York: Viking.

Coontz, S. and Folbre, N. (2002) 'Marriage, Poverty, and Public Policy: A Discussion Paper from the Council on Contemporary Families', *Fifth Annual Council on Contemporary Families Conference*.

Corliss, R. and Steptoe, S. (2004) 'The Marriage Savers', *Time*, 30 January, 73, 66–72.

Costello, P. (2005) Budget Papers, Commonwealth Government.

Cott, N. (2000) *Public Vows: A History of Marriage and the Nation*, Cambridge, MA: Harvard University Press.

Cowan, C. and Cowan, P. (2005) 'Two Central Roles for Couples Relationships: Breaking Negative Intergenerational Patterns and Enhancing Children's Adaptation', *Sexual and Relationship Therapy*, 20, 3, 275–288.

Cretney, S. (2006) *Same Sex Relationships: From 'Odious Crime' to 'Gay Marriage'*, Oxford: Oxford University Press.

Cuthill, M. (2005) 'Capacity Building: Facilitating Citizen Participation in Local Governance', *Australian Journal of Public Administration*, 64, 4, 63–80.

de Beauvoir, S. (1987) *The Second Sex*, Harmondsworth: Penguin.

de Vaus, D. (2004) *Diversity and Change in Australian Families, Statistical Profiles*, Australian Institute of Family Studies, Australian Government.

Dean, H. and Coulter, A. (2006) *Work–Life Balance in a Low-Income Neighbourhood: Preliminary Findings Report*, London: TSO.

Delphy, C. and Leonard, D. (1992) *Familiar Exploitation: A New Analysis of Marriage in Contemporary Western Societies*. Cambridge: Polity Press.

Dench, G., Gavorn, K. and Young, M. (2006) *The New East End*, London: Profile Books.

DeParle, J. (1999) 'The Welfare Dilemma: A Collection of Articles by Jason deParle', *New York Times*, retrieved at www/nytimes.com/library/national/deparleindex.html

Department for Education and Skills (2005) *Every Child Matters Outcomes Framework*, London: TSO.

Department of Education and Skills (2004) 'Results of the 2004–2005 Grant Program – More Support for Families', Marriage and Relationship Support Directory, retrieved at hppt://www.dfes.gov.uk/marriageandrelationshipsupport/famtxtfr.shtml

Department of Employment and Workplace Relations (2005) *WorkChoices – A Simpler, National Workplace Relations System for Australia*, Canberra: AGPS.

Department of Family and Community Services (2003) *Framework for the Review of the Family Relationships Services Program (FRSP) 2003–2004*, Canberra: Commonwealth of Australia.

Dion, R. (2006) 'The Oklahoma Marriage Initiative: An Overview of the Longest-Running Statewide Marriage Initiative in the US', *Office of the Assistant Secretary for Planning and Evaluation Research Brief*, Washington, DC: US Department of Health and Human Services.

Dion, R. and Devaney, B. (2003) *Strengthening Relationships and Supporting Healthy Marriage Among Unwed Parents*, Washington, DC: Mathematica Policy Research.

Dion, R. and Strong, D. (2004) 'Implementing Programs to Strengthen Unwed Parents' Relationships: Lessons from Family Connections in Alabama', Washington, DC: Mathematica Policy Research.

Disney, H. (1999) 'Relationships Australia Celebrates 50 Years of Service', in Relationships Australia, *Papers to Celebrate 50 Years of Relationships Australia*, Deakin: Relationships Australia.

Dixon, M. and Margo, J. (2006) *Population Politics*, London: Institute for Public Policy Research, retrieved at www.ippr.org.uk/publicationsandreports/publication.aspd=341

Dixon, M. and Margo, J. (with Pearce, N. and Reed, H.) (2006) *Freedom's Orphans: Raising Youth in a Changing World*, London: Institute for Public Policy Research.

Doherty, W. and Anderson, J. (2004) 'Community Marriage Initiatives', *Family Relations*, 53, 425–432.

Donovan Research (2001) *Pre-Marriage Education Pilot Project: Final Report to Department of Family and Community Services*, Canberra: Department of Family and Community Services.

Doyle, L. (2001) *The Surrendered Wife: A Practical Guide to Finding Intimacy, Passion, and Peace with Your Man*, New York: Fireside.

Duncan, S., Barlow, A. and James, G. (2005) 'Why Don't They Marry? Cohabitation, Commitment and DIY Marriage', *Child and Family Law Quarterly*, 17, 3, 383.

Edgar, D. (2000) 'Families and the Social Reconstruction of Marriage and Parenthood in Australia', in W. Weeks and M. Quinn (eds) *Issues Facing Australian Families: Human Services Respond*, 3rd ed., Melbourne: Longman.

Edin, K. and Kefalas, M. (2005) *Promises I can Keep: Why Poor Women put Motherhood before Marriage*, Berkeley, CA: University of California Press.

Ellem, B. (2006) 'Beyond Industrial Relations: WorkChoices and the Reshaping of Labour, Class and the Commonwealth', *Labour History*, 90, 211–220.

Elshtain, J. (2006) 'Foreword', in R. George and J. Elshtain (eds) *The Meaning of Marriage: Family, State, Market, and Morals*, Dallas: Spence.

Equal Opportunities Commission (2006) *Sex Equality and the Modern Family: The New Political Battleground*, London: Equal Opportunities Commission.

Eskridge, W. and Spedale, D. (2006) *Gay Marriage: For Better or for Worse? What We've Learned from the Evidence*, Newyork: Oxford University Press.

Eskridge, W. (2003) 'The Same-Sex-Marriage Debate and Three Conceptions of Equality', in L. Wardle, M. Strasser, W. Duncan and D. Coolidge (eds) *Marriage and Same-Sex Unions: A Debate*, Westport: Praeger, 47–59.

Eurostat (2006a) 'Population and Social Conditions – Marriages', retrieved at http://epp.eurostat.ec.europa.eu

Eurostat (2006b) 'Population and Social Conditions – Divorces', retrieved at http://epp.eurostat.ec.europa.eu

Evans, M. (2003) *Love: An Unromantic Discussion*, London: Polity.

Evans, M. (1998) '"Falling in Love with Love is Falling for Make Believe" Ideologies of Romance in Post-Enlightenment Culture', *Theory, Culture and Society*, 15, 3–4, 265–275.

Fagan, P. (2006) 'Why Religion Matters Even More: The Impact of Religious Practice on Social Stability', *Backgrounder*, 1992, Washington, DC: Heritage Foundation.

Fagan, P. (2002) 'Restoring a Culture of Marriage: Good News for Policymakers from the Fragile Families Survey', *Backgrounder*, 1560, 1–7, Washington, DC: Heritage Foundation.

Families Australia (2005) *Submission to the Commonwealth Parliamentary Inquiry into Balancing Work and Family*, retrieved at familiesaustralia.org.au

Family and Parenting Institute (2006) 'Marriage Alone won't Deliver Family Stability', 11 December, retrieved at http://www.familyandparenting.org

Featherstone, B. (2006) 'Rethinking Family Support in the Current Policy Context', *British Journal of Social Work*, 36, 5, 5–19.

Fein, D. and Ooms, T. (2005) *What Do We Know about Couples and Marriage in Disadvantaged Populations? Reflections from a Researcher and a Policy Analyst*, revised version of a paper prepared for presentation at the *Annual Research Conference of the Association for Public Policy Analysis and Management*, Washington, DC, 3–5 November.

Fincham, F., Stanley, S. and Beach, S. (2007) 'Transformative Processes in Marriage: An Analysis of Emerging Trends', *Journal of Marriage and Family*, 69, 2, 275–292.

Fineman Albertson, M. (2004) *The Autonomy Myth: A Theory of Dependency*, New York: The New Press.

Fineman M., Mink, G. and Smith, A. (2003) 'No Promotion of Marriage in TANF!', a position paper, retrieved at http://falcon.arts.cornell.edu/ams3/npmposition.html

Firestone, S. (1970) *The Dialectic of Sex: The Case For Feminist Revolution*. New York: Morrow.

First Things First (2006) *First Things First Strategy*, retrieved at http://www.first things.org

Folbre, N. (2004) 'Disincentives to Care: A Critique of U.S. Family Policy', in D. Moynihan, T. Smeeding and L. Rainwater (eds) *The Future of the Family*, New York: Russell Sage.

Folbre, N. (2001) *The Invisible Heart: Economics and Family Values*, New York: The New Press.

Fragile Families (2002) 'The Living Arrangements of New Unmarried Mothers', Fragile Families Research Brief 7, Princeton University and Columbia University.

Fragile Families Survey, *Backgrounder*, 1560, 1–7, Washington, DC: The Heritage Foundation.

Fraser, N. (1997) *Justice Interruptus: Critical Reflections on the 'Postsocialist' Condition*, New York: Routledge.

Freedom from Religion Foundation (2005) 'McManus Feeds at Public Trough', *State/Church Bulletin*, 22, 2.

Furstenberg, F. (2007a) 'Should Government Promote Marriage?', *Journal of Policy Analysis and Management*, 26, 4, 956–961.

Furstenberg, F. (2007b) 'Response to Amato', *Journal of Policy Analysis and Management*, 26, 4, 963–964.

Gallagher, M. (2006) '(How) Does Marriage Protect Child Well-Being?' in R. George and J. Elshtain (eds) *The Meaning of Marriage: Family, State, Market, and Morals*, Dallas, TX: Spence.

Gallagher, M. (2003) 'Normal Marriage: Two Views', in L. Wardle, M. Strasser, W. Duncan and D. Coolidge (eds) *Marriage and Same-Sex Unions: A Debate*, Westport, CT: Praeger.

Gallagher, M. (2002) 'Marriage and Public Policy: What Can Government Do?' Policy Brief, New York: Institute for American Values.

Gallagher, M. (1996) *The Abolition of Marriage: How We Destroy Lasting Love*, Washington, DC: Regnery.

Gaze, B. (2006) 'Work Choices or No Choices? The Impact of the New Industrial Relations Laws on Work and Family', in J. Teicher, R. Lambert and A. O'Rourke (eds) *WorkChoices: The New Industrial Relations Agenda*, Frenchs Forrest, NSW: Pearson Education.

George, R. and Elshtain J. (eds) (2006) *The Meaning of Marriage: Family, State, Market, and Morals*, Dallas, TX: Spence Publishing.

Giddens, A. (1992) *The Transformation of Intimacy: Sexuality, Love and Eroticism in Modern Societies*, Cambridge: Polity Press.

Gilding, M. (2001) 'Changing Families in Australia, 1901–2001', *Family Matters*, 60, 6–11.

Gillis, J. (2004) 'Marriages of the Mind', *Journal of Marriage and Family*, 66, 988–991.

Gillis, J. (1985) *For Better, For Worse: British Marriages, 1600 to the Present*, Oxford: Oxford University Press.

Golder, H. and Kirkby, D. (1995) 'Marriage and Divorce Law Before the *Family Law Act 1975*', in D. Kirkby (ed.) *Sex Power and Justice, Historical Perspectives of Law in Australia*, Melbourne: Oxford University Press.

Goodison, L. (1983) 'Really Being in Love Means Wanting to Live in a Different World', in S. Cartledge and J. Ryan (eds) *Sex and Love: New Thoughts on Old Contradictions*, London: The Women's Press.

Gottman, J. (1994) *Why Marriages Succeed or Fail*, New York: Simon and Schuster.

Goward, P. (2005) *Striking the Balance: Women, Men, Work and Family, Discussion Paper 2005*, Sydney: HREOC Sex Discrimination Unit.

Goward, P. (2002) *A Time to Value: Proposal for a National Paid Maternity Leave Scheme*, Canberra: HREOC Sex Discrimination Unit.

Graff, E. (1999) *What is Marriage For?* Boston: Beacon Press.

Greater Grand Rapids Community Marriage Policy (2003) 'Healthy Marriages Grand Rapids', retrieved at http://www.ggrcmarriagepolicy.org

Greer, G. (1971) *The Female Eunuch*, London: Paladin.

Grymes, P. (1996) *The Romance Trap*, Kerry, Ireland: Brandon.

Hacker, A. (2003) *Mismatch: The Growing Gulf Between Women and Men*, New York: Scribner.

Hahlweg, K. and Markman, H. (1988) 'Effectiveness of Behavioral Marital Therapy: Empirical Status of Behavioral Techniques in Preventing and Alleviating Marital Distress', *Journal of Family Psychology*, 12, 543–556.

Halford, K. (2004) 'The Future of Couple Relationship Education: Suggestions on How It Can Make a Difference', *Family Relations*, 53, 5, 559–566.

Halford, K. (2000) *Australian Couples in Millennium Three*, Department of Family and Community Services: Commonwealth of Australia.

Halford, K. and Simons, M. (2005) 'Couple Relationship in Australia', *Family Process*, 44, 2, 147–159.

Halford, K., Markman, H., Kline, G. and Stanley, S. (2003) 'Best Practice in Couple Relationship Education', *Journal of Marital and Family Therapy*, 29, 385–406.

Halford, K., Moore, E., Wilson, K., Dyer, C. and Farrugia, C. (2004) 'Benefits of a Flexible Delivery Relationship Education: An Evaluation of the Couple CARE Program', *Family Relations, 53*, 469–476.

Hansard UK (2007) 'Social Exclusion Debate – More "Lies" and Statistics – More "Earache" for MPs', retrieved at www.publications.parliament.uk/pa/cm 200607/cmhansrd/cm070111/debtext/70111–0006.htm

Hansard (2000) 'Family Law Amendment Bill' (second reading), *Commonwealth of Australia Parliamentary Debates*, House of Representatives, 17 August.

Harris, R., Simons M., Willis P. and Barrie A. (1992) *Love, Sex and Waterskiing: The Experience of Pre-Marriage Education in Australia*, Adelaide: University of South Australia, Centre for Human Resource Studies.

Hart, G. (1999) *The Funding of Marriage Support: A Review*, London: Lord Chancellor's Department.

Hartinger, B. (2001) 'A Case for Gay Marriage', in K. Scott and M. Warren (eds) *Perspectives on Marriage: A Reader*, New York: Oxford University Press.

Hartog, J. (2000) *Man and Wife in America: A History*, Cambridge, MA: Harvard University Press.

Haskins, R. (2006) *Work over Welfare: The Inside Story of the 1996 Welfare Reform Law*, Washington, DC: Brookings Institution.

Haskins, R. (2005) 'The Case for Federal Programs to Promote Marriage', *Senate Committee on Appropriations*, 6 October.

Hawkins, A., Carroll, J., Doherty, W. and Willoughby, B. (2004) 'A Comprehensive Framework for Marriage Education', *Family Relations*, 53, 5, 547–558.

Hawkins, A., Nock, S., Wilson, J., Sanchez, L. and Wright, J. (2002) 'Attitudes About Covenant Marriage and Divorce: Policy Implications from a Three-State Comparison', *Family Relations*, 51, 166–175.

Hendrick, S. and Hendrick, C. (1992) *Romantic Love*, Newbury Park, CA: Sage.

Hinsliff, G. and Temko, N. (2007) 'Row over Family Values Splits Cabinet', *Observer*, 25 February.

Home Office (1998) *Supporting Families, a Consultation Document*, London: The Stationery Office.

Horn, W. (2004) 'Marriage, Family, and the Welfare of Children: A Call for Action', in D. Moynihan, T. Smeeding and L. Rainwater (eds) *The Future of the Family*, New York: Russell Sage.

House of Representative Standing Committee on Family and Community Affairs (2003) *Every Picture Tells a Story: Report on the Inquiry into Child Custody Arrangements in the Event of Family Separation*, Canberra: Commonwealth of Australia.

House of Representatives Standing Committee on Family and Human Services (2006) *Balancing Work and Family: Report on the Inquiry into Balancing Work and Family*, Canberra: Commonwealth of Australia.

House of Representatives Standing Committee on Legal and Constitutional Affairs (1998) *To Have and to Hold: Strategies to Strengthen Marriage and Relationships*, Canberra: Commonwealth of Australia.

Howard, J. (2005) 'Australian Families: Prosperity, Choice and Fairness', Address to Menzies Research Centre Westin Hotel, Sydney, 3 May.

Howard, J. (2004a) 'Announcement of Family Law Package, Anglicare Western Australia, Perth', transcript of speech presented on 29 July.

Howard, J. (2004b) 'Address to the National Marriage Forum, Parliament House, Canberra', transcript of speech presented on 2 August.

Hughes, B. and Cooke, G. (2007) 'Children, Parenting and Families: Renewing the Progressive Story', in N. Pearce and J. Margo (eds) *Politics for a New Generation*, Basingstoke: Palgrave Macmillan.

Hughes, C. (2004) *Marriage Promotion: Will it Work?*, The Roundtable on Religion and Social Welfare Policy, Washington, DC: Rockefeller Institute of Government.

Human Rights and Equal Opportunity Commission (2007) *It's About Time: Women, Men, Work and Family*, Sydney.

Human Rights and Equal Opportunity Commission (2002) *Valuing Parenthood: Options for Paid Maternity Leave*, Sydney.

Huston, T. and Melz, H. (2004) 'The Case for (Promoting) Marriage: The Devil is in the Details', *Journal of Marriage and Family*, 66, 4, 943–958.

Hymowitz, K. (2006) *Marriage and Caste in America: Separate and Unequal Families in a Post-Marital Age*, Chicago: Ivan R. Dee.

Illouz, E. (1997) *Consuming the Romantic Utopia: Love and the Cultural Contradictions of Capitalism*, Berkeley, CA: University of California Press.

Ingraham, C. (1999) *White Weddings: Romancing the Heterosexuality of Popular Culture*, New York: Routledge.

Institute for American Values (2004) *Why Marriage Matters: Twenty-Six Conclusions from the Social Sciences*, retrieved at http://www.americanvalues.org

Institute for American Values (2002) *Why Marriage Matters: Twenty-One Conclusions from the Social Sciences*, retrieved at http://www.americanvalues.org

Institute for American Values (2000) *The Marriage Movement: A Statement of Principles*, retrieved at http://www.americanvalues.org

Jackson, S. (1999) *Heterosexuality in Question*, London: Sage.

Jackson, S. (1995) 'Women and Heterosexual Love: Complicity, Resistance and Change', in L. Pearce and J. Stacey (eds) *Romance Revisited*, New York: New York University Press.

Jackson, S. (1993) 'Love and Romance as Objects of Feminist Knowledge', in M. Kennedy, C. Lubelska, and V. Walsh (eds) *Making Connections: Women's Studies, Women's Movements, Women's Lives*, London: Taylor and Francis.

Johnson, M. (1991) 'Commitment to Personal Relationships', in W. Jones and D. Perlman (eds) *Advances in Personal Relationships*, London: Jessica Kingsley.

Johnson, M., Caughlin, J. and Huston, T. (1999) 'The Tripartite Nature of Marital Commitment: Personal, Moral, and Structural Reasons to Stay Married', *Journal of Marriage and the Family*, 61, 160–177.

Joint Select Committee on Certain Aspects of the Operation and Interpretation of the Family Law Act (1992) *Certain Aspects of the Operation and Interpretation of the Family Law Act*, Canberra: Parliament of the Commonwealth of Australia.

Jolly, G., Green, P. and Dunne, J. (2006) 'Workchoices: A Practical Guide to the Changes in Workplace Law', *Employment Law*, February.

Jones-DeWeever, A. (2002) 'Marriage Promotion and Low-Income Communities: An Examination of Real Needs and Real Solutions', Briefing Paper D450, Washington, DC: Institute for Women's Policy Research.

Karvelas, P. (2006a) 'Politicians Want to Get between Your Sheets', *The Australian*, 14 February, 17.

Karvelas P. (2006b), 'Feuding Couples Embrace Free Talks', *The Australian*, 23 December, 12.

Kaye, M. and Tolmie, J. (1998) 'Discoursing Dads: The Rhetorical Devices of Fathers' Rights Groups', *Melbourne University Law Review*, 22, 162–194.

Kearney, S. (2000) 'Mismatch Weddings? No Can Do', *The Sunday Mail*, 29 October, 4.

Kerin, T. (2003) *A Short History of Marriage and Relationship Education in Australia*, Melbourne: Catholic Society for Marriage Education.

Kiernan, K. (2006) 'Unmarried Parents: The UK Context', in *The Edith Dominian Memorial Lecture 2006, Fragile Families and Child Wellbeing*, presented by S. McLanahan and I. Garfinkel, London: One Plus One.

Kiernan, K. (2004) 'Redrawing the Boundaries of Marriage', *Journal of Marriage and Family*, 66, 4, 980–987.

Kiernan, K., Land, H. and Lewis, J. (2004) *Lone Motherhood in the Twentieth Century: From Footnote to Front Page*, reprint of 1998, Oxford: Clarendon Press.

Kiernan, K. and Mueller, G. (1999) 'Who Divorces?' in S. McRae (ed.) *Changing Britain: Families and Households in the 1990s*, Oxford: Oxford University Press.

Kilkey, M. (2006) 'New Labour and Reconciling Work and Family Life: Making it Fathers' Business?' *Social Policy and Society*, 5, 2, 167–175.

Kingdon, J. (1995) *Agendas, Alternatives and Public Policies*, Boston: Harper Collins.

Kipnis, L. (2003) *Against Love: A Polemic*, New York: Pantheon Books.

Kohm, L. (2003) 'Marriage by Design', in L. Wardle, M. Strasser, W. Duncan and D. Orgon Coolidge (eds) *Marriage and Same-Sex Unions: A Debate*, Westport, CT: Praeger, 81–90.

Kotlowitz, A. (2002) 'Are the Conservatives Right?' *Frontline*, PBS, retrieved at http://www.pbs.org/wgbh/pages/frontline/shows/marriage

Kuo, D. (2006) *Tempting Faith: An Inside Story of Political Seduction*, New York: Free Press.

Larson, A. and Olsen, D. (1989) 'Predicting Marital Satisfaction Using PREPARE: A Replication Study', *Journal of Marital and Family Therapy*, 15, 311–322.

Larson, J. (2004) 'Innovations in Marriage Education: Introduction and Challenges', *Family Relations*, 53, 5, 421–424.

Lee, C. (2007) 'NOW Demands Access to Program Geared to Fathers', *Washington Post*, 29 March.

Leiwant, S. (2003) 'Testimony of NOW Legal Defense and Education Fund on Welfare Reform Reauthorization', *US Senate Finance Committee*.

Lerman, R. (2002) 'Should Government Promote Healthy Marriages?' Policy Brief, Washington, DC: Urban Institute.

Lewin, E. (2004) 'Does Marriage Have a Future?' *Journal of Marriage and Family*, 66, 4, 1000–1006.

Lewis, J. (2005) 'Perceptions of Risk in Intimate Relationships: The Implications for Social Provision', *Journal of Social Policy*, 35, 1, 39–57.

Lewis, J. (2002) *The End of Marriage? Individualism and Intimate Relations*, Cheltenham: Edward Elgar.

Lister, R. (2003) 'Investing in the Citizen-Workers of the Future: Transformations in Citizenship and the State Under New Labour', *Social Policy and Administration*, 37, 5, 427–443.

Luhmann, N. (1986) *Love as Passion*, Cambridge: Polity Press.

Mace, D. (1948) *Marriage Crisis*, London: Delisle.

Mace, D. (1945) *The Outlook for Marriage*, London: Marriage Guidance Council.

Mace, D. (1943) *Does Sex Morality Matter?* London: Rich and Cowan.

Mack, D. and Blankenhorn, D. (2001) 'Why This Book?' in D. Mack and D. Blankenhorn (eds) *The Book of Marriage: The Wisest Answers to the Toughest Questions*, Grand Rapids, MI: Eerdmans.

Mackay, H. (1999) 'Is Marriage Going Out of Fashion?' in Relationships Australia *Papers to Celebrate 50 Years of Relationships Australia*, Melbourne: Relationships Australia, Deakin, 47–53.

Macomber J., Murray J. and Stagner M. (2005) *Service Delivery and Evaluation Design Options for Strengthening and Promoting Healthy Marriages*, Washington, DC: Urban Institute.

Maher, B. (2004) *Why Marriage Should be Privileged in Public Policy*, Washington, DC: Family Research Council.

Maley, B. (2001) *Family and Marriage in Australia*, St Leonards: Centre for Independent Studies.

Mansfield, P. (2006) 'Marital Relationships: Someone Who is There For Me', in A. Buonfino and G. Mulgan (eds) *Porcupines in Winter: The Pleasures and Pains of Living Together in Modern Britain*, London: The Young Foundation.

Mansfield, P. (2005) 'Better Partners, Better Parents', *Sexual and Relationship Therapy*, 20, 3, 269–273.

Mansfield, P. (2000) 'From Divorce Prevention to Marriage Support', in Rt Hon Lord Justice Thorpe and E. Clarke (eds) *No Fault or Flaw: The Future of the Family Law Act 1996*, paper delivered to the *Third Inter-Disciplinary Conference on Family Law*, Bristol: Family Law, 29–33.

Marquardt, E. (2005) *Between Two Worlds: The Inner Lives of Children of Divorce*, New York: Crown Publishers.

Marriage and Relationship Educators' Association of Australia (2007) 'Capacity Building: Relationships Help to Fit Pieces of the Puzzle Together', retrieved at http://www.mareaa.asn.au/Capacity%20Building/front%20page.asp

Marriage Savers (2007) 'About Marriage Savers', retrieved at www.marriage savers.com

Marshall, J. (1996) *Fifty Years of Marriage Care*, London: Catholic Marriage Care.

Marshall, J., Lerman, R., Whitehead, B., Horn, W. and Rector, R. (2006) 'The Collapse of Marriage and the Rise of Welfare Dependence', *Heritage Lectures*, Washington, DC: Heritage Foundation.

Marshall, W. and Sawhill, I. (2004) 'Progressive Family Policy in the Twenty-First Century', in D. Moynihan, T. Smeeding and L. Rainwater (eds) *The Future of the Family*, New York: Russell Sage.

Martin, N. (2003) *Marriage on MARS: How the Government's MARS Programme Provides Resources to Organisations that Do Not Support Marriage*, London: Civitas.

Martos, J. (2001) 'Marriage in the Western Churches', in K. Scott and M. Warren (eds) *Perspectives on Marriage: A Reader*, New York: Oxford University Press, 29–44.

McClain, L. (2006) *The Place of Families: Fostering Capacity, Equality, and Responsibility*, Cambridge, MA: Harvard University Press.

McLanahan, S. and Garfinkel, I. (2006) *The Edith Dominian Memorial Lecture 2006: Fragile Families and Child Wellbeing*, London: One Plus One.

McLanahan, S. and Sandefur, G. (1994) *Growing up with a Single Parent: What Hurts, What Helps*, Cambridge, MA: Harvard University Press.

McLanahan, S., Donahue, E. and Haskins, R. (2005) 'Introducing the Issue', *The Future of Children*, 15, 2, 3–12.

McLanahan, S., Garfinkel, I., Reichman, N., Teitler, J., Carlson, M. and Audigier, C. (2003) 'Baseline National Report', *Fragile Families and Child Wellbeing Study*, retrieved at http://www.fragilefamilies.princeton.edu/documents/national report.pdf

McManus, M. (2003) *A Manual to Create a Marriage Savers Congregation* (2nd edn.), Potomac, MD: Marriage Savers.

Melbourne Institute of Applied Economics and Social Research (2004) *HILDA Survey Annual Report 2004*, University of Melbourne: Melbourne Institute of Applied Economics and Social Research.

Mettler, P. (2003) 'Three Organizations in West Michigan Will Use Federal Grant of $999,000 to Develop a Child Support Demonstration Project', Grand Rapids, MI: Pine Rest Christian Mental Health Services.

Morgan, P. (2007) *The War Between the State and the Family: How Government Divides and Impoverishes*, London: Institute of Economic Affairs.

Morgan, P. (2000) *Marriage-Lite: The Rise of Cohabitation and its Consequences*, London: Institute for the Study of Civil Society.

Morse, J. (2006) 'Why Unilateral Divorce Has No Place in a Free Society', in R. George and J. Elshtain (eds) *The Meaning of Marriage: Family, State, Market, and Morals*, Dallas: Spence.

Muehlenberg, B. (2004) 'The Marriage Legislation Amendment Bill', retrieved at www.family.rog.au/Article_Index/ammendment_bill.htm

Mulholland, H. (2007) 'Johnson Attacks Tory "Moralizing" on Marriage', *Guardian*, 27 February, retrieved at http://www.guardian.co.uk/uk_news/story/0,,2022595,00.html

National Council on Family Relations (2006) *Standards and Criteria for the Certified Family Life Educator (CFLE) Designation*, Minneapolis, MN: National Council on Family Relations.

National Fatherhood Initiative (2005) *With This Ring…A National Survey on Marriage in America*, retrieved at www.fatherhood.org

National Marriage Coalition (2004) *Joint Statement by Major Denominational and Church Leaders*. Media Release, 5 August, retrieved at http://www.marriage.org.au

National Organization for Women (2002) *Executive Summary, National Council of Women's Organizations Domestic Priorities Task Force Recommendations for TANF Reauthorization*, retrieved at http://www.now.org/issues/economic/welfare/principles.html

National Organization for Women (ndp) *Looking for Love in All the Wrong Places: The Case Against Government Marriage Promotion.*

National Statistics (2007) *Social Trends 37*, London: Palgrave Macmillan.

National Statistics (2006) 'Live Births Outside Marriage: Age of Mother and Type of Registration (table 3.2)', *Health Statistics Quarterly 32*, National Statistics.

Newman, J. (2000) 'Pre-marriage Education Kits Launched', Media Release, 21 June.

Newman, J. (1999) 'Launch of Pre-Marriage Education Pilot Project', Media Release, 16 October.

Newman, J. (1998) 'Families the Bedrock of Society', Media Release, 25 November.

Nock, S. (2005) 'Marriage as a Public Issue', *The Future of Children*, 15, 2, 13–36.

Nock, S. (2003) 'The Future of Public Laws for Private Marriages', *The Good Society*, 11, 3, 7478.

O'Connor, J., Orloff, A. and Shaver, S. (1999) *States, Markets, Families, Gender, Liberalism and Social Policy in Australia, Canada, Great Britain and the United States*, Cambridge: Cambridge University Press.

Okin, S. (1998) 'Gender, the Public, and the Private', in A. Phillips (ed.) *Feminism and Politics*, Oxford: Oxford University Press.

Oklahoma Marriage Initiative (2003) 'Workshops', retrieved at http:www.okmarriage.org/marriage workshops.htm

One Plus One (2002) 'Changing Marriage', in *Relationships Today*, London: One Plus One.

Ooms, T. (2007) 'Adapting Healthy Marriage Programs for Disadvantaged and Culturally Diverse Populations: What are the Issues?' Policy Brief, Washington, DC: Center for Law and Social Policy.

Ooms, T. (2005) 'The New Kid on the Block: What is Marriage Education and Does it Work?' Policy Brief, Washington, DC: Center for Law and Social Policy.

Ooms, T. (2002) 'Marriage-Plus', Policy Brief, Washington, DC: Center for Law and Social Policy.

Ooms, T. (2001) 'The Role of the Federal Government in Strengthening Marriage', *Virginia Journal of Social Policy & the Law*, 9, 1, 163–191.

Ooms, T., Boggess, J., Menard, A., Myrick, M., Roberts, P., Tweedie, J. and Wilson, P. (2006) *Building Bridges Between Healthy Marriage, Responsible Fatherhood, and Domestic Violence Programs*, Washington, DC: Center for Law and Social Policy and the National Conference of State Legislatures.

Ooms, T., Bouchet, S. and Parke, M. (2004) *Beyond Marriage Licenses: Efforts in States to Strengthen Marriage and Two-Parent Families – A State-by-State Snapshot*, Washington, DC: Center for Law and Social Policy:

Orenstein, C. (2002) *Little Red Riding Hood Uncloaked, Sex, Morality and the Evolution of a Fairy Tale*, New York: Basic Books.

Painter, M. and Pierre, J. (eds) (2005) *Challenges to State Policy Capacity: Global Trends and Comparative Perspectives*, Basingstoke: Palgrave Macmillan.

Parke, M. (2003) 'Marriage-Related Provisions in Recent Welfare Reauthorization Proposals: A Summary,' Policy Brief, Washington, DC: Center for Law and Social Policy.

Parke, M. and Ooms, T. (2002) 'More Than A Dating Service? State Activities Designed to Strengthen and Promote Marriage', Policy Brief, Washington, DC: Center for Law and Social Policy.

Parker, R. (2007) 'Recent Progress in Marriage and Relationship Education in Australia', Australian Family Relationships Clearinghouse Briefing No. 3, 1–9.

Parker, R. (1999) 'A Framework for Future Research in Premarriage Education', Australian Family Briefing No. 8, retrieved at http://www.aifs.gov.au/institute/pubs/briefing8.html

Pateman, C. (2005) 'Another Way Forward: Welfare, Social Reproduction, and a Basic Income', in L. Mead and C. Beem (eds) *Welfare Reform and Political Theory*, New York: Russell Sage.

Paul, S. (2000) *The Conscious Bride: Women Unveil Their True Feelings about Getting Hitched (Women Talk About)*, Oakland, CA: New Harbinger.

Pearce, L. and Wisker, G. (1998) 'Rescripting Romance: An Introduction', in L. Pearce and G. Wisker (eds) *Fatal Attractions: Re-scripting Romance in Contemporary Literature and Film*, London: Pluto Press.

Penman, R. (2005) 'Current Approaches to Marriage and Relationship Research in the United States and Australia', *Family Matters*, 70, 26–35.

Perkins, J. (ed.) (2004) *Defense of Marriage: Does it Need Defending?* New York: Novinka Books.

Perkins, T. (2004) 'Take a Stand for Marriage', Washington, DC: Family Research Council.

Peters, G. (2005) 'Policy Instruments and Policy Capacity', in M. Painter and J. Pierre (eds) *Challenges to State Policy Capacity: Global Trends and Comparative Perspectives*, Basingstoke: Palgrave Macmillan.

Peters, G. (1996) *The Policy Capacity of Government*, Canadian Centre for Management Development.

Pew Forum on Religion and Public Life (2002) 'Conference Proceedings: Religion, the Marriage Movement and Marriage Policy', Washington, DC: The Pew Forum on Religion and Public Life.

Pocock, B. (2003) *The Work Life Collision: What Work Is Doing to Australians and What to Do About It*, Leichhardt: Federation Press.

Pocock, B. and Masterman-Smith, H. (2005) 'WorkChoices and Women Workers', *Journal of Australian Political Economy*, 56, 126–144.

Pocock, B., Skinner, N. and Williams, P. (2007) *Work, Time and Life, the Australian Work and Life Index*, Adelaide: Hawke Research Institute, University of South Australia.

Polikoff, N. (2003) 'Ending Marriage as We Know It', *32 Hofstra Law Review*, 201–232.

Popenoe, D. (2007) *The State of Our Unions: The Social Health of Marriage in America*, Piscataway, NJ: Rutgers, the State University of New Jersey.

Popenoe, D. (1996) *Life without Father*, Martine Kessler: New York.

Power, K. (2005) 'Parents under Pressure', *About the House*, November, 23–25.

Radway, J. (1991) *Reading the Romance: Women, Patriarchy, and Popular Literature*, Chapel Hill, NC: University of North Carolina Press.

Raley, R. and Bumpass, L. (2003) 'The Topography of the Divorce Plateau: Levels and Trends in Union Stability in the United States after 1980', *Demographic Research, 8,* 245–259.

Rauch, J. (2004) *Gay Marriage: Why It Is Good for Gays, Good for Straights, and Good for America,* New York: Time Books.

Rector, R. and Pardue, G. (2004) 'Understanding the President's Healthy Marriage Initiative', *Backgrounder,* 1741, Washington DC: Heritage Foundation.

Relate (2006) '"Breakdown Britain" report – Relate clarification', 18 December, retrieved at http://www.relate.org.uk/mediacentre/pressreleases

Relate (2005) 'Relationships Skills for Love, Family and Life', retrieved at http://www.relate.gov.au

Relate Institute (2007) *Relate Institute Inaugural Lecture,* retrieved at http://www.relateinstitute.ac.uk

Relationships Australia (2006) *Relationship Indicators Survey 2006,* Canberra: Relationships Australia.

Relationships Australia (2005) *Submission in Response to 'A New Approach to the Family Law System: Implementation of Reforms',* Canberra: Relationships Australia.

Relationships Australia (2003) *2003 Relationship Indicators Survey,* Canberra: Relationships Australia.

Relationships Australia (1999) *Papers to Celebrate 50 Years of Relationships Australia,* Canberra: Relationships Australia.

Rhodes, H. (2005) 'Family Welfare and Couple Support: A View from the Bridge', *Sexual and Relationship Therapy,* 20, 3, 289–297.

Richards, S. (2006) 'Who Wants to Hang around in Matrimonial Hell for the Sake of a Few Extra Pounds?' *The Independent,* 12 December, 29.

Roberts, C. (1997) 'Reforming Divorce and Strengthening Marriage: Recent Changes in the United Kingdom', Family Impact Seminar *Strategies to Strengthen Marriage: What Do We Know? What Do We Need to Know?* papers presented at a Roundtable Meeting, Washington, DC.

RPR Consulting (2006) *Family Relationships Program (FRSP) Development of an Integrated Performance Management Framework: Stage 2 Consultation Paper,* Australian Government, Canberra: Department of Families, Community Services and Indigenous Affairs.

Ruddock, P. (2006) 'Official Launch Sutherland Family Relationship Centre', Canberra: Attorney-General's Department.

Russell, B. (2007) 'PM attacks Tory "Moralising" Over Marriage', *The Independent,* 12 August.

Sarsby, J. (1983) *Romantic Love and Society,* Middlesex: Harmondsworth.

Sawhill, I. (2002a) 'Is Lack of Marriage the Real Problem?' *The American Prospect,* 13, 7, 1–3.

Sawhill, I. (2002b) 'The Perils of Early Motherhood,' *The Public Interest,* Winter, 146, 74–85.

Schramm, D. (2006) 'Individual and Social Costs of Divorce in Utah', *Journal of Family and Economic Issues,* 27, 1, 133–151.

Schwartz, P. (1994) *Love between Equals: How Peer Marriage Really Works,* New York: The Free Press.

Scruton, R. (2006) 'Sacrilege and Sacrament', in R. George and J. Elshtain (eds) *The Meaning of Marriage: Family, State, Market, and Morals,* Dallas, TX: Spence.

Seltzer, J. (2004) 'Cohabitation in the United States and Britain: Demography, Kinship, and the Future', *Journal of Marriage and Family*, 66, 4, 921–928.

Senate Legal and Constitutional Legislation Committee (1995) *The Family Law Reform Bill 1994 and the Family Law Reform Bill (no 2) 1994*, Canberra: The Parliament of the Commonwealth of Australia.

Shanley, M. (2004) 'Just Marriage: On the Public Importance of Private Unions', in M. Shanley (ed.) *Just Marriage*, New York: Oxford University Press.

Sharma, A. (2006) 'Family Relationship Centres: Why We Don't Need Them', *Issue Analysis: The Centre for Independent Studies*, 70, 1–11.

Shumway, D. (2003) *Modern Love: Romance, Intimacy and the Marriage Crisis*, New York: New York University Press.

Simons, M. and Parker, R. (2002) *A Study of Australian Relationship Education Activities*, Canberra: Department of Family and Community Services.

Simons, M., Harris, R. and Willis P. (1994) *Pathways to Marriage: Learning for Married Life in Australia'*, Adelaide: Centre for Research in education and Work, University of South Australia.

Smart Marriages (2005) 'Legislation', retrieved at http://www.smartmarriages.com/legislation.html

Smeeding, T., Moynihan, D. and Rainwater, L. (2004) 'The Challenge of Family System Changes for Research and Policy', in D. Moynihan, T. Smeeding and L. Rainwater (eds) *The Future of the Family*, New York: Russell Sage.

Smith, A. (2001) 'The Politicization of Marriage in Contemporary American Public Policy: The Defense of Marriage Act and the Personal Responsibility Act', *Citizenship Studies*, 5, 3, 303–320.

Smock, P. (2004) 'The Wax and Wane of Marriage: Prospects for Marriage in the 21st Century', *Journal of Marriage and Family*, 66, 4, 966–973.

Smock, P. and Manning, W. (2004) 'Living Together Unmarried in the United States: Demographic Perspectives and Implications for Family Policy', *Law & Policy*, 26, 87–117.

Social Justice Policy Group (2006) *Breakdown Britain: State of the Nation Report – Fractured Families*, Westminster, UK: The Centre for Social Justice.

Social Justice Policy Group (2007) *Breakthrough Britain: Ending the Costs of Social Breakdown, Volume 1: Family Breakdown*, Westminster, UK: The Centre for Social Justice.

Stacey, J. (1996) *In the Name of the Family: Rethinking Family Values in the Postmodern Age*, Boston: Beacon Press.

Stacey, J. and Pearce, L. (1995) 'The Heart of the Matter: Feminists Revisit Romance', in L. Pearce and J. Stacey (eds) *Romance Revisited*, New York: New York University Press.

Stanley, K. (2005) (ed.) *Daddy Dearest? Active Fatherhood and Public Policy*, London: Institute for Public Policy Research.

Stanley, K. and Williams, F. (2005) 'Relationships between Parents', in K. Stanley (ed.) *Daddy Dearest? Active Fatherhood and Public Policy*, London: Institute for Public Policy Research.

Stanley, S. (2005) *The Power of Commitment: A Guide to Active, Lifelong Love*, San Fransico: Jossey-Bass.

Stanley, S. (2001) 'Making a Case for Premarital Education', *Family Relations*, 50, 272–280.

Stanley, S. and Markman, H. (1997) *Can Governments Rescue Marriages?* University of Denver: Center for Marital and Family Studies.

Stanley, S., Markman, H. and Jenkins, N. (2002) 'Marriage Education and Government Policy: Helping Couples Who Choose Marriage Achieve Success', *Smart Marriages*, retrieved at http://www.smartmarriages.com

Stanley, S., Amato, P., Johnson, C. and Markman, H. (2006a) 'Premarital Education, Marital Quality, and Marital Stability: Findings from a Large, Random, Household Survey', *Journal of Family Psychology*, 20, 117–126.

Stanley, S., Rhoades, G. and Markman, H. (2006b) 'Sliding Versus Deciding: Inertia and the Pre-Marital Cohabitation Effect', *Family Relations*, 55, 499–509.

Stanley, S., Markman, H., Prado, L., Olmos-Gallo, A., Tonelli, L., St. Peters, M., Leber, D., Bobulinski, M., Cordova, A. and Whitton, S. (2001) 'Community-Based Premarital Prevention: Clergy and Lay Leaders on the Front Lines', *Family Relations*, 50, 1, 67–76.

Stone, L. (1977) *The Family, Sex and Marriage in England 1500–1800*, London: Weidenfeld and Nicolson.

Struening, K. (2007) 'Do Governments Sponsored Marriage Promotion Policies Place Undue Pressure on Individual Rights?' *Policy Sciences*, 40, 241–259.

Summers, A. (2003) *The End of Equality: Work, Babies and Women's Choices in 21st Century Australia*, Sydney: Random House.

Tennant, R., Taylor, J. and Lewis, J. (2006) *Separating from Cohabitation: Making Arrangements for Finances and Parenting*, London: Department for Constitutional Affairs.

Tronto, J. (2004) 'Marriage: Love or Care?' in M. Shanley (ed.) *Just Marriage*, New York: Oxford University Press.

Ulrich, N. (ndp) *First Things First Strategy*, retrieved at http://www.firstthings.org

United States Conference of Catholic Bishops (1998) *NFP Forum Diocesan Activity Report*, 9, 1 and 2.

Urban Institute (2007) 'Should the Government Promote Marriage', Pressroom June 18, retrieved at http://www.urban.org/Pressroom/otherevents/vsmarriage govt.cfm

Urbis Keys Young (2004) *Family Relationships Services Program Client Input Consultancy*, Canberra: Department of Family and Community Services.

US Census Bureau (2003) *Statistical Abstract of the United States: 2000*, Washington, DC: Government Printing Office.

US Census Bureau (2006) *2005 American Community Survey*, retrieved at http://factfinder.census.gov/home/

van Acker, E. (2005) 'Relationship Education and Responses to Government Policy Initiatives', paper presented at the *Family Services Australia Conference*, Adelaide, 28–30 September.

van Acker, E. (2003a) 'Regulating Relationships: Marriage and the State', in I. Holland and J. Fleming (eds) *Government Reformed: Values and New Institutions*, London: Ashgate.

van Acker, E. (2003b) 'Administering Romance: Government Policies Concerning Pre-Marriage Education Programs', *Australian Journal of Public Administration*, 61, 1, 15–23.

van Acker, E. (2001) 'Contradictory Possibilities of Cyberspace for Generating Romance', *Australian Journal of Communication*, 28, 3, 24–62.

Waite, L. and Gallagher, M. (2000) *The Case for Marriage: Why Married People Are Happier, Healthier, and Better Off Financially*, New York: Doubleday.

Walker, A. (2004) 'A Symposium on Marriage and Its Future,' *Journal of Marriage and Family*, 66, 4, 843–847.

Walker, J. (2000) 'Whither the Family Law Act II?' in Rt Hon Lord Justice Thorpe and E. Clarke (eds) *No Fault or Flaw: The Future of the Family Law Act 1996*, paper delivered to the *Third Inter-Disciplinary Conference on Family Law*, Bristol: Family Law, 3–10.

Walter, M. (2005) 'Exploring Mothers' Relationship to the Labour Market', *Just Policy*, 35, 13–21.

Wardle, L., Strasser, M., Duncan, W. and Coolidge, D. (eds) (2003) *Marriage and Same-Sex Unions: A Debate*, Westport, CT: Praeger.

Waring, P., De Ruyter, A. and Burgess, J. (2005) 'Advancing Australia Fair: The Australian Fair Pay and Conditions Standard', *Journal of Australian Political Economy*, 56, 105–125.

Weitzman, L. (1985) *The Divorce Revolution: The Unexpected Social and Economic Consequences for Women and Their Children in America*, New York: Free Press.

Weston, R., Qu, L. and de Vaus, D. (2003) 'Partnership Formation and Stability', paper presented at the *Ninth Australian Institute of Family Studies Conference*, 9–11 February, Melbourne.

Wetzstein, C. (2006) 'Marriage Advocates Key Federal Funding', *The Washington Times*, 25 August.

White House (ndp) *Guidance to Faith-Based and Community Organizations on Partnering with the Federal Government*, Washington, DC: The White House.

Whitehead, B. (1997) *The Divorce Culture*, New York: Knopf.

Whitehead, B. and Popenoe, D. (2006) *The State of Our Unions: The Social Health of Marriage in America*, Piscataway, NJ: Rutgers, the State University of New Jersey.

Whitehead, B. and Popenoe, D. (2005) *The State of Our Unions: The Social Health of Marriage in America*, Piscataway, NJ: Rutgers, the State University of New Jersey.

Whitehead, B. and Popenoe, D. (2004) *The State of Our Unions: The Social Health of Marriage in America*, Piscataway, NJ: Rutgers, the State University of New Jersey.

Whitehead, B. and Popenoe, D. (2003) *The State of Our Unions: The Social Health of Marriage in America*, Piscataway, NJ: Rutgers, the State University of New Jersey.

Whitehead, E. and Whitehead, J. (2001) 'The Meaning of Marriage', in K. Scott and M. Warren (eds) *Perspectives on Marriage: A Reader*, New York: Oxford University Press, 106–115.

Whitehouse, G. (2005) 'Policy and Women's Workforce Attachment', *Just Policy*, 35, 22–35.

Wilcox, B. (2006) 'Suffer the Little Children, Marriage, the Poor, and the Commonweal', in R. George and J. Elshtain (eds) *The Meaning of Marriage: Family, State, Market, and Morals*, Dallas: Spence.

Wilcox, B. (2002) *Sacred Vows, Public Purpose: Religion, the Marriage Movement and Marriage Policy*, Yale, CT: Yale University, The Institute for the Advanced Study of Religion.

Williams, D. (2001) 'A New Era for Marriage Celebrants', News Release, 3 October, Canberra: Parliament House.

Williams, D. (2000a) *Marriage Celebrants are Important to Long, Healthy Marriages*, News Release, 1 November, Canberra: Parliament House.

Williams, D. (2000b) *Proposals Paper: Reform of the Marriage Celebrants Program*, Canberra: Parliament House.

Williams, D. (1997) *Discussion Paper: Civil Marriage Celebrants Program*, Canberra: Parliament House.

Williams, L. and Jurich, J. (1995) 'Predicting Marital Success after Five Years: Assessing the Predictive Validity of FOCCUS', *Journal of Marital and Family Therapy*, 21, 141–153.

Wilson, E. (1983) 'A New Romanticism', in E. Phillips (ed.) *The Left and the Erotic*, London: Lawrence and Wishart.

Wilson, J. (2002) *The Marriage Problem: How Our Culture Has Weakened Families*, New York: Harper Collins.

Witte, J. (2003) 'The Tradition of Traditional Marriage', in L. Wardle, M. Strasser, W. Duncan and D. Coolidge (eds) *Marriage and Same-Sex Unions: A Debate*, Westport, CT: Praeger, 47–59.

Wolf, D. (2004) 'Demography, Public Policy, and "Problem" Families', in D. Moynihan, T. Smeeding and L. Rainwater (eds) *The Future of the Family*, New York: Russell Sage.

Wolfson, E. (2003) 'Enough Marriage to Share: A Response to Maggie Gallagher', in L. Wardle, M. Strasser, W. Duncan and D. Coolidge (eds) *Marriage and Same-Sex Unions: A Debate*, Westport, CT: Praeger.

Wood, R., Goesling, B., Avellar, S. (2007) *The Effects of Marriage on Health: A Synthesis of Recent Research Evidence*, Princeton, NJ: Mathematica Policy Research.

Zedlewski, S. and Loprest, P. (2001) 'Will TANF Work for the most Disadvantaged Families?' in R. Blank and R. Haskins (eds) *The New World of Welfare*, Washington, DC: Brookings Institution.

Zeigler, J. (2005) 'Welfare Policy Analyst, Cato Institute before the Subcommittee on Human Resources of the House Committee on Ways and Means', 10 February.

Zipes, F. (1983) *Fairy Tales and the Art of Subversion: The Classical Genre for Children and the Process of Civilization*, London: Heinemann.

Index